Human–Computer Interaction Series

Editors-in-chief
Desney Tan, Microsoft Research, USA
Jean Vanderdonckt, Université catholique de Louvain, Belgium

HCI is a multidisciplinary field focused on human aspects of the development of computer technology. As computer-based technology becomes increasingly pervasive – not just in developed countries, but worldwide – the need to take a human-centered approach in the design and development of this technology becomes ever more important. For roughly 30 years now, researchers and practitioners in computational and behavioral sciences have worked to identify theory and practice that influences the direction of these technologies, and this diverse work makes up the field of human-computer interaction. Broadly speaking it includes the study of what technology might be able to do for people and how people might interact with the technology. The HCI series publishes books that advance the science and technology of developing systems which are both effective and satisfying for people in a wide variety of contexts. Titles focus on theoretical perspectives (such as formal approaches drawn from a variety of behavioral sciences), practical approaches (such as the techniques for effectively integrating user needs in system development), and social issues (such as the determinants of utility, usability and acceptability).

Titles published within the Human–Computer Interaction Series are included in Thomson Reuters' Book Citation Index, The DBLP Computer Science Bibliography and The HCI Bibliography.

More information about this series at http://www.springer.com/series/6033

Guy André Boy

Tangible Interactive Systems

Grasping the Real World with Computers

 Springer

Guy André Boy
School of Human-Centered Design,
   Innovation and Art
Florida Institute of Technology
Florida, USA

NASA Kennedy Space Center
Florida, USA

ISSN 1571-5035
Human–Computer Interaction Series
ISBN 978-3-319-30269-0   ISBN 978-3-319-30270-6   (eBook)
DOI 10.1007/978-3-319-30270-6

Library of Congress Control Number: 2016936565

Printed on acid-free paper

This Springer imprint is published by Springer Nature
The registered company is Springer International Publishing AG Switzerland

Preface

"Are you a psychologist, a philosopher, or an engineer?" This is the question several people, who I met during the last three decades, repeatedly asked me. For sure, I have an engineering background, mostly automatic control, computer science, and aerospace engineering. Therefore, I am supposed to do tangible engineering. Incidentally in the early 1980s, I started working on the two-crewman cockpits and the fly-by-wire technology. I was research scientist at ONERA (the French Aerospace Research Administration) working with flight test pilots and engineers at Airbus.[1] The problem was for us to certify commercial transport aircraft with two crewmen instead of three. The FAA rules required us to take into account human factors. Very few specifications were provided in the FAA Rules PART 25 Appendix D (a little bit more than half a page—see P25-D in the reference list). They were described in the form of criteria for determining minimum flight crew, and more specifically 10 workload factors such as accessibility to flight instruments and controls, number, urgency, and complexity of operating procedures, mental and physical efforts, systems monitoring, degree of automation, communication and navigation workload, emergency workload management, and crewmember incapacitation.

We then studied human factors and ergonomics. Our first attempt was centered on physiological measures, such as ECG[2] and EEG.[3] Indeed, engineers liked "objective" measures! We could measure electric physiological signals coming from people, in this case pilots. However, the main problem was the interpretation of these signals. Interpretation is always subjective because it requires opinions and judgments from experts. Physiologists were able to provide models, but these models were very context dependent and did not provide meaningful-enough explanations of what was really going on when pilots were flying and, at the same time, trying to manage a failure recovery process (e.g., engine failure). We then decided to use methods that were based on subjective assessment from the start. A good example

---

[1] Called *Airbus Industrie* at that time.

[2] Electrocardiogram.

[3] Electroencephalogram.

is the Cooper-Harper workload assessment method that pilots had to learn in order to self-assess their own workload on a 1-to-10 subjective scale (Cooper and Harper 1969). Pilots' subjective assessments were correlated to workload subjective assessments of an observer located in the cockpit on the jump seat behind them. This approach worked perfectly. This was when I decided to formally attend psychology classes at the University of Toulouse. I learned cognitive psychology, got deeply interested in cognitive science and artificial intelligence, and actively participated in the making of cognitive engineering and human-centered design (HCD) since then (Boy 2003, 2011).

Tangibility: From the User Interface View to the Systems View

Thus, for the last four decades, I learned how and modestly contributed to articulate engineering with human and social sciences when designing life-critical systems,[4] more specifically aerospace systems. After a few years of practice, I understood that human factors were discovered too late during the life cycle of a product to be taken into account seriously. What human factors specialists produced for a long time was mostly informative for training, but cosmetic and not really effective for design. They contributed to the design of user interfaces and operational procedures to improve human adaptation to engineered systems. Since the 1980s, user interfaces became almost exclusively supported by computers and software. Consequently, Human-Computer Interaction (HCI) progressively became the inevitable solution to increasingly computerized Human-Machine Systems (HMS).

The **HCI-HMS distinction** is major. The early conference series on Human-Machine Interaction and Artificial Intelligence in Aerospace was renamed Human-Computer Interaction in Aeronautics (HCI-Aero) in 1998. The term "machine" was used in the HMS community to denote a mechanical system. Pilots were interacting with mechanical devices (e.g., maneuvering the yoke that was mechanically linked to the flight control surfaces of the aircraft). Today, when we talk about an **interactive cockpit**, we mean interacting with computers using a graphical "point-and-click" display system (i.e., pilots interact with a software that itself interacts with the flight control mechanisms). When I first heard about the term "interactive cockpits," I asked: "weren't aircraft cockpits interactive before?" Indeed, pilots were used to interact with mechanical surfaces of the aircraft directly and physically through mechanical control devices. Today with the fly-by-wire, pilots interact with computers that themselves interact with the mechanical systems of the aircraft.

---

[4]Life-critical systems (LCSs) are defined as an integrated set of people and interactive systems that have three main emerging properties, i.e., safety, efficiency and comfort. For example, aircraft, power plants, cars, hospitals, houses and cities are LCSs. New types of LCSs involve security because they are software-based networked and open to the world with little protection. For example, when you loose your smartphone, you realize how life-critical it is. We created this kind of LCS. Consequently, we also created the need to deal with their specific life-criticality. This is a complexity issue because emerging LCS issues are very hard to discovered before use time.

Therefore, the concept of interaction shifted from human-mechanical systems interaction to human-computer interaction.

Consequently, we need to be careful when we talk about interactivity. Human-computer interaction is not only a matter of cognition, but also a matter of tangibility. We are facing the paradox of information overload and information access as well as loosing the sense of physical things. This is why tangibility has become a central focus of current socio-technical evolution.

HCI was born during the early 1980s as a specific branch of computer science. The Special Interest Group on Computer-Human Interaction (SIGCHI) of the Association for Computing Machinery (ACM) created a famous conference series called CHI (Conference on Human Factors in Computing Systems). The first CHI conference was held in Gaithersburg, Maryland, USA in 1982. It was, and still is, a **design** conference more than anything else. CHI focuses on the design of human-centered computing systems (i.e., the whole thing is a computer, even cell phones that populated CHI conferences since the late 1990s). However, **domains**, such as nuclear power plants, aircraft, spacecraft, and other mechanical systems where software was progressively embedded, were never well integrated in the CHI community. For a long time, most HCI solutions and methods were developed with office automation in mind. Today, even if HCI diversified in various application domains, tangibility is still only focused on user interfaces, and not on large complex socio-technical systems.

The concept of user interface is already a concept of the past when it is considered as an add-on. I explained in my previous book (Boy 2013) that systems were designed and developed from **inside-out** (i.e., technological means are engineered without taking into account people who will use them; consequently, when they are fully developed, artifacts such as user interfaces and operational procedures need to be designed and developed). This was the necessary approach of the twentieth century, where engineered systems required human factors and ergonomics specialists to be usable. Since the beginning of the twentieth century, modeling and simulation capabilities enable the development of virtual prototypes that can be tested by appropriate end users. Consequently, systems can be designed from **outside-in** (i.e., usage purposes can be designed taking into account people who will use them from the beginning; people's activity can be tested; emerging behaviors can be discovered and seriously considered in the design process; user interfaces and operational procedures are integrating components of the system from the beginning). Inside-out engineering was about developing technological means requiring user interface development in the end to finally find out technology capabilities and usefulness purposes. Outside-in design is about purposes from the beginning and integration of appropriate technology to fulfill them, involving the participation of potential end users. This is what HCD is about.

User interface and automation are concepts of the twentieth-century bridging the gap between technology-centered engineering and users.

Virtual engineering and tangibility are concepts of twenty-first century bridging the gap between human-centered design, systems engineering, and people.

When I wrote this book, I also started to be in charge of the Human-Systems Integration Working Group of INCOSE.[5] Indeed, systems engineering and human-systems integration, coming from two different approaches (i.e., technology-centered engineering and HCD, respectively), developed independently. I was looking for an integration of these two approaches.

Many colleagues have encouraged and collaborated in my efforts to develop and demonstrate the value of tangibility in virtual engineering and human-centered design of current interactive systems. I am indebted to Mike Conroy, Ondrej Doule, Nikki Hoier, Christophe Kolski, Jason Miller, Jen Narkevicius, and Lucas Stephane for active discussions and provision of helpful comments on this integration. I also want to thank all my students and research scientists at the School of Human-Centered Design, Innovation and Art of Florida Institute of Technology, and NASA Kennedy Space Center who directly or indirectly helped me in shaping the concept of tangible interactive systems developed in this book.

Melbourne, FL, USA   Guy André Boy
December 6, 2015

References

Boy GA (2003) (ed) L'Ingénierie Cognitive: interaction Homme-Machine et Cognition (The French handbook of cognitive engineering). Hermes Sciences, Lavoisier
Boy GA (2011) (ed) Handbook of human-machine interaction: a human-centered design approach. Ashgate, UK. ISBN 978-0-7546-7580-8
Boy GA (2013) Orchestrating human-centered design. Springer, London
Cooper G, Harper R (1969) The use of pilot rating in the evaluation of aircraft handling qualities. Technical report TN D-5153, NASA
P25-D. Part 25: airworthiness standards: transport category airplanes, Appendix D to Part 25, page 163. Docket No. 5066, 29 FR 18291, 24 Dec 1964; as amended by Amdt. 25–3, 30 FR 6067, 29 Apr 1965

[5] International Council on Systems Engineering.

Contents

Chapter 1
Introduction

The real voyage of discovery consists not in seeking new landscapes, but in seeing with new eyes. – Marcel Proust[1]

Hiroshi Ishii was the first human-computer interaction (HCI) scientist to design seamless interfaces between humans, digital information, and the physical environment. He and his team were seeking to change the "painted bits" of graphical user interfaces to "tangible bits" by giving physical form to digital information (Ishii and Ullmer 1997). We need to **distinguish** between this purely HCI concept of **tangible user interfaces** (TUIs)[2] (Ullmer and Ishii 2001) and **tangible interactive systems** (TISs) taking into account the tangibility of systems and not only the user interface enabling interaction with digital information through the physical environment. In addition, TISs are presented as a grounding concept for **human-centered design (HCD) and systems engineering**. The concept of TIS goes far beyond the concept of TUI and addresses large complex systems. Within the context of aerospace complex systems design and management, I recently proposed the shift from automation to tangible interactive objects (Boy 2014). In fact, the concept of "system" is more appropriate than the concept of "object" because it encapsulates objects, processes, and people. Systems can be abstract or concrete and have functions and structures; they include software and hardware. In addition, HCD that puts humans at the center of the design process differs from traditional human factors and ergonomics (HFE) that are commonly taken into account after the engineering process.

---

[1] This quote comes from "A la recherche du temps perdu" (In search for lost time), a novel in seven volumes by Marcel Proust (1871–1922). This work was published in France between 1913 and 1927 (first volume by the Grasset Publishers and then by many others).

[2] https://en.wikipedia.org/wiki/Tangible_user_interface

© Springer International Publishing Switzerland 2016
G.A. Boy, *Tangible Interactive Systems*, Human–Computer Interaction Series,
DOI 10.1007/978-3-319-30270-6_1

Automation, Activity, and Cognitive Functions

We created and are still creating systems that have very sophisticated functions, which were previously handled by people. In Aeronautics, **automation** was, and still is, typically developed incrementally by accumulating layers upon layers of software—progressively isolating pilots from actual mechanical systems. This approach requires constant revisions and repairs to most often adapt people to systems and rarely systems to people. Instead of repairing when it is too late, it is always better to incrementally improve solutions at design time. For this reason, an HCD environment should be available where **both end users and designers learn from each other**. On one side, designers should learn what end users (e.g., pilots) need, can and cannot do in order to design and develop appropriate technology (e.g., aircraft). On the other side, end users should learn how to use new technology. Today, end users need to understand and practice software-intensive systems management (i.e., a very new endeavor in the history of humanity). Pathways for feedback should be provided to end users for continuous improvement to take place.

During the mid-1990s, when I was studying aircraft automation, I realized that it was important to develop the **cognitive function** representation to analyze function allocation between humans and life-critical systems. From this perspective, this book is a follow-up of my 1998 book on Cognitive Function Analysis (CFA), when I tried to understand and rationalize the relationship between **task** (i.e., what is prescribed to the human operator) and **activity**[3] (i.e., what this human operator can effectively do when he or she executes the task). I decided then to call this relationship between task (i.e., an input) and activity (i.e., an output), a "cognitive function." CFA was developed within the context of aircraft cockpit automation (Boy 1998a, b) and based on the concept of agent. We will consider that an agent is a system that is capable of acting on its environment. An agent has at least one cognitive function.

> **Tasks are prescriptions that people use to do things.**
>
> **Activities are what people really do when they execute tasks.**
>
> **Cognitive functions are processes that enable people to transform tasks into activities.**

---

[3] People's activity is taken in the ethnomethodology sense (i.e., what people actually do) and not on tasks (i.e., what people are prescribed to do). This distinction between task and activity was already described to define the cognitive function representation for the implementation of cognitive function analysis (Boy 1998b, 2011, 2013), as well as activity theory (Leont'ev 1981; Kaptelinin 1995). The concept of activity is related to Ochanine's concept of operative image (Paris I Seminar on D. Ochanine's Operative Image 1981). More recently, exploring the social aspects of interactive systems, Paul Dourish proposed the foundations of a phenomenological approach to human-computer interaction through embodied interaction (Dourish 2004). The concept of activity has then to be understood as both cognitive and embodied.

In the past, activity analysis was only carried out on existing, but not yet formalized, **practice**.[4] Applied to actual design and engineering work, this kind of approach reinforced what people were doing with old technology, and inference of possible practice using new technology was somehow deemed hazardous. Of course, the value of analyzing current activity led to considering **continuity** between current and new practices. It also created some kind of evolution viscosity and in some cases prevented radical changes, precisely for continuity purposes.

Indeed, the difficulty in the use of CFA is in the observation of activity. You must have a fully developed system to observe what people can do using it. Until recently, this was only possible at the end of the manufacturing process (e.g., during flight tests in aeronautics). Today, things have changed. We have simulation capabilities that enable us to test the system being designed very early during the design process. Consequently, activity can be observed and further analyzed. Therefore, CFA has become possible at design time. This is great progress because we can test both deliberatively designed and emerging cognitive functions.

Cognitive functions are cognitive in the sense that they are capable of information processing. Consequently, **automation** can be viewed as cognitive function transfer from humans to systems. This kind of transfer has been incremental during the last decades of the twentieth century. Of course, a system cognitive function (SCF) is different from an equivalent human cognitive function (HCF). They are not generated in the same way (i.e., the software engineering process of making SCFs is certainly very different from the human cognitive process of learning HCFs). However, they both should have (or must have) a similar **role**, a similar **context** of validity, and a similar set of allocated **resources** that enable their execution (Boy 1998b). Resources can be physical or cognitive. At this point, we can see that a resource can be a cognitive function. Therefore, the concept of cognitive function is recursive. This is also true for a physical function. The irony is that when they are well designed and manufactured, SCFs can be more effective and reliable than their equivalent HCFs, when they are of course used within their context of validity. In this book, we will see how cognition plays an important role in the interaction between humans and software-based systems and how we need to better understand the orchestration of human and system cognitive functions. Cognition however is not the only factor that we need to consider; emotions and social factors are also crucial in this framework.

> **Human and system cognitive functions are both represented by a role, a context of validity, and resources that enable their execution.**

---

[4] The term "practice" is used in this book to talk about activity. This interpretation is based on practice theory. Practice theory focuses on how people's purposes and intentions contribute to shape and change their environment. It is strongly based on Pierre Bourdieu's sociological work (Bourdieu 1980), and more specifically the notion of "habitus" (i.e., permanent embodiment of social order). Practice theory is intimately related to ethnography. I will use the same meaning when I will introduce the "maturity of practice" concept.

From Automation to Tangible Interactive Systems

Back in the 1980s, when conventional fly-by-the-seat-of-your-pants technology was replaced by fly-by-wire technology in commercial aircraft, pilots had difficulties using innovative onboard computing systems, such as the Flight Management System (FMS), doing several flying tasks for them. They had to learn how to delegate—not an easy task! When you delegate, you do not control all tasks at the finest grain level. Pilots incrementally adapted to this new way of thinking and doing things. This computerization evolution never stopped and is still not ready to stop. Today, there are two main issues. The first issue is related to **complacency** due to good performance and reliability of these systems, hence new habits of pilots to trust them (often too much trust nowadays). When an unexpected situation occurs, pilots may not be in the control loop any longer—we talk about lack of situation awareness and control awareness. The second issue is related to the **virtual** life induced by the use of these systems—pilots need to learn how to deal with the real world through computers. Unlike pilots of the 1980s who were used to dealing with physics and mechanics, and (some of them) hated computers, young pilots of today are more familiar with virtual worlds (i.e., they are coming from the computer-game generation) and may have some problems dealing with real-world events that include physics. **Tangibility** becomes a major issue. Something tangible is, by definition, capable to be physically graspable, touched, or discernible by the touch. It is also understood as real or actual, rather than imaginary or visionary.[5] Tangible can be thought as the opposite of vague. In other words, flying highly automated aircraft requires understanding of classical flight handling qualities and flying tasks handled by onboard systems. Today, people need to be able to **grasp the real world using computers**.

Let's take the example of *TangiSense* (Kubicki et al. 2013; Lebrun et al. 2015), which consists in a set of tangible objects, considered as agents, moving or moveable on an interactive tabletop. Each tangible object has a behavior and a role. TangiSense was used to support the simulation of road traffic management. Authors, located around TangiSense interactive tabletop, were able to interact with other people (decision-makers) in a simultaneous and collaborative way during a simulation session.

During the twentieth century, we automated mechanical machines, i.e., we incorporated software into hardware (Fig. 1.1). This automation was done because we could do it (i.e., human-centered purposes were too often investigated once technological means were already developed).

Many research efforts were developed to investigate benefits and drawbacks of automation (Bainbridge 1983; Billings 1991; Sarter et al. 1997). Since the beginning of the twenty-first century, we have been designing systems by developing software programs that lead to human-in-the-loop simulations, which enable us to test various kinds of purposes. Today, the question is less investigating drawbacks of automation as we did during the last decades of the twentieth century, than discovering emerging properties of **Tangible Interactive Systems, or TISs** (Fig. 1.2).

---

[5] http://dictionary.reference.com/browse/tangible

Fig. 1.1 Automation as the "old" shift from mechanical engineering to information technology: the inside-out approach (Boy 2014)

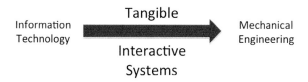

Fig. 1.2 Tangible interactive systems as the "new" shift from information technology to mechanical engineering: the outside-in approach (Boy 2014)

The concept of tangible interactive system extends the concept of tangible user interface already developed in human-computer interaction. TISs are useful bricks for **virtual systems engineering** (VSE). VSE is based on modeling and simulation. It enables human-in-the-loop simulations (i.e., VSE support human-centered design). Let's take the office automation revolution example, which drastically changed cognitive functions dealing with office tasks. Until the end of the 1970s, computers were big machines used by a few specialists in very constrained environments. The development of **microcomputers** started to democratize information technology at work and at home. The first leading type of application became word (text) processing. When I prepared a PhD in the end of the 1970s, I wrote my dissertation by hand and, as everybody else in this situation did, I had the secretary of my department type it. Nobody at that time thought that we would type our research reports or dissertations by ourselves. Today, we all use our favorite text processing applications and hardly think that someone else would type it for us. Computer-supported writing cognitive functions have become sustainable, and the role of dactylograph secretaries obsolete. Text processing became tangible because it enabled us to easily produce information content, share it, and use it as a collaborative support system thanks to email and Internet.

A major distinction: tangible interactive systems are in virtual systems engineering what tangible user interfaces are in human-computer interaction.

Virtual systems engineering is model based and supports human-in-the-loop simulations.

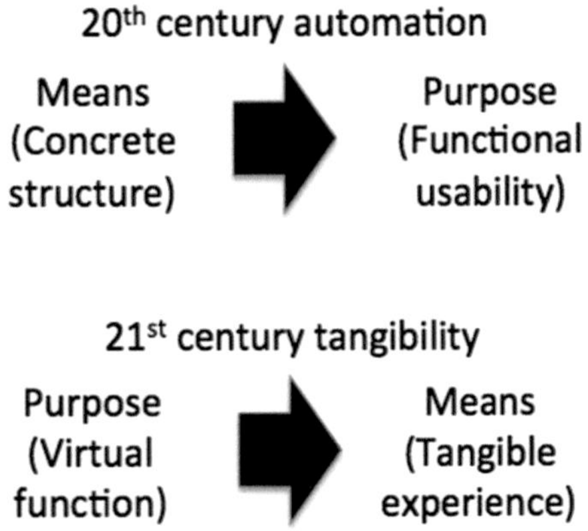

Fig. 1.3 Paradigm shift: from "means-to-purpose" to "purpose-to-means"

20ᵗʰ century automation

Means
(Concrete
structure)

Purpose
(Functional
usability)

21ˢᵗ century tangibility

Purpose
(Virtual
function)

Means
(Tangible
experience)

More recently, mobile devices were developed. New cognitive functions emerged to satisfy the need of always being connected. Several categories of information transfer were developed such as texting, emailing, and speaking directly. Smartphones are excellent TIS examples, which are integrated systems providing such capabilities.

One of my graduate students proposed that HCD should be called Human-Centered Engineering. She said: "When I tell people my field of study, I get very similar reactions – what they hear is 'design' and assume it is like 'Interior Design' for example. This becomes most evident especially when a person is pseudo-listening, which many people do – you pick out the words you know or remember the last word spoken… It seems I have to explain *what* my field is before I can even explain what I am even doing in the field itself." My reaction was to say that this debate is indeed purposeful and, yes, we need to explain what HCD is about.

The distinction between HCD and Technology-Centered Engineering (TCE) should be put forward. HCD goes **from purpose to means** (i.e., the architect view), instead of traditional engineering that mostly goes from means to purpose (i.e., the builder/mason view). This shift from twentieth-century automation issues that attempted to provide functional usability to concrete structures to twenty-first-century tangibility that requires looking for tangible experience of human-centered designed virtual functions, as illustrated in Fig. 1.3.

The Authority Issue: Being in Charge and Accountable

TISs have cognitive functions that now can be identified early on during the design process. These cognitive functions can be either deliberately chosen to satisfy the purpose of the system being designed or discovered as emergent properties of the system being used. All these cognitive functions can also be characterized in terms of **control, responsibility, and accountability**. TISs can provide tremendous power to their users. Spreadsheets, for example, are TISs that provide an enormous amount of power to finance specialists. When spreadsheets and connectivity became available and stable, top managers suddenly were able to financially control their various enterprises safely, efficiently, and comfortably, like pilots control their airplanes in their cockpits. Consequently, top managers and stakeholders learned how to master these technologies to control companies and institutions by using a single independent variable, which is money! They enabled reinforcement and stabilization of finance-driven management. However, there are other independent variables that have to be considered if we want to develop and maintain a human-centered philosophy in socio-technical systems. For example, these independent variables can be well-being, health, liberty, and pursuit of happiness.

> **Designing and using tangible interactive systems involves control, responsibility, and accountability.**

For example, Volkswagen is the most profitable automobile manufacturer in the world, which maintained a solid reputation of reliability until the International Council for Clean Transportation (ICCT), a non-governmental organization specialized in clean transportation, decided to test gas emissions of some diesel cars in the United States. ICCT requested the support of the Center for Alternative Fuels Engines and Emissions of West Virginia University to perform the tests. *The Economist* (September 26, 2015) reports that "emissions of nitrogen oxides (NOx) and other nasties from cars' and lorries' exhausts cause large numbers of early deaths — perhaps 58,000 a year in America alone, one study suggests. So the scandal that has engulfed Volkswagen (VW) this week is no minor misdemeanor or victimless crime… The German carmaker has admitted that it installed software on 11 million of its diesel cars worldwide, which allowed them to pass America's stringent NOx-emissions tests. But once the cars were out of the laboratory the software deactivated their emission controls, and they began to spew out fumes at up to 40 times the permitted level." This kind of practice is of course illegal, but more fundamentally VW main motivation, purpose, and goal were financial and not human centered.

In the Orchestra framework sense (Boy 2013), current socio-technical world's music theory is centered on the single money dimension. This is why we see many catastrophes, in the **complexity** science sense (i.e., in René Thom's catastrophe theory sense — Thom 1976). Indeed, complexity science tells us that when we project a multidimensional space onto a space of lower dimensions, a fortiori one dimension, we should expect **catastrophes**. For example, we have projected our multidimensional world (e.g., that includes human rights variables such as life, liberty, and pursuit of happiness) onto a single dimension world of finance (i.e., money being the single variable). HCD, as a philosophy and a set of methods and tools trying to harmonize technology, organizations, and people, has the mission to bring back all these variables that make our **humanity**[6] more livable, sustainable, and richer in the human sense. Therefore, in addition to being visionary, human-centered designers need to be responsible. Indeed, HCD is about design and use. Therefore, human-centered designers should investigate the various kinds of use of, and possible futures induced by, systems that they design.

Creativity and Emergence Rationalization

HCD is about **creativity**, in the sense of **synthesis** and **integration**. HCD is prior to engineering and should lead engineering. The main reason HCD is possible today, and not before, is because we have modeling and simulation tools that enable it to be done. We can work with product's actors (e.g., designers, end users, maintainers, trainers, and so on) because we can work on very realistic models and simulations from the start and carry out effective participatory design. In other words, modern computing means are crucial.

Software and computer networks have created new types of **complexity** in our everyday life. The best example is the Internet. However, connectivity will quickly expand far beyond the Internet, as we know it today. For example, the rapid growth of aircraft density in some zones of airspace requires special attention (i.e., 4.5 % growth per year average for the last 30 years). Current investigations show that we should anticipate a regulated growth instead of a global growth as we typically thought during the last decade (Challenge of Growth, 2013[7]). This means there could be a decrease of growth rate, and EUROCONTROL Statistical Reference Area (ESRA) already calculated a 1.8 % average annual growth during the period 2012–2035. In any case, some big airports are already saturated and require an integrated approach to solving the problem of delays. For example, the concept of New York Integrated Control Complex (NYICC) was proposed for improving the efficiency of operations by "integrating terminal and en-route airspace to expand the use of 3-mile separation procedures and improve communication and coordination" (FAA 2007). This kind of process integration involves creativity and complexity analysis. The combined problem of density, capacity, and safety requires search for solutions on the ground and onboard airplanes. There are basically three solutions to this problem. First, we could build more airports. Economy and ecology currently tend to dictate not to do this. Second, we can build bigger commercial aircraft. Airbus took the lead and built the A380, capable of transporting up to 800 passengers. The small number of these aircraft is far from solving the problem yet. Third, we could automate the sky! This means that instead of keeping implicit connectivity among aircraft, we could make it explicit (i.e., making each aircraft aware of the

---

[6] Humanity should be understood in the sense of human condition, that is human existence in harmony with nature and our growing sociotechnical world.

[7] http://www.eurocontrol.int/sites/default/files/article/content/documents/official-documents/reports/201306-challenges-of-growth-2013-task-4.pdf

traffic around it and developing capabilities that keep the overall airspace safe). This third solution is currently studied within programs such as NextGen[8] in the United States and SESAR[9] in Europe. When we analyze this new problem, it turns out that the current centralized air traffic control system is very limited for the management of high-density traffic. Therefore, a decentralized solution should be found. This means that aircraft flows should be considered as flocks of birds where each bird is aware of the presence of the other birds around it and act accordingly. Consequently, each aircraft should be equipped with specific cognitive functions that automatically detect other aircraft around it, infer appropriate actions, and act appropriately. There are new types of **multi-agent** complex systems. Understanding of the complexity of **Human-Systems Integration** (HSI) in such highly dynamic multi-agent environment can be supported by use of the cognitive function representation that enables better understanding of **emergent behaviors and properties**. An example of cognitive function orchestration will be provided in this book when the association of HCD and systems engineering are described in Chap. 3.

> **Creativity is about synthesis and integration.**
>
> **Designing a new TIS is about understanding the complexity of induced human-systems integration through the discovery of emergent behaviors and properties using HITLS.**

Software prototypes can be developed very early during the design process. Consequently, usefulness and usability tests are possible during the design process also (as opposed to traditional human factor studies when products are fully developed). This is a radical shift. These prototypes enable us to co-adapt technology to people and organizations, at least functionally speaking. More specifically, **human-in-the-loop simulations** (HITLS) are now possible using very realistic simulated environments, which enable observation of people using systems being designed, and eventually discovery of emerging patterns and properties (Fig. 1.4).

More specifically, the use of CFA combined with HITLS enables us to discover emergent cognitive functions. During the early 1980s, the main issue was the difficult adaptation of people to information technology and its integration in various domains (e.g., pilots adaptation to new generation of fly-by-wire aircraft). I remember old pilots trying to adapt to the use of Cathode Ray Tubes (CRT) displays and later to the Flight Management System (FMS). Today, technology has evolved to present different challenges to the end user. People know more about information technology (IT) in their everyday life, and the main issue is adaption in our real physical world using IT. Young people do not generally seem to have difficulty living in the virtual world provided by Internet, social networks, smart phones, and

---

[8] Next Generation Air Transportation System.
[9] Single European Sky Air Traffic Management Research.

Fig. 1.4 Human-in-the-loop simulation in HCDi (Human-Centered Design Institute, School of Human-Centered Design, Innovation and Art, Florida Institute of Technology.) cockpit research lab

tablets. However, they may have issues with relating this virtual world with the physical world. This is why we need to find out more about the tangibility of software interactive systems that are currently developed. This tangibility knowledge could be effectively used at design time, ideally in the form of supporting models and assessment metrics.

Orchestrating Tangible Interactive Systems

Moving further, what we commonly call today a software application, or **App**, is typically developed as a piece of software designed to satisfy a specific purpose. An App is commonly integrated with a hosting platform (e.g., servers on Internet). Anybody can easily download an App on his or her tablet or smartphone. It typically supports either very simple or very sophisticated functions. An App can become life critical when it is physically integrated in our everyday life (e.g., a GPS-based navigation App on a smartphone used in a car). It becomes tangible (i.e., a TIS) when it fulfills a real tangible need, as well as is understood and used as such. Apps range from newspaper applications where you can read updated information on what is going on in the world to your favorite airline application where you can consult the status of and departure time of your next flight. These Apps can be considered as **software agents** (Bradshaw 1997). Today, they can be, and some of them are, interconnected. Video chat Apps (e.g., Skype, Google + and VSee) can be interconnected with other applications. They enable you to orally and visually communicate with other people.

It follows that we need appropriate organizational models that enable us to handle new endeavors of the information-intensive planetary metamorphosis of our various societies and cultures. I already introduced the **Orchestra** framework that supports multi-agent organization analysis, modeling, and simulation (Boy 2013). In this book, I will further develop this model and provide examples of its operationalization. In particular, the cognitive function paradigm introduced in the CFA book (Boy 1998b) will be extended to multi-agent interaction using the Orchestra framework to analyze, model, and simulate organizations of both humans and software-based systems. This framework is clearly intended to support organization design and management (ODM). Indeed, HCD cannot be seriously implemented without an appropriate HCD-based organization, which has in mind a target organization that will receive and operationalize the technology being designed.

> **The Orchestra model provides a usable framework for human-systems integration. It requires definition of a common frame of reference (music theory), human-centered designers, and systems architects (composers) providing coordinated requirements (scores), highly competent socio-technical managers (conductors) and performers (musicians), and well-identified end users and involved stakeholders (audience).**

In fact, we need to constantly keep in mind the **TOP model**, where **Technology** should be designed together with changing **Organizations** and **People**'s jobs at the same time (Fig. 1.5). The TOP model also has to be used with **culture** in mind. Culture is to people what water is to fish! We need to understand it in order to innovate correctly. This will be discussed using the cognitive function representation in Chap. 3.

What we have in front of us is the same as organizing ourselves to go and explore another planet. We need to learn how to deal with an unprecedented socio-technical development that breaks "the continuity of the relationship between people, artifacts,

Fig. 1.5 The TOP Model

which they build, their environment and societies" (Boy and Doule 2014). Charles Darwin explained a great deal of human kind evolution (Darwin, 1859). Today, we are experiencing a new type of evolution that involves human-systems integration (Boy and Narkevicius 2013). Human adaptation is crucial and needs to be better understood in this new type of environment. What does habitability mean in a highly technological environment? Human-centered design of such technology takes a different flavor from traditional ergonomics principles and requirements. We need to better understand what the underlying socio-technical economy is and should be, when we observe our constantly **increasing global demography, degraded ecology, and chaotic economy**. How can we model and further explain these integrated mechanisms that inter-relate technology, organizations, and people. We need to better understand human limitations and capabilities in both natural and artificial worlds, in order to develop **sustainable** human-systems integration. Sustainability is a matter of strong high-level requirements. This is why HCD plays a crucial role in the definition of these requirements. Modeling and simulation, in particular, provide major tools for their development.

A great amount of research and innovation is already available in the field of tangible user interfaces, but I would like to **break with the concept of user interface**, which is a notion of the twentieth century when engineers and HFE research scientists were focusing on adapting people to machines—even if they said that they were doing the opposite! This book provides an introduction to the TIS concept, coming from the development of our immersive information technology and society. Today, virtual objects are familiar for young people who were born with computer games in their hands. They manipulate software-based devices "naturally." Actually, many adults are included in this group of natural handlers too! Many questions have to be answered, such as: How can we make these virtual objects more tangible? How can we use this actual "virtuality" to grasp abstract concepts and transform them into tangible interactive systems? How can we teach or learn mathematics by using tangible things? I believe that TISs are new solutions for improving our understanding of the physical world and abstract concepts that help us understand it, like books were solutions in the past. TISs can augment our mental and physical capabilities to explore worlds that were barely accessible before.

> **Human-centered designers should take into account appropriate dimensions that shape the complexity of the TOP model (technology, organizations and people) they are making concrete by designing new tangible interactive systems.**

Current Socio-Technical Evolution

Tangible interactive systems are growing everywhere, and depending on the community where they are designed, developed and manufactured, they may take different kinds of names and their underlying concepts could be slightly different. This being said, this book emphasizes the crucial revolution introduced by TISs in design and other parts of our lives. Two communities are adjacent to TIS's development: Internet of Things and Cyber Physical Systems.

Kevin Ashton, an English entrepreneur, coined the term, **Internet of Things**, which captures the concept of integration between computer-based systems and the physical world (Guardian 1999). Think about using your smartphone! You are connected to other people who have the same kind of device via a computer network. Your smartphone can be considered a smart interconnected "thing." It belongs to the Internet of Things (IoT). Chapter 9 will present the difficult aspect of sustainability, and we will see how a good mix of software and hardware is crucial to develop sustainable TISs. For example, the development of sustainable energy (e.g., wind, solar and tidal based technologies) does not only require taking into account very advanced knowledge and know-how on how to build and operate these technologies in isolation; it requires taking into account their specificities in the framework of people's needs. More specifically, wind may not be available for some periods of time, as solar or tidal could be. Therefore, a combination of the three sources then becomes a smarter solution. This combination associated with people needs necessarily leads to the concept of a "smart grid," which could be extended to almost any kind of socio-technical problems with today's technology.

> **Two TIS perspectives: Internet of Things that attempts to provide physical structures to software things, and Cyber Physical Systems that attempts to provide embedded functions into physical things.**

In the Internet of Things, things can be represented by concrete systems that have sensors and effectors and are capable of information processing (e.g., wireless washing machine, smart houses, and smart cities where transportation means are highly interconnected to improve urban life). The Internet of Things cannot be contemplated without both local and global considerations. Locally, people need to be able to handle things that they are using. This is related to usability, usefulness, and other individual human factors. Globally, the societal complex system resulting from the integration of these smart interconnected things should be flexible, mature, stable, and self-sustainable. In this book, we will review these properties and show the importance and usefulness of the TIS concept in the Internet of Things.

> **Virtual versus tangible: orchestrating the duality.**

TISs can also be considered as embedded systems (Wolf 2014) and therefore include some kind of automation. Embedded systems typically satisfy control purposes and are part of a generic class called **Cyber Physical Systems** (CPSs). CPSs constitute a National Science Foundation (NSF) key area of research. CPSs are engineered systems that are built from, and depend upon, the seamless integration of computational algorithms and physical components (Lee 2008). Embedded systems were designed as standalone systems. In this book, I will consider CPSs as systems of systems. The concept of CPS is not new. Most avionics systems in aircraft can be qualified as CPSs. We can find the same kinds of systems in chemical and energy process industries, medicine, automotive, road infrastructure, robotics, and entertainment, for example.

In manufacturing, the concept of "digital twins" was introduced and further developed to emphasize the importance of digital modeling and simulation (Grieves 2014). Grieves advocated "the concept of a 'Digital Twin' as a virtual representation of what has been produced. Compare a Digital Twin to its engineering design to better understand what was produced versus what was designed, tightening the loop between design and execution." This book takes the Digital Twin concept a step further, extending it to incremental human-in-the-loop test support.

For a long time, prior to putting together the first operational (i.e., flyable) aircraft prototype, the "iron bird" was developed and tested. An iron bird is a set of interconnected pieces of an aircraft distributed in a large hangar and interconnected. Some parts are the exact physical replicates of the parts on the aircraft itself. The reason these parts are distributed on the floor of the hangar is to better observe their behavior at pre-operations time. These physical and electronics parts are all related to a flight deck, where professional pilots can fly the iron bird. Therefore, the iron bird is a very interesting CPS for pre-flight tests, as well as a great verification tool for in-detail testing of things that may not go as required during the real flight tests. Today, the concept of iron bird can be extended to Internet-related connection to weather information sources, which enable more realistic pre-tests or verification tests.

Both the Internet of Things and Cyber Physical Systems provide concrete approaches and tools for the development of TISs. The former starts for computer science and information technology premises. The latter starts from physical engineering and automation premises. It is interesting to follow the evolution of TISs from both perspectives, and they will cross-fertilize each other.

Finally, What Is the Purpose of This Book?

The central concept of tangible interactive system is proposed as the atomic architectural element and can be extended to TISs of TISs. Main TIS properties will be provided. We will also focus on the following questions:

- What happens when a new TIS is integrated into or with an existing TIS?

- What are the behaviors, phenomena, and properties that emerge from this integration?
- What are the repercussions in the design of the new TIS itself?
- How should we evaluate the resulting integration?

These questions should be answered within the twenty-first-century context where designers use virtual tools to make ideas concrete. Virtual design and engineering, supported by modeling and simulation (M&S), enable human-in-the-loop simulations, which therefore involve potential users of technologies being designed and developed. These means enable human-centered design to be possible from the beginning of the design process. The question is: how can we make sure that virtual concepts, designed and tested that way, are tangible? It has become clear that 3D printing is a real solution for us to test tangibility.

Organization of the Book

Chapter 2 describes the emergence of the **tangibility** concept and the shift from twentieth-century automation issues brought by technology-centered engineering to twenty-first-century TISs issues induced by digital HCD supported by powerful M&S capabilities. Tangibility will be considered as physical and figurative. A distinction will be made between inside-out tangibility based on automation and outside-in tangibility based on TISs.

Chapter 3 presents a few **concepts and tools for designers**, including the SFAC model (Structure/Function versus Abstract/Concrete) that support collaborative work in an HCD team. Any TIS has a structure and a function, which can be decomposed into intertwined sub-structures and sub-functions. Each structure and function can be described in an abstract way and a concrete way. The design team then collaboratively generates four types of things: declarative knowledge (i.e., abstract structures), procedural knowledge (i.e., abstract functions), static objects (i.e., concrete structures), and dynamic processes (i.e., concrete functions). The "multiple V model" (MVM) is introduced as an agile framework for HCD and TIS production toward human-systems integration.

Chapter 4 links HCD to **innovation**, as well as **empathy** to help stating correctly human-centered problems/challenges and **creativity** as integration of TISs in our society. Innovation is described as use of current knowledge and technology to foster creativity, considered as synthesis and integration. This chapter will be illustrated using the example of the city of the future.

Chapter 5 introduces the **complexity** factor created by current interconnectivity and TISs integrated in our constantly evolving society. We will see how to handle the concept of emergence in TIS design and interpret the concept of affordances. More generally, human-centered designers need to more deeply understand the TIS revolution and, more specifically, the incremental integration of TISs into our socio-technical environments.

Chapter 6 discusses the need for **flexibility** in both design and development of TISs and their subsequent use and evolutionary redesign. Anytime an artifact is developed, it introduces some kind of rigidity because it fixes some life activities that were previously handled by people only. The same artifact also creates new possibilities that are discovered incrementally and therefore eventually provide flexibility.

Chapter 7 discusses and details the importance of **maturity** of TISs and more generally all kinds of currently designed products. Any product or technology has a birth, a life, and a death. The first issue in this life cycle is for us to bring the product to maturity. We will become familiar with the concepts of technology maturity, maturity of practice, and organizational maturity.

Chapter 8 describes the concept of **stability** of TISs. Anytime a TIS is in use, it may fail and therefore could cause instability around it. We will discuss the distinction between passive and active stability of TISs. The question of resilience is crucial and will be discussed.

Chapter 9 brings the longer-term problem of **sustainability** of TISs, supported by the "TOP model for sustainability." Lots of gadgets are being developed today. They come and go! We have installed a disposable socio-technical society where objects are created and thrown away when they do not work. Technology is produced around three main domains: communication, energy, and transportation. All of them have very similar multi-agent interconnectivity properties (e.g., communication has the Internet, energy will soon have the grid, and transportation tries to design new intermodal systems).

Chapter 10 is devoted to **art**. It proposes a reconciliation of art, science, and engineering toward design creativity. TIS design not only involves cognitive and social issues, but also emotions and aesthetics. We will see how the art of defining "purpose" can guide the entire design process.

The conclusion of the book is devoted to the promotion of TISs that support and are generated by HCD as a grounding and leading discipline based on modeling and simulation, advanced interaction media, complexity analysis, life-critical systems, organization design and management, creativity and design thinking, industrial design and engineering, user experience and, of course, cognitive engineering (Boy 2013).

There are several repetitions in the book that are left intentionally because each chapter can be used independently of the others (even if they are sometimes cross-referenced).

Thanks for reading this book!

References

Bainbridge L (1983) Ironies of automation. Automatica 19(6):775–779. International Federation of Automatic Control, Pergamon Press

Billings CE (1991) Human-centered aircraft automation: a concept and guidelines, NASA technical memorandum 103885. NASA-Ames Research Center, Moffett Field

Bourdieu P (1980) The logic of practice. Stanford University Press, Stanford

Boy GA (1998a) Cognitive function analysis. Greenwood/Ablex, Stamford. ISBN 1567503764

Boy GA (1998b) Cognitive function analysis for human-centered automation of safety-critical systems. In: Proceedings of CHI'98, the ACM conference on human factors in computing systems, Los Angeles. Published by ACM Press, New York. ISBN:0-201-30987-4

Boy GA (2013) Orchestrating human-centered design. Springer, London. ISBN 978-1-4471-4338-3

Boy GA (2014) From automation to tangible interactive objects. Ann Rev Control.:1–11. doi:10.1016/j.arcontrol.2014.03.001, Elsevier

Boy GA, Doule O (2014) How can space contribute to a possible socio-technical future on Earth? Le Travail Humain Journal. Presses Universitaires de France, Paris

Boy GA, Narkevicius J (2013) Unifying human centered design and systems engineering for human systems integration. In Aiguier M, Boulanger F, Krob D, Marchal C (eds) Complex systems design and management. Springer, London, 2014. ISBN-13: 978-3-319-02811-8

Bradshaw JM (1997) Software agents. MIT Press, Cambridge

Darwin C (1859) On the origin of species by means of natural selection, or the preservation of favored races in the struggle for life. See more at http://www.darwins-theory-of-evolution.com/#sthash.SBaOIh7k.dpuf and http://www.literature.org/authors/darwin-charles/the-origin-of-species/preface.html

Dourish P (2004) Where the action is: the foundations of embodied interaction. MIT Press, Cambridge. ISBN 9780262541787

Grieves M (2014) Digital twin: manufacturing excellence through virtual factory replication. White paper. Michael W. Grieves, LLC. Retrieved on August 30, 2015. http://innovate.fit.edu/plm/documents/doc_mgr/912/1411.0_Digital_Twin_White_Paper_Dr_Grieves.pdf

FAA (2007) Integrated arrival/departure control service (big airspace) concept validation. Federal Aviation Administration – Air Traffic Organization Operations Planning, Research & Technology Development Office, Air Traffic System Concept Development, AJP-66. Technical report. http://tg.hfes.org/astg/Big%20Airspace%20Final%20Report_FINAL_Sept%2007.pdf

Guardian (1999) The internet of things is revolutionising our lives, but standards are a must. Retrieved on July 5, 2015. http://www.theguardian.com/media-network/2015/mar/31/the-internet-of-things-is-revolutionising-our-lives-but-standards-are-a-must

Ishii H, Ullmer B (1997) Tangible bits: towards seamless interfaces between people, bits and atoms. In: Proceedings of the ACM SIGCHI conference on human factors in computing systems (CHI'97), pp 234-241. ACM Digital Library

Kubicki S, Lebrun Y, Lepreux S, Adam E, Kolski C, Mandiau R (2013) Simulation in contexts involving an interactive table and tangible objects. Int J Simul Model Pract Theory 31:116–131, Elsevier

Lebrun Y, Adam E, Mandiau R, Kolski C (2015) A model for managing interactions between tangible and virtual agents on an RFID interactive tabletop: case study in traffic simulation. Journal of Computer and System Sciences 81:585–598

Lee EA (2008) Cyber physical systems: design challenges. Retrieved on May 10, 2015. http://www.eecs.berkeley.edu/Pubs/TechRpts/2008/EECS-2008-8.html

Paris I Seminar (1981) Operative Image (in French). Actes d'un séminaire (1-5 juin) et recueil d'articles de D. Ochanine. Université de Paris I (Panthéon-Sorbonne), Centre d'éducation Permanente, Département d'Ergonomie et d'Ecologie Humaine

Sarter N, Woods DD, Billings CE (1997) Automation surprises. In: Salvendy G (ed) Handbook of human factors and ergonomics, 2nd edn. Wiley, New York, pp 1926–1943

Thom R (1976) Structural stability, catastrophe theory, and applied mathematics: the John von Neumann lecture. SIAM Review 19(2):189–201 (Apr., 1977)

Ullmer B, Ishii H (2001) Emerging frameworks for tangible user interfaces. In: Carroll JM (ed) Human-computer interaction in the new millenium. Addison-Wesley, New York, pp 579–601

Wolf M (2014) High-performance embedded computing, second edition: applications in cyber-physical systems and mobile computing. Morgan Kaufmann, 2nd edn. ISBN-13: 978-0124105119

Chapter 2
Looking for Tangibility

Today, drones (i.e., autonomous or remotely piloted flying machines) are being built and start to be used. Military operations using drones are now becoming better established. However, drones are still under-regulated in the civilian world. Main questions are about safety and security. Therefore, drone operations have to be seriously considered by commercial and general aviation regulatory institutions, such as ICAO[1] at the international level, FAA[2] in the USA, and DGAC[3] in France. More generally, this kind of issue always comes into play when new life-critical technology is integrated in our everyday life. In other words, this new technology has to be tangible for use (i.e., we need to demonstrate that use of technology makes sense from various relevant points of view).

Something is tangible when it is **graspable** in the **physical** sense, but also **believable** in the **figurative** sense (e.g., an idea or a concept that cannot be grasped by the mind). In the case of drones, they will become operationally tangible when they will be safely, efficiently, and comfortably usable and useful for tasks, such as package delivery, image capture for news purposes (e.g., television), and disaster management support. In addition, new technology brings new properties that need to be explored. For example, drones become birds that can see what people cannot see. They create new supports to situation awareness and other functions that were impossible before. In addition to regulatory framework (the safety issue), important concerns that need to be taken into account are privacy (the ethical issue), unfair competition (the economic development penalization issue), and the toy effect (the use-for-fun issue). Technology design has shifted from mechanical engineering to information technology. For example, mechanical and aerospace engineers created and developed aircraft the way they are today; information technology specialists, who do not have professional aviation training, already started to be the designers and developers of a new generation of drones (e.g., for 3D movie making). Some of

---

[1] International Civil Aviation Organization.

[2] Federal Aviation Administration.

[3] Direction Générale de l'Aviation Civile.

© Springer International Publishing Switzerland 2016

G.A. Boy, *Tangible Interactive Systems*, Human–Computer Interaction Series,

DOI 10.1007/978-3-319-30270-6_2

the drones are 3D printed! As already stated before, making tangible software-based things becomes the prominent issue over the previous automation issue brought by the twentieth century engineering practice. Therefore, new certification rules need to be developed.

> **Tangibility can be physical and/or figurative**.
>
> **Systems become tangible when they can be used safely, efficiently, and comfortably**.

(HITLSs) and, ultimately, human-centered design (HCD). On a broader perspective, combined with systems engineering (SE), HCD is currently maturing as useful and effective support for human-systems integration (HSI) (Boy and Narkevicius 2013). More specifically, TIS design and development highly contribute to HSI and conversely!

A Short History of Automation

This section addresses the mutual influence of engineering sciences and life sciences, more specifically regarding the difficult question of understanding automation processes, as well as control, regulation, and autonomy concepts.

In the end of the eighteenth century, James Watt, a Scottish mechanical engineer, invented the steam engine and, most importantly for the sake of the content of this book, a centrifugal flyball governor, which proportionally controls engine speed by regulating the amount of fuel admitted into an engine. Watt offered the world one of the first automatons based on mechanical engineering theory and practice. Mechanical engineering started to really develop during the nineteenth century, with the development of steam machines and trains in particular. It was essentially technology centered until the end of the twentieth century. However, machines that were produced needed to be controlled. Consequently, control mechanisms and theories were developed.

In the end of the nineteenth century, Claude Bernard, a French physiologist,

> **The automation concept constantly swapped from hard sciences to life and social sciences back and forth**.

coined the term *milieu intérieur* (i.e., internal environment), which Walter Cannon[4] named "homeostasis" later on. The regulating process insures consistency of the internal environment of the human body and preserves it from external aggressions.

---

[4]The term "homeostasis" was coined by Walter Cannon in 1930, referring to any process that living organisms use to actively maintain stable conditions necessary for survival (Cannon 1932).

It is considered as the main continuous compensating process, which maintains life of the whole body.

It is interesting to observe that, working totally independently, Watt and Bernard produced scientific results that led to a common theoretical and practical field currently called automatic control or automation. These two tracks (i.e., engineering sciences and life sciences) required more than one and a half century to reconcile and give a consistent theory of control.

In the first part of the twentieth century, Arturo Rosenblueth Stearns, a Mexican physician and physiologist and Cannon's student at Harvard University, continued to develop homeostasis and wrote papers together with Norbert Wiener, the father of cybernetics (Rosenblueth and Wiener 1945). They greatly contributed to explain the feedback control loop of regulated systems. They showed that combining life sciences and mathematics was a powerful mix. In this case, their joint enterprise led to the formalization of mathematical control theories and more specifically automatic control. This kind of models enabled later development in industry and research. Aircraft autopilots were rationalized using these theories.

More generally, human sciences and STEM[5] never stopped developing together. Until the 1980s, autopilots were developed using electric and electronics components. Then software started to become prominent, and a new kind of automation emerged. We were able to design and develop more complex algorithms. During the mid-1980s, the flight management system (FMS) was developed on top of autopilots to handle aircraft navigation automatically. The pilot's job shifted from control of flying quality parameters to management of avionics systems: a big step!

The era of mechanical/physiological control, even assisted by an autopilot, shifted to a new era of **cognitive management** of artificial agents.[6] Designing and developing these new software-intensive systems, we needed to rethink the classical validation and certification rules and invent new ones more appropriate for operational tests for these new information-based technologies. Cognitive psychology and cognitive anthropology became important reference disciplines for studying human-computer interaction, which led to cognitive engineering.

In the beginning of the 1980s, office automation started to penetrate our everyday lives. Text processors were developed and massively used to the point that jobs drastically changed. Until the end of the 1970s, we were using paper and pencil to write letters, documents, and reports. Some used typewriters. Most people did not

---

[5] Science, Technology, Engineering, and Mathematics.

[6] During the 1980s, computer science strongly developed and led to the extension of two new disciplines that are artificial intelligence (AI) and human-computer interaction (HCI). Creating the term "artificial intelligence" in 1955, John McCarthy and Marvin Minsky wanted to denote the science and engineering of making intelligent machines. An intelligent system, sometimes called an intelligent agent, should be able to perceive external signals, process them, and act on its environment with respect to three main principles that are safety, efficiency, and comfort. AI has the long-term vision of designing and developing intelligent robots capable of some degrees of autonomy. Human-computer interaction (HCI) was more short term, focusing on user interfaces and usability of systems. HCI led to deeper scientific developments of the concept of interaction design (we will see this later in this chapter).

think about typing their own text. There were people assigned for professional typing. A few years after, almost all of us typed, copied, and pasted our own texts and were reluctant to delegate this task to someone else. In addition to text processing, office automation led to the development of spreadsheets, computer-supported cooperative work, the Internet, and more recently sociomedia. People adopted these technologies because they became tangible (i.e., they are purposeful, usable, and useful in the society where we live).

From Control to Management

Basic automata exist for a long time. The clock is probably the oldest one. Air conditioning was used in ancient Egypt. Egyptians understood that the process of evaporation was producing negative enthalpy, and they exploited it by hanging moistened rugs in a location where there was enough air circulation to generate this evaporation process. More recently, mechanical and electromechanical refrigeration was invented. The thermostat[7] was developed as an **automatic control** system, which has a set point and an output. The output (e.g., the temperature of the room to be cooled) is sensed and compared to the set point (i.e., the temperature that you assigned on the thermostat), and the difference between the output and the set point minimized. This regulation principle is generic for all electrical regulators. Of course, there are various types of homeostatic processes that enable to minimize the difference between the output and the set point.

During the twentieth century, many automated machines were developed, starting by the washing machine, refrigerator, and automated transmission on cars. People have adapted to these kinds of automation now. In the beginning of the 1980s, a new type of automation started to be developed, supervisory control. Thomas Sheridan, Professor at MIT in the Department of Mechanical Engineering and Department of Aeronautics and Astronautics, coined the term of **supervisory control** to denote a process that involves several basic controllers whether they are humans or machines (Sheridan 1984). Supervisory control contributed to shift human work from manual control and basic automatic control to (automated) systems management. Human operators had to move from doing to thinking (i.e., **from control to management**).

---

[7]The term "thermostat" includes two concepts: the concept of "thermos" (i.e., θερμός, in Greek) and the concept of "statos" or stationary (i.e., στατός).

From Analog Signal Processing to Digital Computing

Up to the 1980s, electrical engineering and electronics governed automation. We were in the analog era. Signal processing strongly developed and was extensively used, leading to modern mechatronics today. A major revolution happened during the 1980s; digital computers, and more specifically microcomputers, became operational and massively used. Automation became digital. We entered into the software era. Programming languages evolved toward object-oriented programming, leading to both declarative and procedural programming. Design and development of systems progressively involved more cognitive skills. This is another reason of the emergence of cognitive engineering.

It became very easy to program software supporting the development of new automated systems, sometimes too easy! Software engineering had to keep up with the mandatory certification issues required for safety, efficiency, and comfort in life-critical systems (LCSs). Robust, resilient, and reliable software engineering methods are needed to handle the development of large software-based LCSs. Systems engineering developed such methods and keeps doing so. SCRUM, for example, is a very useful method that enables several design teams to reach a common goal by incorporating "the concepts of continuous improvement and minimum viable products to get immediate feedback from customers, rather than waiting until a project is finished" (Sutherland 2014). It is based on a holistic approach that belongs to the **agile** software development philosophy,[8] which is symbiotic to the HCD approach. It is based on the fact that requirements may change during the development process, and flexibility is required to incrementally modify both high-level and low-level developments. One of the basic assumptions is that the final product is defined incrementally. Agile design and development will be further presented in Chap. 6.

> The evolution from signal processing to digital computing induced the emergence of the shift from the control of a machine to the management of systems.

From User Interface Ergonomics to Interaction Design

For a long time, machines were developed **from inside out** (e.g., engine, chassis, and car body were developed before drivers could start using the integrated product). Users were taken into account after technology was developed. This

---

[8] The Manifesto for Agile Software Development (http://www.agilemanifesto.org) has been written to improve the development of software. It values more individuals and interactions over processes and tools, working software over comprehensive documentation, customer collaboration over contract negotiation, and responding to change (flexibility) over following a plan (rigidity).

philosophy led to the concept of user interface. Indeed, once a machine was developed, a user interface was necessary for the users to operate this machine. The more complex the machine was, the more complex the user interface had to be.

Consequently, human factors and ergonomics (HFE) specialists took the job of designing and developing user interfaces. However, user interfaces cannot compensate all design flaws regarding operational issues. More specifically, when a machine is not fully autonomous, some kinds of (more or less) specialized people have to control or manage it. This engineering/HFE approach is still active today. It requires adaptation: adaptation of the machine to people (i.e., developing a good user interface) and adaptation of people to the machine (i.e., training people). This philosophy is technology centered and necessarily requires iterative adaptation of both humans and user interfaces because machine core technology has already been developed and cannot be, or can be slightly, modified for heavy-financial investment reasons. This approach typically leads to conflicts between engineers and HFE specialists, mostly because there is no real mutual understanding and constructive discussion between them.

The user interface issue emerged from the fact that up to the end of the twentieth century, technology had to be developed from scratch almost all the time. Therefore, engineers had to develop their ideas, try solutions, and could not provide a product to potential test users sooner than after its full development. There was not much choice!

> **Technology-centered engineering is based on an inside-out approach that starts by developing technology and discover human factors and ergonomics issues when technology is developed.**
>
> **Human-centered design is based on an outside-in approach that starts by modeling and simulating technology in its environment together with involved stakeholders (formative evaluations) and incrementally continues by developing TISs.**

Today, the situation is very different. Information technology provides tools and methods, which enable design and development of software-based prototypes that can be tested in HITLS environment very early on during the design process. Current M&S capabilities change everything. In particular, design can be done **from outside in** (e.g., virtual engine, chassis, and car body can be integrated at design time, and the overall virtual integrated product prototype can be tested by real users). End users can be taken into account before technology is developed.

Digital prototypes enable "interaction design" (Bolter and Gromala 2008). Interaction design is often defined as a process that consists in shaping digital things for people's use.[9] Interaction design is deeply rooted in the human-computer interaction (HCI) community. However, it takes insights and techniques from architecture, industrial design, cognitive science, social sciences, and, of course, computer science.

---

[9] https://www.interaction-design.org/

From Interaction Design to Human-Systems Integration

The HCI community started to develop in the early 1980s with the emergence of personal computers and more specifically text processing and office automation (Card et al. 1983; Norman and Draper 1986; Winograd and Flores 1987). User interfaces became digital. HCI started during a period when artificial intelligence (AI) was at its apogee (i.e., AI was very strong, even if it was much too ambitious at that time). HCI was more short term than AI and became a discipline on its own right; HCI and AI were always distinct disciplines (Grudin 2006). This is unfortunate because one can bring to the other and conversely. HCI is centered on interaction design, and AI is centered on content automation, reasoning, and machine learning.

In addition, the HCI community developed itself around user-centered design of friendly computers, which took various tangible forms (e.g., laptops, tablets, and smartphones). The question of tangibility was reduced to the use of a computer targeted toward very well-formatted tasks (e.g., text processing, spreadsheet-based calculation, drawing, telephoning, texting, and so on). Ishii and his team at MIT coined the term "tangible bits" to denote graspable and manipulable everyday physical objects. "The goal of Tangible Bits is to bridge the gaps between both cyberspace and the physical environment, as well as the foreground and background of human activities" (Ishii and Ullmer 1997).

Using computers as user interfaces (i.e., using HCI) and internal control mechanisms (i.e., using AI and control theories) for larger industrial systems, such as aircraft, spacecraft, hospital operating rooms, and nuclear power plants, leads to different kinds of problems. Consequently, specialized communities were created and developed, such as the HCI-Aero community (human-computer interaction in aerospace). In the beginning, HCI-Aero conferences emphasized user interfaces, computer graphics for aircraft cockpits and air traffic control workstations, and other HCI issues and techniques. The shift from inside-out engineering to outside-in design induced a new shift from HCI to **human-systems integration** (HSI), which is the HCI-Aero 2016 conference topic.

The concept of "computer," in terms of software and hardware, is embedded in the concept of "system." System has to be thought within the framework of the TOP (technology, organizations, and people) model (Boy 2013). The concept of "integration" has become fundamental in design and encapsulates the concept of "interaction." The HCI community studied the latter and came up with the already mentioned crucial concept and process of "interaction design" (Rogers et al. 2011). The systems engineering community, the International Council on Systems Engineering (INCOSE) in particular, is currently developing the concept and process of HSI (Boy and Narkevicius 2013). This book emphasizes the shift from HCI to HSI and associated design, integration, and management of tangible interactive systems.

The challenge today is the integration of cyberspace and physical systems into socio-technical environments (Rajkumar et al. 2010). Several attempts are currently developed. They deserve to be compared and further homogenized. The

cyber-physical system (CPS) approach that focuses on embedded systems requires extending the emphasis on human-systems integration. Human-centered design of CPSs has become a contemporary problem that needs to be properly addressed and solved. Again, the main issue is **integration**. We have technology, lots of technology! For example, cost and size of sensors are going down every day as their capabilities are going up. Computing technology is cheaper, more powerful, and more effective in terms of capabilities and dimensions. We now live immersed in the cloud!

Progress is made on alternative energy production, even if this sector needs to be boosted. We now need to work on large-scale problems that our planet Earth poses to us. For example, since most people are still massively migrating to cities, what will be the city of the future? How can we integrate transportation systems? What will be the lower-energy house of the future? Again, this is a problem of integration of existing technology and integration of systems to be created and developed in the sense of the TOP model. Several concepts emerge and are required to be properly addressed such as innovation, complexity, flexibility, maturity, stability, and sustainability (Chaps. 4, 5, 6, 7, 8, and 9 of this book). CPSs attack control and management of life-critical systems (LCSs). Examples of LCS are integrated systems in cities, transportation, health care, crisis management, and alternative energy management and education. This is the reason why HCDi, and now the School of Human-Centered Design, Innovation and Art, were created and developed at Florida Institute of Technology.

The Philosophical Shift from Mechanical Engineering to Information Technology

During the whole twentieth century, mechanical engineering was the top engineering discipline until information technology took progressively the lead. Software incrementally invaded mechanical things at the end of the last century. For example, when I was studying at the university during the 1970s, I was able to repair the engine of my car without any major issues. Today, it is impossible without going to the garage where a garage operator will test the car engine with a diagnostic system, which will display how much the repair will cost! He or she will read the technical reason on his/her computer screen to tell you what it means, just in case you ask! Mechanical parts have been categorized and standardized. This achievement considerably increased structural integration.

However, human-systems integration (HSI) remains a problem. Why? We need to acknowledge the philosophical shift from mechanical engineering to information technology. Up to the end of the twentieth century, engineers put software into hardware. From the beginning of the twenty-first century, we are doing the opposite. We now design hardware using software (e.g., using CAD[10] systems and HITLS environments). Ultimately, we can 3D-print hardware from software (Fig. 2.1).

---

[10] Computer-aided design.

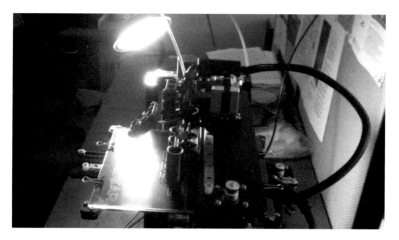

Fig. 2.1 A simple 3D printer that enables printing a CAD model

Consequently, this new information technology approach enables more holistic design and human-systems integration very early during the design process. However, resulting upstream tests rely on software prototypes that require tangibility. The notion of tangibility currently shifts from the previous inside-out philosophy to the outside-in philosophy. In the inside-out philosophy, the HSI burden was put on the end users. In the outside-in philosophy, the HSI burden is now put on the designers. In other words, designers need to understand the various cognitive functions involved in the use of the systems they are designing.

We will develop the cognitive function aspect in the next chapter. However, at this point, it is important to mention that some cognitive functions involved in the use of a system being designed can be deliberately defined by design, but there are other cognitive functions emerging from the use of the system that cannot be anticipated without human-in-the-loop simulations and sometimes real-world operations. Early discovery of emerging cognitive functions is another new possibility provided by information technology that supports HCD. This process of emerging cognitive function discovery is even more crucial in the design of large complex systems (e.g., design of a hospital). This is why complexity science has become crucial support in the design of such large systems.

Evolution, Revolution, and Constant Changes

The HFE tradition often dictates continuity of work practices. I remember the fear of automation when we delivered the first highly automated cockpits (Billings 1991); one of the arguments was the lack of continuity in work practices. This kind of automation was not an evolution; it was a revolution. Whenever work practice changes, it is however reasonable that people fear for their jobs. The main question is acceptability of new technology. We obviously can expect opposition, possible rejection, and, if accepted, possible surprises, when this technology is only technology centered. This is why HCD is necessary.

During the 1980s and 1990s, automation drawbacks emerged from several HFE studies, such as "ironies of automation" (Bainbridge 1983), "clumsy automation" (Wiener 1989), and "automation surprises" (Sarter et al. 1997). These studies did not consider the importance of maturity of technology, maturity of practice, and organizational maturity. These three concepts will be further developed in Chap. 7. Good design can be seen as a matter of function allocation. More specifically, functions cannot be correctly allocated among humans and machines without a thorough identification of **emerging cognitive functions**. In other words, we need to observe **user's activity** and not being limited to prescribed tasks. Only users facing new technology will be able to make emerge cognitive functions that were not anticipated by designers.

> **Automation surprises happen when a tangible interactive system is not mature enough and when people become too complacent to work with it**.

Sometimes socio-technical evolution transforms into a revolution. This was the case of the revolution of the fly-by-wire that led to what we call today "interactive cockpits." The accumulation of software-based systems in aircraft transformed pilots into aircraft system managers. Pilots' jobs now require them to know not only how to fly an airplane but also aircraft systems and how to manage them. It is clear that this is more than an evolution. In addition to knowing about mechanical systems of an airplane, pilots now need to know about systems controlling them (i.e., this requires more cognitive capacities in addition to flying skills).

This distinction between evolution and revolution has now to be considered as a dynamic process. Technology is changing faster than before. This is due to the extensive use of software both in the design of systems and in the systems themselves. Information technology increases connectivity at a very large scale, transforming socio-technical systems into biological-like systems. By analogy to Nobel Prize Jacques Monod's thesis in molecular biology, the constant changes that we experience today can be seen as **chance and necessity** (Monod 1970). Current information technology (IT) happened as a chance. It is also a necessity in many cases. For example, IT is both a chance and a necessity in air traffic management. Increasing connectivity among aircraft to handle high density and airport capacity progressively appears to be a necessity. However, in this case, IT also brings new problems such as cybersecurity. This is why the evolution of related socio-technical systems brings us into a new era, like *Homo sapiens* emerged as a distinct species of hominids.

Summarizing, for the last 60 years, HCD socio-technical evolution can be decomposed into three phases (Fig. 2.2):

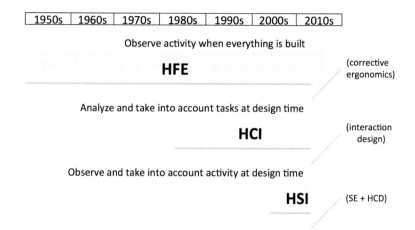

Fig. 2.2 Human-centered design evolution

- Human factors and ergonomics (HFE) that was developed after the World War II to correct engineering productions and had generated the concepts of human-machine interfaces or user interfaces.
- Human-computer interaction (HCI) that started to be developed during the 1980s to better understand and master interaction with computers; it contributed to shift from corrective ergonomics to interaction design.
- Human-systems integration (HSI) that emerged from the need of taking into account human factors in systems engineering (SE); SE and HCD combined incrementally lead to HSI.

In other words, the TOP (technology, organization, and people) model shifted from interface to interaction to integration. It also could be seen as a shift from engineering to information technology to systems, where systems include people and complex interactive artifacts. Finally, another interpretation is the shift from mechanical machines to computers to tangible interactive systems.

The Progressive Issue of Tangibility

Ray Kurzweil claims that information technologies grow exponentially, but our brain grows linearly (Kurzweil 2013). They double their power (i.e., price performance, capacity, and bandwidth) every year. Kurzweil advocates that our societies will evolve toward "super-intelligence, and with it, humans/machines expanding into the Universe.[11]" He predicts that by 2029, we will be able to reverse engineer our brain and make machines that will be far more powerful than our brains. He also

---

[11] http://bigthink.com/the-nantucket-project/ray-kurzweil-the-six-epochs-of-technology-evolution

predicts that we will stop aging and dying. If this kind of prediction is true, how will we regulate our planetary population growth? Knowing that we have gone from two billion people in the beginning of the twentieth century to more than seven billion now and possibly ten billion in 2060. A logical answer would be to say that we will be obliged to explore the universe and find other planets to live on. Why not?

Even if I currently observe this technology exponential growth (Emmott 2013), I also observe lots of troubles on and around our planet that need to be fixed, global warming, freshwater issues, diseases due to starving, and other serious problems due to the growth of our worldwide population and the distribution of wealth. Technology and its benefits for a small number of people are growing. These are facts! But how can we continue to develop this technology for the sake of everyone on planet Earth? Are there alternative ways of thinking? Information technologies provide crucial means to solve Earth problems, but they need to be used properly for the right purposes. Taking a HCD approach, I came to the point that the most important issue is tangibility (i.e., we need to be able to grasp these information technologies for dedicated specific purposes as well as integrate them together for bigger endeavors). Now let's figure out in more details what TISs are and could be.

Tangible Things Suddenly Emerge from Failing Virtual Things

I had an interesting experience planning to go to a country where I went several times. The procedure about getting a visa was very straightforward. I usually sent my passport to a broker company that took care of it. The delegation process always went perfectly in the past. They always did their job extremely well. This time, starting the procedure on their Web site, I suddenly discovered that they could not handle the visa process for French citizens any longer. In other words, I had to go to the consulate of the targeted country and do the paper work in person. I had to go through the whole process myself. In particular, I had to fly to the consulate and spend 2 days there. I realized that the process that was virtual to me before became very tangible in terms of time, money, travel, and concentration spent on details that were not familiar to me. This story shows that our society developed services that removed perception, understanding, and action on things that are very tangible if you had to do them by yourself. When these virtual services fail, we need to handle lower grain tangible things.

This is the same thing for any automated processes that fail. Human operators have to handle lower grain tangible things, in the physical sense. Consequently, it becomes crucial that everybody understands what tangible interactive systems are about. In the past, this visa company, which I was talking about, was a black box for me. I did not know people in this company. This company was therefore tangible for me, in the figurative sense, because it was able to satisfy my visa needs. Although I ignored the way it was working internally, I trusted it. This story made me realize that our consumer society tends to take for granted virtual services until they fail (i.e., in my visa story, the failure was an exception that forced me to analyze, understand, and execute the various elementary tasks involved). Indeed, when these services become unavailable, we need to handle directly things that were usually handled for us in the background. Indeed, I considered the visa company as a very useful TIS until this exception came out. More generally, a TIS should stay tangible (i.e., easy to understand and operate) when it fails.

Summarizing, during the twentieth century and before, we had to directly handle tangible physical objects, but now other people and systems are doing them for us in the background, except when they fail. Consequently, citizens of the twenty-first century will need to have deeper knowledge of what is going on in the background of services they are using or have services handling exceptions. In other words, education should take into account this requirement seriously. At this point, tangibility becomes a matter of acquaintance between people and systems.

From Inside-Out to Outside-In Tangibility

A distinction will be made between inside-out tangibility based on automation (i.e., the product of integrating software into hardware) and outside-in tangibility based on tangible interactive systems (i.e., the product of shaping hardware from and around software). As already mentioned, layers of automation were added to physical things as a solution for users' safety, efficiency, and comfort. The inside-out approach to engineering was initially based on technology development and human factor care after full development. We then ended up investigating tangibility of automation and figured out that well-done automation introduced considerably better usability in nominal situations, but rigidity in unexpected situations. Tangibility of automation in nominal situations corresponds to invisibility of automation (i.e., human operators forget that the system is automated and enjoy its use). Tangibility of automation in off-nominal situations is another story. It deals with new types of situation awareness, decision-making, and action taking. It requires that human operators know about how (automated) systems work, how to override them, and what they have done prior to shifting into the off-nominal situations. Human operators also need to know how to operate systems without automation (i.e., manual reversion). For example, pilots need to keep their flying skills on the most advanced highly automated aircraft. Therefore, inside-out tangibility of automated systems is context sensitive. An automated system will be said **inside-out tangible** when automation is invisible to its user in nominal situation and self-explanatory in off-nominal situations. Of course, complexity of an automated system will define the level of training of its users, especially in off-nominal situations.

> **Technology-centered engineering is means driven. It leads to automation and inside-out tangibility**.

The outside-in approach characterizes HCD. It promotes human-systems integration from the beginning of the design process by using M&S capabilities, creativity and design thinking, as well as incremental formative evaluations. Basic components of the outside-in approach to design and engineering are TISs. TISs should be tested individually as well as integrated in their environments. HCD includes scenario-based design (i.e., scenarios need to be defined and developed to support analysis, design, and evaluations) and evaluation/validation principles and criteria. Scenarios are typically both declarative scenarios (i.e., systems configurations) and procedural scenarios (i.e., scripts and chronologies of use cases). Two categories of scenarios can also be distinguished: nominal scenarios and off-nominal scenarios. HITLS are used to test systems being developed based on scenarios and evaluation criteria. HCD is an incremental process that progresses with TISs' maturity. Chapter 7 is devoted to maturity of TISs. Therefore, outside-in tangibility of human-centered systems is also **context sensitive**, but, unlike inside-out tangibility, context sensitivity is tested from the very beginning of the design process. A human-centered system will be said **outside-in tangible** when its TISs are well integrated both among them and with their users. Complexity of a human-centered system will be investigated during the design process, and along the life cycle of systems being developed and operated. In other words, M&S will be used to support both creativity (i.e., TIS synthesis and integration) and rationalization (i.e., comprehension and validation of human-systems integration). We can expect a progressive standardization of TISs.

> **Human-centered design is purpose driven. It leads to TISs and outside-in tangibility**.

Summarizing: What Can We Say on Tangibility at This Point?

Tangibility can be understood in the physical sense as well as in the figurative sense. In the physical sense, systems that we create and build should be graspable and well integrated in their physical environment. In the figurative sense, we often say, "I don't buy this idea; it is not tangible!" What does the term "tangible" means in the case of an idea? It means that you can or cannot grasp the concept behind the argument. It means that you can or cannot accept this idea using your own frame of reference.

Even if we developed great human-computer interaction capabilities based on cognitive engineering principles, cognitive factors are not the only human factors that need to be taken into account. Sensory-motoric factors are still there and require much attention. Our hands are effectors and also sensors. Gestures are incredible means for interaction. Considering our five senses, HCI mostly focused on central vision, providing computer screens where almost the whole underlying interaction is managed. Interaction devices, such as the mouse, enabled quick interaction with

Fig. 2.3 3D printed a handheld rocket pointing device

these screens. We are manipulating virtual objects on screens. The role of our hand (i.e., only one hand) has been standardized and reduced to specific horizontal movements and clicks. The use of TISs will bring different directions for interactivity. For example, we recently developed an interaction device that enable to quickly and purposefully display camera views around a rocket during the countdown period before a launch. We 3D printed a handheld mock-up of the rocket, equipped it with sensitive sensors, and tested it with a few cameras located around the actual rocket (Fig. 2.3). This TIS enables its user to point where he or she wants to see details on the rocket surface, and the system automatically provides the desired view from the closest camera. Experimentations showed that this is a very powerful and meaningful tangible interactive system.

Interaction with the physical environment using computers requires meaningful artifacts. For example, if we want to improve the quality of life in a large city such as Paris, transportation system integration is a real issue. How can we study such integration to better design new systems? First, we need to know about people's mobility in such a city. Is traveling more than 2 h in the morning tangible? The first answer that comes to mind is no! However, when you look carefully at what Parisians do, you immediately realize that they have adapted to the city system by necessity, either for money reasons or because they want to live in a specific area of the town and their work requirements bring them elsewhere. Information technology can propose new ways of working such as teleworking from home and working in the transportation system itself. This requires new technologies and most importantly infrastructures that are capable of handling mobility and work at the same time. On this very brief example, you can see that nothing is possible without creativity and an interdisciplinary approach.

Tangibility has also to be taken at the conceptual level. We communicate using advanced interaction media much more than a few years ago. For example, we use Skype, VSee, or Google Hangouts to communicate among friends but also at work.

In other words, we use virtual media to perform human-human interactions. For the last two decades, the computer-supported cooperative work (CSCW) community designed and developed technology to this end. Within this framework, what do we mean by tangible interaction? Sometimes it is difficult to perceive tangibility of ideas being discussed because we do not grasp clear physical attitudes of people remotely located. This is a physical (or physiological) tangibility issue. On the other hand, people can add text to oral interactions using chat capabilities. This increases credibility of what is being said, just because written arguments can be kept and further used (in the legal sense). This is a figurative tangibility issue.

Summarizing, tangibility is intimately related to physical sensing capabilities, personal desires, life management, infrastructure availability, human attitudes, and conceptual credibility. We often talk about tangible evidence. Let's provide a list of synonyms for tangible: current, authorized, assured, authentic, certain, concrete, consistent, demonstrated, effective, established, exact, existent, founded, unquestionable, undisputed, incontestable, indubitable, evident, concrete, objective, palpable, real, serious, solid, truthful, and true.

References

Bainbridge L (1983) Ironies of automation. Automatica 19(6):775–779. International Federation of Automatic Control, Pergamon Press

Billings CE (1991) Human-centered aircraft automation: a concept and guidelines, NASA technical memorandum 103885. NASA-Ames Research Center, Moffett Field

Bolter JD, Gromala D (2008) Windows and mirrors: interaction design, digital art, and the myth of transparency. MIT Press, Cambridge, MA. ISBN 0-262-02545-0

Boy GA (2013) Orchestrating human-centered design. Springer, London. ISBN 978-1-4471-4338-3

Boy GA, Narkevicius J (2013) Unifying human centered design and systems engineering for human systems integration. In: Aiguier M, Boulanger F, Krob D, Marchal C (eds) Complex systems design and management. Springer, UK. ISBN 978-3-319-02811-8

Cannon WB (1932) The wisdom of the body. Reprinted by W.W. Norton & Company, New York; Rev. and Enl. Ed edn (17 Apr 1963). ISBN-13: 978-0393002058

Card S, Moran TP, Newell A (1983) The psychology of human computer interaction. Lawrence Erlbaum Associates, Hillsdale. ISBN 0-89859-859-1

Emmott S (2013) Ten billion. Vintage Books, New York. ISBN: 978-0-345-80647-5

Grudin J (2006) Turing maturing: the separation of artificial intelligence and human–computer interaction. Interactions 13(5):54–57

Ishii I, Ullmer B (1997) Tangible bits: towards seamless interfaces between people, bits and atoms. Proceedings of CHI'97, 22–27 Mar. ACM Digital Library

Kurzweil R (2013) How to create a mind: the secret of human thought revealed. Penguin Books, New York. ISBN 978-0143124047

Monod J (1970) Chance and necessity: essay on the natural philosophy of modern biology (in French: Le Hasard et la Nécessité: Essai sur la Philosophie Naturelle de la Biologie Moderne). Seuil. ISBN-13: 978-2020028127

Norman DA, Draper SW (eds) (1986) User centered system design: new perspectives on human-computer interaction. Lawrence Erlbaum Associates, Pub, Hillsdale

Rajkumar R, Lee I, Sha L, Stankovic J (2010) Cyber-physical systems: the next computing revolution. Design Automation Conference 2010, Anaheim, California, USA. ACM Digital Library.

Rogers Y, Sharp H, Preece J (2011) Interaction design: beyond human – computer interaction, 3rd edn. Wiley, Chichester, U.K. ISBN-13: 978-0470665763

Rosenblueth A, Wiener N (1945) The role of models in science. Philos Sci 2(4):316–321

Sarter NB, Woods DD, Billings CE (1997) Automation surprises. In: Salvendy G (ed) Handbook of human factors & ergonomics, 2nd edn. Wiley, New York

Sheridan TB (1984) Supervisory control of remote manipulators, vehicles, and dynamic processes. In: Rouse WB (ed) Advances in man-machine research. JAI Press, New York, pp 49–137

Sutherland J (2014) Scrum: the art of doing twice the work in half the time. Crown Business, New York. ISBN-13: 978-0385346450

Wiener EL (1989) Human factors of advanced technology ("Glass Cockpit") transport aircraft. NASA Contractor Report 177528. NASA Ames Research Center, Moffett Field, CA

Winograd T, Flores F (1987) Understanding computers and cognition: a new foundation for design. Addison-Wesley Reading, MA, USA. ISBN-13: 978-0201112979

Chapter 3
Concepts and Tools for Designers

Human-centered design (HCD) should not only take into account end users but all the stakeholders dealing with the product being designed, including designers themselves. This is one of the reasons why I prefer to talk about human-centered design instead of user-centered design. This chapter is devoted to a few concepts, models, and tools for teams involved in human-systems integration.

Redefining Human-Systems Integration

Traditional systems engineering (SE) is technology centered. If we represent the traditional V model that consists in a left hand-side part for design and development and a right hand-side part for evaluation and validation, the V is not uniform. The V model looks more like a check mark (i.e., we spend less time and money in the beginning and waste a lot of money in the end because we did not care about purposes and people involved early enough; consequently, engineers need to compensate for requirement flaws). HCD adopts the opposite perspective (i.e., spending more time in the beginning to state well the problem to be solved). In practice, by spending a little more time and money stating problems well, we can gain lots of time and money in the end. This is why I propose to combine HCD and technology-centered engineering to make human-systems integration (Fig. 3.1).

Human-systems integration (HSI) was already defined in Chap. 2. Shifting from the traditional positivist approach of engineering (i.e., the materialistic builder approach) to a more phenomenological approach of design (i.e., the humanist architect approach), HSI architects can no longer restrict their investigations to using open-loop linear methods, exploring HSI complexity (Boy 2014).

The combination of HCD and SE leads to HSI (Boy and Narkevicius 2013). Design is iterative by nature. Therefore, several experience feedback loops (i.e., agile design and development that involves formative evaluations) are necessary to discover emergent properties. It is not by asking people what they want in the first

© Springer International Publishing Switzerland 2016
G.A. Boy, *Tangible Interactive Systems*, Human–Computer Interaction Series,
DOI 10.1007/978-3-319-30270-6_3

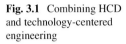

Fig. 3.1 Combining HCD and technology-centered engineering

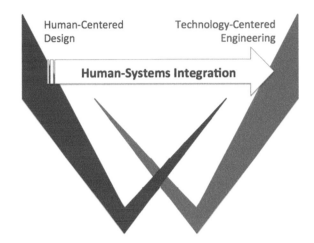

place that we define good high-level requirements for a product. It is by developing prototypes from the very beginning of the design process and testing them (using human-in-the-loop simulations) with potential users that we obtain good requirements. In other words, prescriptions are not sufficient; human-system interaction experience observation and analysis are necessary.

Conventional systems engineering starts with high-level technology-centered requirements, establishes a rigid work plan, and executes it. This approach leads to inside-out tangibility, always fixing the repercussions of design flaws, often too late. HCD goes the other way. It uses methods that provide **flexibility** and support creativity at all stages of a project. Human-centered requirements are incrementally generated from prototyping and formative evaluation. This means that we spend more time and money in the beginning of the project, but gain a lot in the end. In addition, human-centeredness should not be focused on potential end users only, but we also need to observe and find out how designers and developers work, not how they say they work. In other words, we need to be human centered (i.e., not only centered on the end users but on all involved stakeholders including the designers themselves). Knowing how designers and developers work enables to better manage their activity and, therefore, anticipate outside-out tangibility.

Design team members always look for flexibility, easy interaction among themselves, and constant verification that they are on the right track. They address complexity by becoming more familiar with it. In other words, they design and develop mock-ups that they immediately test with appropriate people in the loop. This is an effective way to design for flexibility and accountability. They also incrementally rationalize what they do. This is far from linear planning imposed by a priori rigid Gantt charts!

The Task-Activity Distinction

The V model is based on requirements that are set up (often too lightly from a human-centered point of view) from the beginning, serving as guides for technical specifications for manufacturing and criteria for verification when the product is fully developed. The paradox is that such a "clean" verification-based approach to industrial engineering often delivers products that are verified on the basis of wrong purposes (i.e., requirements). This approach is fundamentally based on the ignorance of the task-activity distinction. Requirements are task based, but they should be activity based. The only way to be able to take into account activity at design time is to develop prototypes and test them with human operators in the loop. This is not compatible with "open-loop" conventional V model approach, which takes into account prescribed tasks only. It requires a close-loop process, which takes into account effective tasks, also called activities.

Until now, most design approaches in human factors and ergonomics (HFE) only focused on the **task** (i.e., what we need or want to do using technology) because it was the only tangible "operational" approach available. In contrast, people using technology produce activity (i.e., what we effectively do using technology), which is the only meaningful thing that will really enable us to grasp usefulness and usability of technology being developed and used. A task is what is prescribed, not what is really performed (Fig. 3.2). We then need to develop means that enable us to observe and understand human **activity** produced in the execution of a task using the system being developed. Today, modeling and simulation (M&S) provide such means. The cognitive function paradigm (i.e., the transformation of a task into an activity) enables a contextual representation of interactivity (the functional part) among various agents (the structural part) of a socio-technical system being designed and developed. This is why I developed the cognitive function representation 20 years ago (Boy 1998a, b).

The problem is how can we observe activity (i.e., what people really do using the system) at design time? This is a HCD fundamental question. Good news is that M&S techniques and tools now enable designers to quickly develop digital proto-

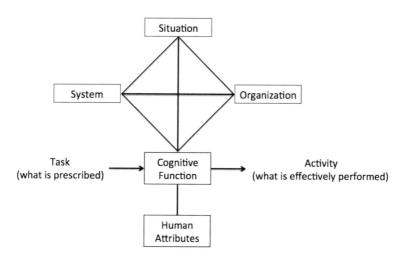

Fig. 3.2 A cognitive function as a transformation of a task into an activity, influenced by human attributes (e.g., fatigue, motivation, competence), the current situation (i.e., the state of the world around), the organization (i.e., the various actors involved in the execution of the task), and the system itself

types that can be almost immediately tested by appropriate users (i.e., perform human-in-the-loop simulations). HCD and M&S enable a design team to incorporate activity-based requirements into their design incrementally. This is often called **virtual engineering**. HCD drastically differs from the traditional HFE approaches because it enables us to take into account human activity at design time and not once a system is fully developed. The solution proposed in this book is the agile approach, which constantly redefines the requirements, and proceeds by steps. It provides more meaning, and proceeds from purpose to means, as HCD is promoting.

> **Human-in-the-loop simulation enables observation of activity resulting from task execution.**

The AUTOS Pyramid

The AUTOS pyramid is a framework that helps rationalize HCD and engineering. It was extensively described in the introduction of the *Handbook of Human-Machine Interaction* (Boy 2011).

The AUT triangle (Fig. 3.3) enables the explanation of three edges: task and activity analysis (U-T), information requirements and technological limitations (T-A), and ergonomics and training (procedures) (T-U).

Artifacts may be aircraft or consumer electronics systems, devices, and parts, for example. Users may be novices, experienced personnel, or experts, coming from and evolving in various cultures. They may be tired, stressed, making errors, old or young, as well as in very good shape and mood. Tasks vary from handling quality control, flight management, managing a passenger cabin, and repairing, designing, supplying, or managing a team or an organization. Each task involves one or several cognitive functions that related users must learn and use.

The organizational environment includes all team players, called "agents," whether humans or artificial systems, interacting with the user who performs the task using the artifact (Fig. 3.4). It introduces three additional edges: social issues (U-O), role and job analyses (T-O), and emergence and evolution (A-O).

The AUTOS framework (Fig. 3.5) is an extension of the AUTO tetrahedron that introduces a new dimension, the "situation," which was implicitly included in the "organizational environment." The four new edges are usability/usefulness (A-S), situation awareness (U-S), situated actions (T-S), and cooperation/coordination (O-S).

The AUTOS pyramid is useful support to human-centered designers in the analysis, design, and evaluation of human-systems integration, by taking into account human factors (i.e., user factors), systems factors (i.e., artifact factors), and interaction factors that combine task factors, organizational factors, and situational factors.

Fig. 3.3 The AUT triangle

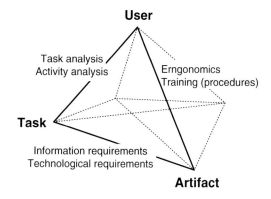

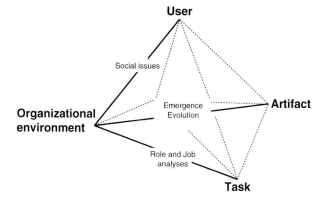

Fig. 3.4 The AUTO tetrahedron

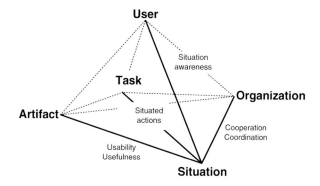

Fig. 3.5 The AUTOS pyramid

The Agile Approach

In the beginning of the 1990s, Jeff Sutherland and Ken Schwaber created SCRUM, an agile development method, to support faster, more reliable, and more effective creation of software in industry (Schwaber 1997; Sutherland 2014). Design and development of tangible interactive systems (TISs) requires the same kind of approach, but for both software and hardware integrated.

Instead of using the classical V model and linear Gantt charts, design teams develop sequences of small-Vs that provide constant feedback loops (Fig. 3.6). In addition, after each small-V—typically a period of 2 weeks—a potential releasable product should be available for testing. Agile software development is based on collaboration of cross-functional teams. It provides flexibility whenever it is necessary. More specifically, both components and processes must be changeable.

> **The agile design and development approach naturally supports observation of activity and formative evaluation**.

The "multiple V model" (MVM) is introduced as an agile framework for HCD and the contribution of TISs in human-systems integration (HSI).

Design and development of TISs requires creativity and management of uncertainty. This is why stating problems well is mandatory. In addition, when we think that problems are well stated, solving them brings new questions and new ways of stating the initial problems. Why? This is because our environment is difficult to grasp in the first place (i.e., this is a question of problem statement tangibility) and changes continuously when we are developing a project (i.e., the world is highly dynamic and requires flexibility for changing perspectives when necessary).

Now that we have seen the coordinated importance of testing activity and agile approach in HCD, we need to better understand the rationale of TISs in terms of structures and functions, as well as intimate relationships among structures and functions.

Articulating Structures and Functions

More than 35 years ago, I was working in control and computer sciences, modeling and simulating thermodynamics and fluid transfer.[1] At that time, I was more interested in modeling and simulation of physical phenomena than in cognitive

---

[1] For the readers who are knowledgeable in mathematics, I was focusing on parabolic and hyperbolic partial differential equations, which enable to simulate diffusion and convection processes at

Fig. 3.6 The agile
"multiple V model"
(MVM)

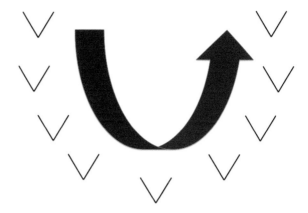

systems. The study of fluid dynamics, for example, necessarily associates structure and function of what we want to model and simulate. More specifically, I was studying fluid dynamics and gas transfer in the human lung.

Human lung's function is to provide oxygen from the air to the blood and exhaust carbon dioxide from the blood to the air. Lung structure is organized into 23 generations of branches going from the trachea to the alveoli (at the bottom of the trachea, there is a first generation of branches, one going to the right part of the lung and another to the left part; each of these branches typically divides into two subbranches and so on 23 times). A generally accepted mean number of alveoli is 480 million with a variation of 37 % among people (Ochs et al. 2004). The total surface area of the cumulated membrane between alveoli and blood capillaries is about 75 square meters (i.e., a surface area as large as half of a tennis court). Weibel's model was commonly used to represent lung geometry (Weibel 1963). Using this model, Fig. 3.7 displays cumulated diameter of the 23 generations of the tracheobronchial tree geometry (vertical axis, going from around 2 cm at the mouth to around 8.7 m at the alveoli level) against the linearized cumulated trajectory from the mouth to blood capillaries (horizontal axis, with a distance from the mouth to the alveoli of around 27 cm) (Soong et al. 1979). It is clear that the first part of the lung structure from the mouth to around the 21st bronchial generation, fluid dynamics is mostly a convective phenomenon. Since the cumulative section is growing exponentially after that, fluid dynamics almost instantly bifurcates to a diffusive phenomenon. Consequently, the structure of the human lung enables air to transfer very quickly from the mouth to the alveoli and leave time for the diffusion process to and from the blood to take place. Of course, there are other factors that enter into play, but they are not essential for the purpose of this book. This is a great example of how nature combines structure and function to provide appropriate phenomena to happen effectively.

----

the same time. I was interested in singularities occurring when hyperbolic phenomena vanish into parabolic phenomena. One of the applications was the airflow within a human lung (Boy 1980, 1981).

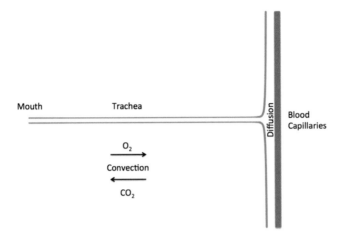

Fig. 3.7 Essential structures and functions of the human lung

> **The structure of a tangible interactive system determines its function and conversely**.

The human lung can be seen as a natural TIS. For this reason, we managed to model and simulate a generic human lung on a computer (Boy 1980, 1981; Boy et al. 1980). As a general principle, structures determine physical functions and conversely. I claim that this is true for any physical architecture. Of course, several functions may take place within a single architecture. Back to HCD, it is important to think in terms of structure and function concurrently anytime we attempt to design a new artifact.

The SFAC Model

TIS design is typically done using digital models that can be simulated as pieces of software. For example, an aircraft model can be fully developed as an integrated piece of software related to a physical cockpit, which in turn can be used to develop human-in-the-loop simulations.

We have seen that a TIS is defined by its structure and function, which can be decomposed into substructures and subfunctions. Each structure and function can be described in an abstract way and a concrete way. The SFAC (structure/function versus abstract/concrete) model supports collaborative TIS design. It is presented in

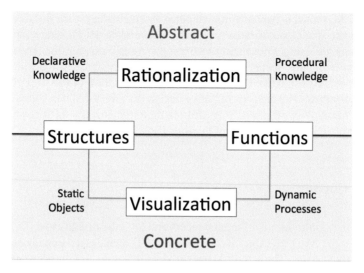

Fig. 3.8 The SFAC model

Fig. 3.8. The design team then collaboratively generates four types of things: declarative knowledge (i.e., abstract structures), procedural knowledge (i.e., abstract functions), static objects (i.e., concrete structures), and dynamic processes (i.e., concrete functions).

The abstract part is a knowledge base representing the rationalization of the system being designed. This rationalization can be represented by a set of concepts related among each other by typed relationships. This kind of representation can be called ontology,[2] semantic network, or concept map. It can take the form of a tree hierarchy in the simplest case or a complex concept graph in most cases.

At design time, the concrete part can commonly be represented using computer-aided design (CAD) software, which enables to generate 3D models of the various components of the system being designed. These 3D models include static objects and dynamic processes that enable the visualization of the way the various components being designed work and are integrated together. Later on during the design and development process, these 3D models can be 3D printed and lead to more graspable appreciation of the components being built and their possible integration. Testing occurs at each step of the design process by taking into account concrete parts together with their abstract counterparts (i.e., their rationalization, justifications, as well as various syntactical and semantic relationships that exist among them).

> **The SFAC model supports both rationalization and visualization of the design process and its solutions, in terms of structure and function.**

---

[2] In philosophy, ontology is the study of what there is, what exists. It is "what the most general features and relations of these things are" (Hofweber 2011).

The SFAC model is typically implemented as a mediating space that design team members can share, collaboratively modify, and validate. HCDi is developing such a tool using the latest information technologies (e.g., software for modeling and simulation, computer game generation, and rationalization development). SFAC also enables the design team to support the **documentation of the design process and its solutions**. The concept of active design document (ADD), initially developed for traceability purposes, is useful for the rationalization of innovative concepts and incremental formative evaluations (Boy 2005).

Design Cards

At this point, I introduce a different concept and tool, the **design card** (DC), which supersedes the ADD concept. Like in the ADD, CD includes a rationalization space and an activity space. The activity space provides dynamic visualization capabilities that enable virtual manipulation of systems being designed and developed. Instead of ADD's task space and the evaluation space, design cards have a structure space and a function space. ADD emphasized HFE issues only; design cards emphasize human-systems integration as a whole concept. This is why structure and function are put to the front. Structure space emphasizes the multi-agent declarative perspective (i.e., the HCD view of modern design), which can be denoted system of systems in systems engineering. Function space emphasizes both physical and cognitive function allocation and supports storytelling (i.e., scenario-based design) from the start of the design process.

As ADD, DC supports the design history of the system being designed. Several versions of a DC are incrementally generated and refined. These versions can be traced at any time by anyone in the design team. This feature increases intersubjectivity in the design team (i.e., mutual understanding among the design team members).

A design card (DC) is defined by four entities (Fig. 3.9):

- A rationalization space where the various components of the system being designed (SBD) are described in terms of design rationale, integration, and requirements; this space includes declarative and procedural descriptions and statements.
- An activity space where the current version of the SBD is displayed; it includes static and dynamic features; this space enables SBD manipulation.
- A structure space where the various components and their interrelations are formally and declaratively described as systems of systems.
- A function space where the various functions of the SBD are described in terms of procedural knowledge and dynamic processes involved; this space includes qualitative and quantitative physical and cognitive models.

A given DC presents the state of the design of a TIS at a given time for a given design team member (DTM). It is formally represented by DC (t, DTM_i), where t is time and DTM_i is the design team member i (could be a person or a group of persons).

Fig. 3.9 Design card (DC)

Structure Space	Rationalization Space
Activity Space	Function Space

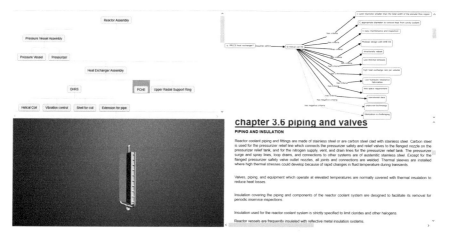

Fig. 3.10 Example of a design card showing a structure space (e.g., describing the various components and their links), an activity space (e.g., visualizing a reactor part), a rationalization space (e.g., QOC (QOC is a method that enables design rationale visualization of various design questions, possible options (or solutions), and criteria used for the choice of the best options (MacLean et al. 1991)), and related functional documentation

The concept of TIS fits very well with the DC concept. A DC enables designers to describe the various components of a system and the integrated whole (i.e., the TIS itself) in the rationalization space, display and manipulate them in the activity space, describe and use the navigation and control features in the operational space, and fill in the evaluation space as required after assessment of the system being designed.

An example of DC is provided for the I²S-LWR design project[3] (Fig. 3.10). The upper-left part is the structure space where the system is described in terms of abstract concepts and their interrelations. The lower-left part is the activity space

---

[3] The Integral Inherently Safe Light Water Reactor (I²S-LWR) nuclear project is funded by the US Department of Energy, in collaboration with several universities and industry partners including Georgia Tech, University of Michigan, Florida Institute of Technology, and Westinghouse.

where the system and/or its components and dependencies can be visualized and manipulated as virtual objects. The upper-right part is the rationalization space where design rationale can be stored and related to the three other parts. The lower-right part is the function space where physical and cognitive functions can be defined, refined, and connected to the three other parts. In addition, any DTM can interact with another DTM using the instant messaging space of the DC. All DC parts are interrelated. For example, a DC user can easily navigate from one part to another.

Using DCs supports solving several problems, such as geographical spread-out of experts of these groups, speed of technology evolution, high personnel turnover, and lack of documentation of the design process. DC generation happens during design. When DCs are documented regularly, they do absorb very little time of the design process. This additional time is compensated by a gain of time due to shared situation awareness of the entire design team. DC quality contributes to the quality of design.

Each DC (t, DTM_i) corresponds to a version of the system being designed and developed. Each time design management has a design review meeting at time t_1 (Fig. 3.11), all DTMs analyze the work done by each DTM and create a synthetic ADD (t_1, DT), where DT is the whole design team. DCs are like scores that musicians use to play a symphony in an orchestra, with the peculiar difference that, unlike scores, DCs are being incrementally defined to get a sound symphony in the end of the design process.

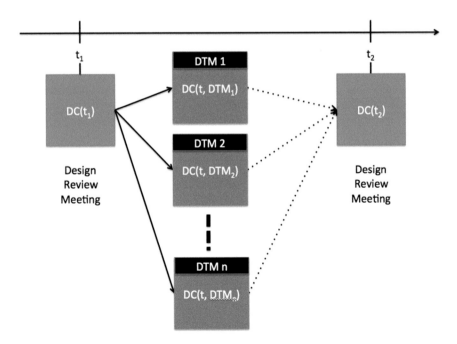

Fig. 3.11 Design card generation

After a design review meeting at time t_1, each DTM_i works on the premises of DC (t_1, DT), and produces their own DC (t, DTM_i) until the next design review meeting is organized at time t_2, where a new DC (t_2, DT) will be produced from the integration of all active design documents created and/or modified by each design team member during the time interval $[t_1, t_2]$.

Each DC is stored into a design database and can be retrieved at any time by any member of the design team (although some restrictions could be implemented and applied if necessary). Various DC traceability mechanisms can be implemented such as via:

- Rationalization space (e.g., creation date, design rationale, requirements)
- Activity space (e.g., evaluation, scenarios, criteria)
- Structure space (e.g., visualization of components)
- Function space (e.g., procedures, checklists, and technical explanations)

Capturing Design Rationale

As already said, HCD goes from purpose to means. Therefore, the first thing to do is to get an initial purpose that tells us what we want to do, knowing that it will evolve with the product being incrementally developed and used. Design team members need to work on meaningful things. Meaning is coming from both rationalization of design rationale (setting up tasks) and formative evaluations (figuring out activities). This is not only important for developing a great product but also creating and keeping a soul in the project. Indeed, design team members need to clearly perceive and understand what they are doing and why, and they need to project themselves into the future to "see" how the product they are developing can be used.

I^2S-LWR design team included about 30 people coming from different backgrounds (e.g., mechanical, nuclear, electrical, and computer engineering). The SFAC model supported the HCD approach. A computer-supported cooperative work (CSCW) system, called SCORE, enabled the rationalization of the various decisions made during the design process and facilitated collaboration among the various DTMs. We also structured the design rationale capture using the QOC formalism (Boy et al. 2016).

HCD promotes documenting design work incrementally during the design process and not only when product manufacturing is completed. An example of such a tool is the Computer Integrated Documentation (CID) system developed at NASA (Boy 1991). Another example can be found in the IMAT (Integrating Manuals and Training) system developed for designing learning material (de Hoog et al. 2002). Also in the WISE (Web-enabled Information Services for Engineering) workspace, the engineer is enabled to make annotations to all different kinds of knowledge objects and choose whether to share them with DTMs or other relevant stakeholders (Boy and Barnard 2003). Crisp and clearly understood design rationale is a good indicator of design maturity of the final product. Formalisms have been developed to describe design rationale such as gIBIS (*graphical Issue-Based Information System*) (Conklin and Begeman 1989) or QOC. QOC stands for questions, options, and criteria (MacLean et al. 1991). They support the elicitation of design rationale and enable the documentation of design decisions, development plans, and systems that are effectively developed.

QOC is a semiformal notation that enables a design team to capture design knowledge and represent the design space around the system being developed. Questions are key design issues (i.e., problem statements). Options provide possible answers to the questions. Criteria guide the assessment and comparison of the options. MacLean and his colleagues defined QOC to develop the Design Space Analysis approach, which enables the documentation of design rationale including possible alternative designs. QOC notation is very useful later on when we need to understand design history and rationale (Moran and Carroll 1996). Design Space Analysis also enables design team members to take into account consistency, models and analogies, and relevant data and theory. Indeed, there are design decisions that are based on experience and expertise and others on theoretical constructs (e.g., on phenomena described by equations in the nuclear domain). QOC enables the documentation of explanations, argumentations, and decisions during the design process.

In practice, design rationale documentation is done using graphical tools such as Cmaps (concept maps), which enable the definition of concepts and their interrelations (Novak and Cañas 2006). There are of course other knowledge management tools, such as Protégé, which enable design and refinement of ontologies that define concepts in a domain and their relationships (Gennari et al. 2003). We choose CmapTools[4] for their simplicity of use. CmapTools provides features for construction and navigation through different concept maps. Theses maps can be shared enabling critical thinking of the knowledge model emerging from the concept maps. A Cmap is typically constructed with the intent to answer a specific question. It is used for modeling "tacit" knowledge captured from experts. Experts know many things that they often cannot express in layman's terms. For example, designers can construct their knowledge models using CmapTools on their local computer, which can then be shared with anyone using Cmap servers. Designers can also create links between different Cmaps and have Web pages created based on the model. They can also edit their Cmaps at the same time. An example of QOC design rationale represented using a Cmap is provided in Fig. 3.12.

Modeling 3D Static Objects

Mainstream engineering traditionally focuses on delivering technologically working products. HCD focuses on engaging people and creating value. Designing static objects, such as an architect would do, is the first step to capture user experience

---

[4] http://cmap.ihmc.us/

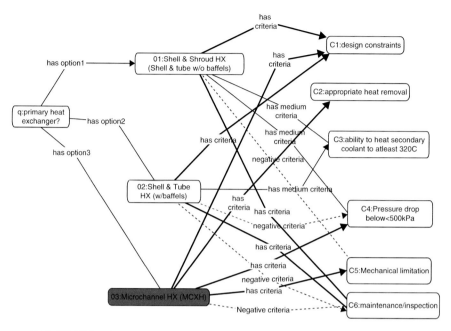

Fig. 3.12 I²S-LWR primary heat exchanger QOC design rationale

(i.e., user's activity). There are many CAD tools that enable designers to produce virtual 3D static objects, such as Dassault Systemes's CATIA, PTC's ProE, Siemens's NX, and Autodesk Inventor. Visualization of concrete objects provides intuitive anticipation of possible activities (i.e., user experience) and impacts on the real world (i.e., emergent properties).

Easy manipulation of 3D static objects provides designers with capability of testing configurations, also called declarative scenarios. They can construct and deconstruct objects, as well as assemble them among each other and disassemble them. For example, a nuclear reactor 3D model, visualized on a screen, can be decomposed into components, such as core assemblies, to geometrical dimensions of rods[5] (Fig. 3.13). This is made possible through the link between visually tangible objects and their formal representations in the corresponding design rationale. Typically, the user typically selects a visually tangible object and gets a description pop-up window that enables selection of subcomponents or attributes.

> **Physical modeling supports visualization and awareness improvement of what is being designed**.

---

[5] This example illustrates a human-centered design student project carried out at the Human-Centered Design Institute of Florida Institute of Technology in the fall 2014, involving the following graduate students, Saad Almesalm, Nicholas Kasdaglis, Joan Savage, Golnoosh Torkashvand, Ruthvik Adloori, and Joseph Torkaman.

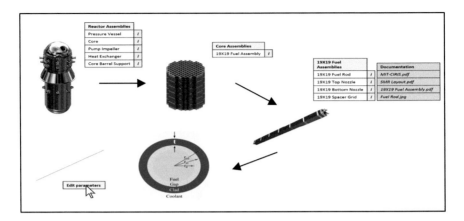

Fig. 3.13 Example of a decomposition of a nuclear reactor into components

This kind of modeling and simulation capability provides design team members with endless trial-and-error possibilities. In addition, when this graphical capability is connected with a design rationale generator, it tremendously increases the production of meaningful tangible interactive objects. This design rationale tool can be implemented as an annotation mechanism on top of the 3D-static-object visualization. This kind of feature provides meaningful interactivity with the objects being designed and enables traceability among the various versions of these objects as well as connectivity among the various components of the systems being designed.

Visually tangible objects enable designers to immediately capture salient features that either confirm design choices or suggest modifications. Design is an iterative process. Visualization suggests confirmations or modifications; design rationale enables rationalization and deeper calculations. Linking visually tangible objects to their abstract descriptions (i.e., design rationale) enables designers to proceed with a convergent process when the design team is proactive, competent, and collaborative.

Modeling Dynamic Processes

Visualization of 3D static objects is an important step for handling their tangibility. However, these objects have also internal and/or external dynamics. In the case of a nuclear power plant, we typically focus on internal fluid dynamics, which includes momentum, mass, and thermal transfers. In the case of aircraft, an important part is their external dynamics (i.e., kinematics of and fluid dynamics around aircraft). Nevertheless, it is also useful to introduce a pseudo-natural dynamics of the way the structure-function duality of the system being designed works.

Dynamic processes are all related to time. The term "time" has several meanings in natural language. The question is the nature of time (Klein 2006). We often think time as a river. This analogy carries several concepts such as speed and even acceleration (e.g., time is going fast, or time is going faster!). We often hear about psychological time. For example, we feel that time is longer when we experience a bad experience and shorter when we experience great experience. However, time has no speed (i.e., what is the derivative of time?). The feeling that we may experience in the case of a great or bad experience is in fact a temporal phenomenon. Therefore, it is important to make a distinction between time and temporal phenomena. A phenomenon is defined by the cause that precedes it. This is called the **causality** principle in physics. If an event happens, then it exists forever (i.e., we cannot change the past). This is true in the real world. However, we can record this event and then replay it from our memory. Current technology enables us to record events and easily replay them. Media, television in particular, uses this capability today.

Aesthetics guides our construction of patterns that help us make sense of the real world. Tufte (2001) describing the visual display of quantitative information wrote, "graphical elegance is often found in simplicity of design and complexity of data." Klein and Lachieze-Rey (2001) claimed, "both Einstein and Dirac[6] felt that the aesthetic mathematical appeal of a physical theory was not just to please the mind. It was also an indication—indeed perhaps the best there is—of its validity." For example, if we see a car, it does not matter from what angle we see the car; we will say that it is a car. This will be true until we see that an attribute of the object we are watching disconfirms the concept of a car, for example. This means that we learn patterns that help us recognize objects (e.g., a car), no matter from what viewpoint we observe them.

The whole question is then eliciting the right patterns that better represent dynamic processes. Indeed, even if we have equations that represent these dynamic processes, the human-centered designer needs to provide the best graphical representation of their complexity. I cannot resist to quote Tufte, "not the complication of the simple; rather the task of the designer is to give visual access to the subtle and the difficult – that is, the revelation of the complex" (Tufte 2001, p. 191).

In addition, the user of the visualization system is part of the problem to be solved. The user should be able to easily manipulate visually tangible objects and associated dynamic processes. This is why gaming software engineering is very useful to this end. An example of visualization of the I^2S-LWR reactor assembly is presented in Fig. 3.14.

The user of this activity space can manipulate the reactor assembly, decompose it, add new components, and so on. Aesthetics is again part of the "game." I claim that aesthetics in human-computer interaction deals with qualitative attributes such as interaction minimality, usability, usefulness, simplicity, and cooperation support. The easier human-system interaction is, in terms of number of interactions, efficiency, success, or pleasure, the more you find the system aesthetic.

---

[6] Paul Dirac was a physicist who contributed to the development of quantum physics.

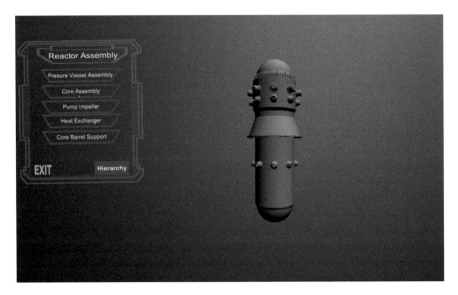

Fig. 3.14 I²S-LWR reactor assembly (activity space of a design card)

Collaborative Work

Collaborative work is a crucial activity in a HCD team. Shared situation awareness (SSA) is a key issue in LCS design. SSA has been, and still is, studied at operations time (Stanton et al. 2006), but it requires more attention at design and development times. People may make errors because they are not aware of the current state of the design process. We should provide solutions to answer the following questions: Is DTM_1 aware of current actions and productions of DTM_2 at any time? Is DTM_1 aware of what DTM_3 did at some point in time on the same topic he/she is currently working on or a similar one? How can we create and maintain the best SSA in the design team? As already mentioned above, the SCORE CSCW system was developed to support SSA. A SCORE overview is provided in Fig. 3.15.

> **Shared situation awareness in a design team can be supported by a common interactive database that includes design cards incrementally generated during the whole life cycle of the system being designed and developed.**

SCORE uses components and procedure models. It is implemented using a Web-based application mechanism, which allows secure and trusted communication via VPN (virtual private network). In addition, effective search mechanisms provide the necessary means to pull appropriate information when needed. It would also be nice

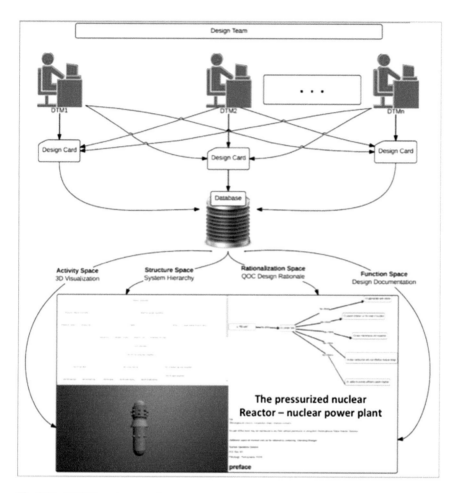

Fig. 3.15 SCORE system overview

to have the appropriate information pushed to the front, so potential users are aware of its existence. In both cases, context-sensitive information should be available at any time.

For this reason, at all stages of the design process, any DTM have access to salient reasons that pushed other people to design systems the way they are. When I carried out an exhaustive study on traceability within a large aircraft manufacturing company (Boy 2001), I found out that traceability not only is information retrieval but also deals with awareness that potential knowledge exists somewhere, and finally when this knowledge is found, it must be understood correctly.

Cognitive and Physical Functions: The NAIR Model

The I²S-LWR example illustrates the design of a pure technological system. Indeed, nuclear power plants are among the most automated systems currently in service. Cognition is therefore in the design process (i.e., technology being developed incorporates designers' cognitive functions), which contributes to produce systems' cognitive functions that human operators will need to understand, monitor, and collaborate with. Concurrently, we also need to take into account cognitive functions of future potential human operators who will need to control, manage, and maintain systems being designed.

Following up on a large experience using CFA since 1998, I want to extend the notion of function to phenomena that are not cognitive but purely physical. One would say that this is what the physicists are already doing for a long long time! They actually did not care about cognitive functions. Consequently, if we want to study and design cyber-physical systems (CPSs), we really need to better understand the distinction between cognitive functions and physical functions. The NAIR (natural/artificial versus cognitive/physical) model is an attempt to rationalize this distinction (Fig. 3.16).

Whether they are natural or artificial, systems can have functions that are either cognitive or reactive. Natural systems include biological systems of any kind, such as people, and physical systems, such as geological or atmospheric phenomena. Artificial systems include information technology, such as aircraft flight management system or the Internet, and mechanical systems such as old mechanical watches.

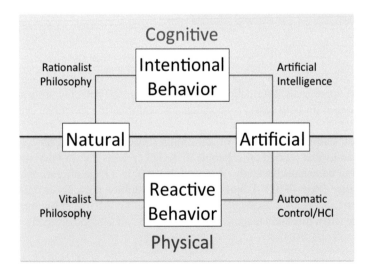

Fig. 3.16 Cognitive and physical functions: the NAIR model

Cognitive functions produce intentional behavior where situation awareness, decision-making, and action taking are the main cognitive resources. Symmetrically, physical functions produce reactive behavior. On the artificial side, artificial intelligence tools and techniques can support intentional behavior (e.g., aircraft FMSs[7] use operations research, optimization techniques, and knowledge-based systems); and control theories and human-computer interaction tools and techniques can support reactive behavior (e.g., aircraft TCASs[8] use radars, control mechanisms, and voice outputs). On the natural side, intentional behavior can be supported by rationalist[9] philosophies (i.e., mainly related to the cortex, including reasoning, understanding, and learning); and reactive behavior can be supported by vitalist[10] philosophies (i.e., mainly related to the reptilian brain, including emotions, experience, and skills). These philosophies will be described in more details later on in the chapter.

Let me take an example. "Planning a trip" is a complex cognitive function, which involves other cognitive functions such as "defining a budget," "choosing transportation means," "defining time constraints," and so on. Each of these CFs involves smaller grain CFs. The concept of cognitive function is therefore recursive (i.e., a CF is an organized set of CFs). However, it may happen that a CF requires the use of a physical tool involving physical functions, such as "using paper and pencil to write down an itinerary." It is practical to extend both concepts of cognitive function and physical function to the generic concept of **resource**. We will then say that a resource can be physical or cognitive.

Articulating Declarative and Procedural Dimensions

The terms "declarative" and "procedural" that respectively refer to knowing what and knowing how are used to describe human memory. Declarative memory includes facts and defines our own semantics of things. Procedural memory includes skills and procedures (i.e., how to do things). We can think declarative memory as an explicit network of concepts, as procedural memory could be thought as an implicit set of know-hows. Declarative memory is typically stored in the temporal cortex of the brain. Procedural memory is stored in the motor cortex. They are both in the cortex and involve learning.

Computer programming started being thought and implemented in the procedural way. Languages such as Fortran were developed on the basis of subroutines, and Pascal used procedures, for example. Subroutines and procedures enable programmers to develop procedural knowledge. Then, artificial intelligence came and

---

[7] Flight management systems.

[8] Traffic alert collision avoidance systems.

[9] Rationalist philosophy (Markie 2013).

[10] Vitalist philosophy was developed by Henri Bergson (1907).

proposed declarative programming, such as Lisp and Prolog (i.e., defining objects, functions, predicates, and methods).

In **theater,** for example, there are actors and scenery, which are declarative entities, as well as scripts and dialogues, which are procedural supports. Brenda Laurel used her education in theater to describe what human-computer interaction is about or should be in terms of multi-agent declarative and procedural descriptions (Laurel 1991, 2013). Theater is about interaction among actors (i.e., in the computer world, we would say agents). A theater play embeds notion like time, change, and dialogue. This is what TISs are about. Brenda Laurel was ahead of her time when she produced her first book in 1991. She was talking about human-computer experience instead of user interfaces. Now, we interact with systems using gestures, voice, and midair interaction, for example. The notion of user interface is no longer a crucial issue; understanding the system in its environment is fundamental issue. In fact, during the twentieth century, user interfaces were developed because we were not capable of doing HCD. Engineers were leading the technological world, and human factors specialists were following by adapting people to machines even if they claimed that we should do the opposite. This adaption was done by developing user interfaces and user's guides (i.e., procedures), which automated human behavior in specific ways.

Today, we have the means to implement HCD. We have modeling and simulation capabilities that enable design teams to test **human-systems integration** very early on. Both human and system functions can be declared, tested, and refined incrementally using human-in-the-loop simulations. We also can figure out what skills, procedures, and knowledge are required on both sides (i.e., humans and systems). At the cognitive level, the cognitive function representation has been defined and successfully used to investigate both human and system functions. However, since this book is about tangibility, physical functions should be better defined on both sides. We will see in the next section that physical functions cannot be dissociated from their structures.

The Problem of Abnormal Situations

The NAIR model presented above (Fig. 3.16) does not take into account abnormal situations. In normal situations, (adult) people learn using their cognitive abilities and incrementally compile their acquired knowledge into situational patterns, very much like a computer program that is compiled into an executable application, which itself is impossible to decompile. If we take this analogy, learning by repetitive training needs to be done correctly; otherwise, we are condemned to live with bad situational patterns (i.e., compiled executable applications). In abnormal situations, people who do not have the appropriate situational patterns need to use their cognitive abilities to solve problems. They may not have the right declarative and procedural knowledge and need to invent (create) ad hoc declarative and procedural knowledge. The question is the following: do they rely on their cognition (the cognitive part of Fig. 3.16) or the "vitalism" they have in them (the physical part of

Fig. 3.16)? Animals use the latter because their cognition is not developed as it is for humans. Some of us react physically using their free will (Bergson written in 1889 a document published in 2001). The French philosopher, Henri Bergson, promoted immediate experience and intuition to forge the **vitalist** approach in philosophy based on observation, as opposed to abstract **rationalism** and science used to understand reality (i.e., rationalize and establish goals before acting).

Bergson's vitalist philosophy emphasizes creativity. He opposed intelligence to intuition. In the NAIR model, intelligence is definitely in the cognitive domain associated with intentional behavior, as intuition is in the physical domain associated with reactive behavior. Bergson criticized Kant's conception of truth (Kant 1781). For Bergson, intelligence is a product of evolution used by people to survive. However, our vitalism[11] might push us to solve real problems, as deep as they could be. For Bergson, freedom is mobility! Henri Bergson is definitively in the camp of the philosophy of life, as opposed to mechanical philosophies of his time. I claim that this statement is still true today.

> **Intentional and reactive behaviors can be interpreted using two different kinds of philosophy: rationalist and vitalist.**

Abnormal situations are usually taken into account using two kinds of behavior. Let's assume that people are engaged into a routine activity guided by procedures, and when they encounter an abnormal situation, they try to find a response either by directly reacting or by developing a problem-solving process. Reaction could be the result of a stimulus-response process based on fear, training, or experience. In the case of fear, the response may not be appropriate. This is why training and gaining experience are crucial (i.e., people need to develop situational patterns related to abnormal situations). When people involved in an abnormal situation try to understand what is going on and try to solve a problem by themselves without training, they do not use a stimulus-response process, but a cognitive problem-solving process. For the people who are trained to follow procedures—let's call them procedure followers—this shift to problem-solving can create difficulties. Conversely, some of them hate procedures and constantly solve problems by themselves. Let's call them problem-solvers. In this case, when an abnormal situation occurs, problem-solvers easily include this new problem-solving task in the flow of the others' problem-solving tasks. Instead, procedure followers may have difficulty in swapping from the procedure-following mode to the problem-solving mode. Of course, once they found the right abnormal procedures, they follow them to the letter! Consequently, when we design applications for human operators involved in the management of

---

[11] Vitalism should be understood as an internal force that pushes us to grow and exit from the mess where we are. The vitalism concept is taken in Nietzsche's Dionysian sense (Nietzsche, translated by Kaufmann and Hollingdale 1968).

life-critical systems, it is important to think concurrently in terms of procedure following and problem-solving.

Tangible Interactive Systems as System Agents

The holistic approach to HCD should be better denoted cognitive function-based design or activity-centered design (Norman 2005). The cognitive function paradigm provides an explicit representation to what is commonly implicitly done in design. It enables us to rationalize both deliberative (i.e., a priori defined) and emergent (i.e., discover when the socio-technical system is put at work) cognitive functions. The concept of cognitive function encapsulates the concept of agent. People can be called human or natural agents, which use natural and artificial cognitive functions. TISs are artificial agents, which also use natural and artificial cognitive functions.

The claim that **people adapt to technology** is not enough to eliminate **tests** that lead to technology improvement and more generally incremental design of natural and artificial cognitive functions. This orchestration of incrementally generated cognitive function networks is the key for harmonious human-systems integration. Orchestrating cognitive and physical functions is the main topic of this book, where a concept map of natural and artificial physical and cognitive phenomena needs to be developed; and cooperation/coordination rules need to be discovered and effectively used. It is like an orchestra where the musicians would have scores that would evolve with time to fix the harmony of the symphony being developed. As an example, the increasing density of air traffic strongly suggests that aircraft cannot be controlled the way they are now, i.e., centralized control. Moving toward **decentralized management** of aircraft in dense air traffic can be compared to a flock of birds, and therefore new types of cognitive functions would need to be discovered and implemented. Such implementation can lead to specific human learning/practice and/or development of TISs onboard aircraft that automatically assist pilots in separation assurance and collision avoidance.

References

Bergson H (1907) L'évolution créatrice, 86th edn. Presses Universitaires de France, Paris, 1959
Bergson H (written in 1889-document published in 2001) Time and free will: an essay on the immediate data of consciousness 1910 (Essai sur les données immédiates de la conscience 1889). Dover Publications: ISBN 0-486-41767-0 – Bergson's doctoral dissertation
Boy GA (1980) Respiratory structure and function: modeling and applications of the analysis of transfer phenomena for the prediction of the human respiratory system behavior. PhD dissertation. ISAE-SUPAERO, University of Toulouse, France
Boy GA (1981) A numerical method for convective and diffusive process simulation, application to respiratory gas transfer. In: Proceedings of the 2nd World Cong. Chem. Engineering, Montreal

Boy GA (1991) Indexing hypertext documents in context. In: Proceedings of the ACM Hypertext'91 conference, San Antonio, December, also in the ACM Digital Library

Boy GA (1998a) Cognitive function analysis. Praeger/Ablex. ISBN 9781567503777

Boy GA (1998b) Cognitive function analysis for human-centered automation of safety-critical systems. In: Proceedings of CHI'98, the ACM conference on human factors in computing systems, Los Angeles, USA. Published by ACM Press, New York. pp 265–272, ISBN:0-201-30987-4

Boy GA (2001) Organizational memory systems. In: Plenary paper, Proceedings of IFAC 2001, Kassel, Germany

Boy GA (2005) Knowledge management for product maturity. In: Proceedings of the international conference on Knowledge Capture (K-Cap'05). Banff, Canada. October. ACM Digital Library

Boy GA (ed) (2011) Handbook of human-machine interaction: a human-centered design approach. Ashgate

Boy GA (2014) From automation to tangible interactive objects. Ann Rev Control:1367–5788. Elsevier. doi:10.1016/j.arcontrol.2014.03.001

Boy GA, Jorda MF, Renun B, Brieussel JM, Caval E, Lareng L (1980) Comparison of different methods of mean alveolar PCO2 measurement during mechanical ventilation. In: Proceedings Computer in Critical Care and Pulmonary Medicine, IEEE, Elsevier, Holland. Presenté à Lund, Sweden

Boy G, Barnard Y (2003) Knowledge management in the design of safety-critical systems. In: Proceedings of the European Cognitive Science Conference (EuroCogSci'03). Osnabrück, Germany, September

Boy GA, Narkevicius J (2013) Unifying human centered design and systems engineering for human systems integration. In Aiguier M, Boulanger F, Krob D, Marchal C (eds) Complex systems design and management. Springer, London, 2014. ISBN-13: 978-3-319 02811-8

Boy GA, Jani G, Manera A, Memmott M, Petrovic B, Rayad Y, Stephane AL, Suri N (2016) HCD improves project management. Ann Nucl Energy, Elsevier, ANE4864

Conklin EJ, Begeman ML (1989) gIBIS: a tool for all reasons. J Am Soc Inf Sci 40:200–213

de Hoog R, Kabel S, Barnard Y, Boy G, DeLuca P, Desmoulins C, Riemersma J, Verstegen D (2002) Re-using technical manuals for instruction: creating instructional material with the tools of the IMAT project. In: Proceedings of ITS'2002 workshop on integrating technical and training documentation, San Sebástian, Spain, pp 28–39

Gennari JH, Musen MA, Fergerson RW, Grosso WE, Crubézy M, Eriksson H, Noy NF, Tu SW (2003) The evolution of protégé: an environment for knowledge-based systems development. Int J Hum Comput Stud, Academic Press, 58(1):89–123

Hofweber T (2011) Logic and ontology. Stanford Encyclopedia of Philosophy. http://plato.stanford.edu/entries/logic-ontology. Retrieved on 24 Mar 2016

Kant I (1781) Critique of pure reason (The Cambridge edition of the works of Immanuel Kant) Paperback – February 28, 1999. Guyer P (Editor, Translator), Wood AW (Editor, Translator). ISBN-13: 978-0521657297

Klein E (2006) Le temps qui passe (French). POMMIER Edition. ISBN-13: 978-2746503076

Klein E, Lachieze-Rey M (2001) The quest for unity: the adventure of physics (trans: Reisinger A). Oxford University Press. ISBN-13: 9780195120851

Laurel B (1991) Computers as theatre. Addison-Wesley, Saddle River, NJ. ISBN 0-201-55060-1

Laurel B (2013) Computers as theatre: a dramatic theory of interactive experience, 2nd edn. Addison-Wesley, Upper Saddle River

MacLean A, Young RM, Bellotti VME, Moran TP (1991) Questions, options, and criteria: elements of design space analysis. Hum Comput Interact 6:201–250, Lawrence Erlbaum Associates, Inc

Markie P (2013) Rationalism vs. empiricism. Stanford Encyclopedia of Philosophy. First published August 19, 2004. Retrieved on September 3, 2015, http://plato.stanford.edu/entries/rationalism-empiricism/

Moran TP, Carroll JM (eds) (1996) Design rationale: concepts, methods and techniques. Erlbaum, Hillsdale

Nietzsche F (1968) Trans. Kaufmann W, Hollingdale RJ (1968) The will to power paperback. Vintage. ISBN-13: 978-0394704371

Norman DA (2005) Human-centered design considered harmful. Interactions 12(4):14–19. Also available at http://jnd.org/dn.mss/human-centered_design_considered_harmful.html

Novak JD, Cañas AJ (2006) The theory underlying concept maps and how to construct and use them. Institute for Human and Machine Cognition, Pensacola. Technical Report IHMC Cmap Tools 2006–01 Rev 2008–01. http://Cmap.ihmc.us/docs/theory-of-concept-maps. Retrieved on 1 May 2015

Ochs M, Nyengaard JR, Jung A, Knudsen L, Voigt M, Wahlers T, Richter J, Gundersen HJ (2004) The number of alveoli in the human lung. Am J Respir Crit Care Med 169(1):120–124, 1

Schwaber K (1997) Scrum development process. In: Sutherland J, Patel D, Casanave C, Miller J, Hollowell G (eds) OOPSLA business objects design and implementation workshop proceedings. Springer, London

Soong TT, Nicolaides P, Yu CP, Soong SC (1979) A statistical description of the human tracheobronchial tree geometry. Respir Physiol 37:161–172, Elsevier/North-Holland Biomedical Press

Stanton NA, Stewart R, Harris D, Houghton RJ, Baber C, McMaster R, Salmon P, Hoyle G, Walker G, Young MS, Linsell M, Dymott R, Green D (2006) Distributed situation awareness in dynamic systems: theoretical development and application of an ergonomics methodology. Ergonomics 49(12–13):288–311

Sutherland J (2014) Scrum: the art of doing twice the work in half the time. Crown Business. ISBN-13: 978-0385346450

Tufte ER (2001) The visual display of quantitative information. Graphics Press, Cheshire. ISBN 0-9613921-4-2

Weibel ER (1963) Morphometry of the human lung. Academic, New York

Chapter 4
Innovation

This chapter presents a framework for innovation and its important attributes and methods that are likely to make a difference. The **innovation-research duality** will be discussed. Traditional research is based on the demonstration of a claim. Similarly, innovation is based on the investigation of appropriate possible futures and the demonstration that they are viable. In addition, I claim that innovation can greatly be supported by incremental **design**, **development, and integration** of tangible interactive systems (TISs) in our society. The city of the future will be taken as an example to illustrate the various concepts, methods, and tools that support innovation.

Innovation always starts from the implementation of intentions and purposes (e.g., John F. Kennedy's intention to go to the Moon and bringing back people safely to Earth). Of course, innovation can be influenced by knowledge generated by research; this is the research loop on innovation. Innovation consists in producing new technology, organizational setups, and people's jobs and activities, which evolve through incremental integration of emerging properties (including emerging cognitive functions). These emerging properties are analyzed and used as experience feedback to eventually modify intentions and purposes; this is the emergence loop on innovation intentions and purposes (Fig. 4.1).

Orchestrating Possible Futures

Innovation is necessary. Let's take the Paris region, Île-de-France, and its 12 million people—population of the city of Paris itself is 2.2 million people. These people constantly move from one location to another every day using various kinds of transportation means including their own feet. People walk, bike, drive, and take the metro, train, and other transportation means. Vehicles and transportation infrastructures need to be adapted to citizen requirements. If we want to improve citizen mobility in an urban environment like the Paris region, we need to investigate

© Springer International Publishing Switzerland 2016   63
G.A. Boy, *Tangible Interactive Systems*, Human–Computer Interaction Series,
DOI 10.1007/978-3-319-30270-6_4

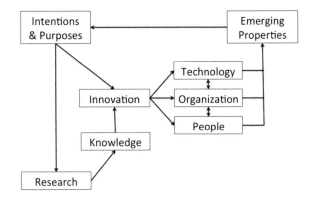

Fig. 4.1 Intentions/ purposes (based on past knowledge), research (producing new knowledge), innovation, and properties that emerge from various impacts of innovation on technology, organization, and people

various kinds of TISs, which altogether need to be **orchestrated**. For example, if you leave your house in the morning to go to work, you may take your car, if you have one and want or need to drive it, or use public transportation. Many Parisians spend more than 2 h commuting to work. Of course, they get used to it. However, they get tired and do not necessarily take advantage of their travel time to work. Do they relax? No! Are they stressed? Most of them, yes! Is it good for their health? No! Therefore, what would be a great human-centered innovation that would improve all of the above?

> **We cannot predict the future, but we can model, orchestrate, simulate and test possible futures.**

Innovation is possible. The main block for rethinking mobility—in a city like Paris and its region, for example—is our persistent cognitive patterns or habits. There are things that we do because they have been learned by repetition, sometimes in a hard way. We do not want to change, or have difficulty to change. In addition, we may not see **possible futures**. Innovation is about looking for possible futures, setting up models of them, evaluating these models using appropriate simulations, and iterating on this cycle until a satisfactory possible future is found. Although stating a goal may result from an unacceptable event, inventing and assessing possible futures is inherently goal driven and could take time. From a cognitive viewpoint, this is the opposite of predicting the future, which is clearly event driven and short term. Looking for possible futures is longer term and visionary. It may take time for maturity reasons. This question of maturity is further developed in Chap. 7.

Continuing on the city of the future as an example, there are two complementary human-centered design (HCD) tasks that need to be developed concurrently and incrementally harmonized:

- The **top-down** HCD task enables us to holistically model the overall interconnectivity of the city (i.e., define a global architecture that leads to integrated city TISs).
- The **bottom-up** HCD task enables us to design, develop, and orchestrate useful and usable TISs (i.e., define necessary structures and functions that will need to be integrated within the architecture).

In this book, the HCD approach proposed for innovation is twofold: top-down and bottom-up. On the one hand, designers need to have a holistic view of the product they want to produce. On the other hand, they need to develop specific TISs structures and functions that will fit the holistic view. Both approaches are incrementally defined through participatory design involving all possible stakeholders who can deal with the product being designed.

It would be great if we could totally redesign a city by redefining all structures and functions, but people would not be prepared to change their habits at once. Main problem is **maturity of practice**. More likely, smaller changes could be incrementally tested and potentially accepted. These changes are typically local, and may have an influence on the whole city. Considering the city as a complex system, local changes may cause tremendous modifications at the global level. However, like in any complex system, we need to find out what are the main attractors related to local changes, in the complexity science sense. Modeling and simulation (M&S) can help in figuring out these attractors or organizational patterns.

Smartphones, for example, contributed to change people's habits in their everyday lives. Today, people text, telephone, and exchange emails. In addition, they use these modalities for specific purposes. Telephone is most often used for emergencies or confidential discussions for example. Text is preferred for short messages, as email typically enables longer developments. This contextual categorization of communication support modalities is still incrementally and socially constructed toward maturity of practice.

HCD is about **context**, i.e., social context, knowledge management context, people's maturity-of-practice context, and technology maturity context. For this reason, HCD should be supported by incrementally upgraded prototypes and recurring scenario-based evaluation. HCD recommends that we focus on people by constantly asking them what they think about the new prototype and observe their activity while using and testing the prototype. We should observe what they do with this prototype. We should listen to them. We should learn from them. HCD provides a way of seeing the world, where participation and caring for stakeholders are key. Stakeholders include designers themselves, certifiers, maintainers, and trainers, in particular.

Top-down and bottom-up HCD tasks can be put into practice in three steps:

1. Create problem statements through empathy (i.e., this step requires better explanation of what **empathy** is about in HCD—this will be done in the next section).

2. Abduct possible solutions (i.e., this step requires that we master the **abduction** inference process).
3. Deliver products (i.e., this step requires understanding the **delivery** process and, more specifically, practice in evaluating and communicating the value of the developed product).

Empathy

Innovation starts with empathy. HCD cannot be done without developing deep connections with the people who will use and interact with the products being designed. For a long time, designers, writers, and artists have been using introspection to produce concepts. Some of the best ones were, and currently are, excellent observers. A good human-centered designer should be able to observe the world and perceive salient features of the system being designed. He/she should also be able to understand these features, contest them against current culture, and project possible futures where the system being designed could be integrated and used. This capacity to observe the external world is called **outrospection** (Krznaric 2014). Roman Krznaric argues, "Our brains are wired for social connection. Empathy, not apathy or self-centeredness, is at the heart of who we are." He associates empathy and creativity.

Meaningful innovations cannot be created without enough knowledge about potential users. You need to care about how they live. Finding the right solution strongly depends on the way the problem is framed. In addition, the right solution is more likely to pop up from a large set of solutions than from an ideal single solution. You need to visualize solutions, make them as concrete as you can, in order to think about them and test them. You will learn a lot by testing them, and also about potential users involved in the test.

> **Empathy is about knowing how to observe outside of us, the others, and our environment and act accordingly.**
> **Empathy is about how to tell the right story at the right time.**

Empathy plays a key role in discovering and stating meaningful problems. Hard and messy design problems, which need to be solved, emerge from careful **observation** of the world around us. This would not be possible without being sensitive to others. It requires us to cultivate attention and awareness. Sometimes technology could help, such as audio and videotaping or more simply picture taking. Indeed there are features that are difficult to capture in the real life, but that could be discovered in a quiet environment replaying recorded scenes. Appropriate observations provide datasets for investigating why people act the way they act. Accessing the rationale for the various interactions among agents, whether they are people or systems, is crucial to create the sense of **purpose**. Purpose is key in HCD to infer means for developing possible solutions. Indeed, purpose is likely to evolve with time since it is based on observation. We continue to observe the use of technology being developed and therefore identify emerging properties that need to be taken into account to reformulate the initial purpose.

Empathy is also about knowing how to tell the right story at the right time with the right attitude. For a long time, storytelling is an excellent way of transferring information and knowledge. Taking a constructivist approach, good stories tend to incrementally reformulate concepts in our memory by assimilation and accommodation (Piaget 1985). Assimilation consists in using current schemes to interpret the external world (i.e., fitting practice to theory), as accommodation consists in creating new schemes and/or adjusting old ones after noticing that current thinking does not capture the environment completely (i.e., fitting theory to practice). This is because it mixes cognition and **emotion**. You also need a lot of empathy to tell a good story. You need to know your audience if you really want to have an impact. Therefore, empathy is a crucial cognitive and emotional function for all of us who want to live in harmony on our planet. Empathy is about understanding another person's motivation, feelings, and activity rationale. Let's analyze these two empathy aspects dealing with emotion and cognition.

People's emotional attitudes can be observed using predefined features such as Robert Plutchik's wheel of emotions (Fig. 4.2).

Emotional attributes are easy to observe when people are extroverted. Conversely, they are difficult to observe when people are introverted. Introverted people develop defense mechanisms. Plutchik proposed that eight defense mechanisms were manifestations of the eight core emotions. Defense mechanisms are generally unconscious (innate) and reactive to some external events. Unconscious defense mechanisms are distinguished from conscious strategy copping, in Sigmund Freud's sense (Kramer 2010).

Even if emotion is key in design, **cognition** is often playing a tremendous role. I already defined the cognitive function representation by three attributes (i.e., a role, context of validity, and resources that are needed to accomplish the role). For example, can we talk about empathy when people communicate remotely via Skype or Google Hangouts? In other words, can we detect enough features on the face of the utterer on a 2D screen instead of a 3D face-to-face interaction? Cognition has to interpret the image that the interaction media provides. Emoticons are now used to express emotions in such virtual interactions. Before these kinds of interaction media existed, we had the "regular" telephone that provided even less interaction channels, only voice. Therefore, it is very difficult to define what remote empathy could be. This does not prevent us to define cognitive empathy as an intersubjectivity resource in remote synchronous or asynchronous communications. For example, cognitive empathy can emerge from a very well-written text read by a very advanced reader. In fact, reading provides features that can be transformed into emotional empathy.

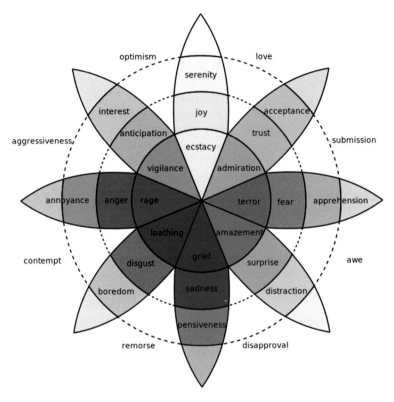

Fig. 4.2 Robert Plutchik's wheel of emotions (Plutchik 2002)

Abduction

Alan Kay stated the maxim: "The best way to predict the future is to invent it."
Prediction is related to short-term event-driven thinking. Indeed, a causal prediction
in mathematics is modeled by a derivative based on a projection of the immediate
past. Therefore, if we do not want to commit errors, we need to stay in the short term
(i.e., close to the point where the derivative is calculated). We cannot predict a too
far future!

> **Abduction is one of the three logical inference mechanisms that people
> use to project themselves into the future and act accordingly to prove the
> relevance of their projection**.

In contrast, inventing a possible future is related to longer-term goal-driven thinking. The underlying logical inference process is abduction, which assumes a possible future and requires demonstration that it is reachable. Abduction is an inference process that is based on heuristics (i.e., something that you learn from experience). Therefore, anyone using abduction requires a minimum level of experience and expertise in the domain where the inference is made. Design thinking is an abductive process, made of trials and errors, incrementally using creativity and rationalization.

Abduction consists of projecting a possible future B, and then proving the inference (A → B) leading from where we are now, i.e., A to B. The mental process of abduction, notably the choice of the correct hypothesis, is closely linked to pragmatism, intuition, expertise, and skill. Charles Peirce defined abduction as the process of constructing an explicative hypothesis and claimed that it is the only logical operation by which to introduce a new idea. Airbus's fly-by-wire technology was revolutionary in transport aircraft. The designers at the time set up a process of abduction. Of course, this choice gave rise to a number of deductive processes, which contributed to rationalizing and proving the pertinence and viability of the system. For instance, one might seek to deduce how to make an aircraft lighter, facilitate operator training, protect against external events or human error. Initial abductive processes, and the rational deduction processes which follow, are guided by general objectives related, for example, to operational economics, safety, performance, comfort, and training. It is the state of knowledge at a given moment, which provides the basis for the choice and implementation of these processes. In practice, the definitive choice of fly-by-wire controls resulted from reasoned and deductive choices with respect to specific objectives such as weight reduction, simplicity, advantages of protecting the flight envelope, and homogeneity of the different training courses (Boy and Brachet 2010).

Risk-taking is about abduction. Design thinking is about taking risks in choosing possible futures. Therefore, good design thinkers should know about abduction.

The fact that risk in aeronautics is very low (less than 10^{-7} losses per hour of flight) is largely supported by the use of procedures. In surgery, as in aeronautics, procedures enable a surgeon to benefit from the experiences of thousands of other surgeons. Surgery safety made tremendous progress thanks to procedures. However, procedures followed by mediocre pilots or surgeons are likely to induce disastrous problems. This is true for all life-critical systems. Procedures (i.e., automating people's activities) or automation (i.e., automating systems) improve human operators' productivity and overall human-system safety, but cannot work without human operators' domain competence and knowledge. Great surgeons and pilots break free of procedures when necessary, because they know that procedures cannot solve everything and are context sensitive. They know about context of validity of the cognitive functions that are implanted in the procedures. They also know when a situation is not "right." Progress in technology clearly reduces risk. However we should overcome the myth that technology does not eliminate risk. Technology cannot provide absolute safety. Life-critical domain skills and experience have to be preserved with new technology in mind.

Abduction is a key process in design, more specifically in TIS design. Design always starts with a first mock-up (i.e., a projection), which we test (i.e., verify the validity of the project). We eventually fail. As a matter of fact, the more difficult is the task and the more complex is the artifact being designed, the more we may fail in the first place. However, failing is great for learning. We learn about things that cause failures. Consequently, we improve the various elements of the AUTOS pyramid[1] (i.e., artifact being designed, users interacting with it, tasks being executed, as well as related organizations and situations). We then test again. We may fail again! In this case, we analyze again and improve again, and so on until we succeed. This is what agile design is about (Agile Manifesto 2015). Of course, this approach requires competence, perseverance, patience, vision, and great management. In other words, taking care of people and team spirit are key.

It may happen that failures are catastrophic. For example, the three astronauts of Apollo 1 lost their lives on the launchpad at Cape Canaveral because of a cabin fire during a launch rehearsal test on January 27, 1967. Astronauts' deaths were attributed to a wide range of lethal design and construction flaws in the early Apollo command module. Manned Apollo flights were suspended for 20 months while these problems were corrected. The first successful manned Apollo mission was flown by Apollo 1's backup crew on Apollo 7, launched on October 11, 1968. The rest is history! Apollo 11 landed on the Moon on July 20, 1969. This was one of the most extraordinary accomplishments of human kind. Without such an abductive approach, NASA would not have done what we know today. More generally, goal-driven programs require competent people and great team spirit.

Apollo 13: "Houston, we've got a problem!" Competence could be seen at the individual level, but also at the collective level. Apollo 13 "successful accident" is a good example of great ground-crew cooperation. Apollo 13 was launched on April 11, 1970, from Kennedy Space Center, Florida. Two days after launch, an oxygen tank exploded, crippling the service module (SM) upon which the command module (CM) depended (Fig. 4.3). Lunar landing was aborted.

Ground engineers managed to solve the problem by making a carbon dioxide removal system using various kinds of things available on board. They made it and sent procedures to astronauts who managed to build such a system. Finally, the crew succeeded to put together the system and returned safely to Earth on April 17. This is an example of creativity (i.e., integration of existing equipment to create something) and cooperation (i.e., ground people and space crew collaborated to make a system in real time). This is what design thinking is about.

---

[1] The term "AUTOS" stands for Artifact, User, Task, Organization, and Situation. It defines a framework useful for human-centered designers (see Chap. 3 of this book; and Boy, 2011, 2013).

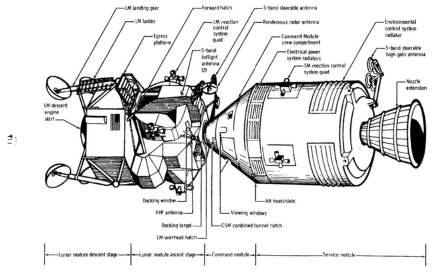

LM landing gear — Forward hatch — S-band steerable antenna
LM ladder — LM reaction control system quad — Rendezvous radar antenna — Environmental control system radiator
Egress platform — Command Module crew compartment — S-band steerable high gain antenna
S-band inflight antenna (2) — Electrical power system radiators — SM reaction control system quad
— Nozzle extension
LM descent engine skirt
Docking window — Aft heatshield
VHF antenna — Viewing windows
Docking target — CSM combined tunnel hatch
LM overhead hatch —

|←—Lunar module descent stage—→|←—Lunar module ascent stage—→|←—Command module—→|←————Service module————→|

Apollo 13 space vehicle configuration.

Fig. 4.3 Apollo 13 configuration

Delivery

Innovators usually think that once a good product is made, delivery will follow without difficulty. This is far from the truth. Product delivery is a long process. Marketing is part of it. In fact, delivery is a communication process that consists in convincing people to buy a product. In our market economy, anything can be sold, even if it is not human centered. The recurring question is: what do we mean by human-centered products? HCD is based on elicitation, integration, and communication of people's needs.

Apple, for example, clearly understood these three processes. More specifically, the iPod music player is based on people's needs for easy access to music anytime anywhere. Consequently, the iPod was designed using an outside-in approach going from the purpose (i.e., easy access to music anytime anywhere) to means (i.e., easy-to-use interface, mp3, and iTunes). Everything started when Tony Fadell, a former Philips engineer, convinced Steve Jobs about the iPod idea.[2] Steve Jobs gave him 30 brilliant designers, programmers, and hardware engineers (12-month development), and the rest is history.

Creativity is integration! Knowing how to integrate ideas from various sources is key. Vinnie Chieco was a copywriter who Apple asked for advice on how to introduce the new player to the public. After he saw the prototype, he thought about the

---

[2] It should be noted that, prior to connecting with Apple, Tony Fadell went to Microsoft, and his proposal was turned down because they did not believe that idea could make any money.

phrase "Open the pod bay door, Hal!" in Stanley Kubrick's movie "2001: A Space Odyssey."

However, the iPod would not be the iPod without constant efforts in design, tests, assessments, and improvement. Everything is important, from user interface, color, reliability, size, and weight to battery life. Refinement went very far. Apple integrated latest technology such as the revolutionary touch interface developed for the iPhone and transferred it to the iPad.

One of the main reasons for the success of the iPod is its immediate total adoption by young people. Of course, as all Apple products, iPod's use is easy, intuitive and appealing, and consequently easy to adopt. Aesthetics was also an important factor for delivery. The iPod is a beautiful object. Conventional marketing was not used. iPod's values were communicated by word of mouth. When customers are happy, they tend to communicate their happiness. This is exactly what happened. Apple did not make any conventional marketing! The genius comes from the vision, the projection into the future, betting on mobility and easy access to music.

Summarizing, iPod delivery success was not a matter of marketing, but a matter of great ideas, solid integration, and constant attention of people's needs in terms of music and mobility.

Back to Top-Down and Bottom-Up Design Strategies

Design is about getting the big picture as well as mastering details.

The distinction between top-down and bottom-up design strategies is not new in information processing, software design, and organization design and management (Pereira et al. 1993). Human-centered designers and engineers cannot separate these two design strategies. They usually go from one to the other with respect to design purposes and constraints. For example, a composer designing a symphony continuously swaps from one to the other. We will use the Orchestra metaphor to illustrate how these design strategies can be used.

The **top-down** design strategy consists in decomposing from the big picture into components. It is used when most components are custom designed. It induces constraints such as testing can only be done when everything is developed. Top-down developments require definition of specific syntax and semantics of the product being developed. In software engineering, for example, top-down developments involve complete understanding of what the system will be and planning in consequence. No coding can start before everything is well understood.

The **bottom-up** design strategy consists in composing from seed elements, described and elaborated in great detail, into a whole that progressively make sense, cognitive and emotionally. It is used when costs need to be minimized. It uses off-the-shelf components. Of course, this approach requires standardization. For example, you can build a system using Lego components, and the resulting system will be Lego-based. Bottom-up developments are based on reusability of components. This is the case in software engineering, where old programs can be reused and modified to make new ones. Testing needs to be done from the beginning of the design process.

Top-down design requires a hierarchical organization from the start. Bottom-up design requires orchestration of several contributions (e.g., like orchestrating in real time a free jazz band). A composer has also to be a musician (i.e., a design team should be able to operate the system being designed). Each design team member has a role. For example, some of them are in charge of testing the system being designed.

Various types of organizations play complementary roles. For example, governmental institutions manage public health using a top-down strategy (i.e., health care is organized with respect to planned global objectives, which are translated into laws that must be followed). In contrast, nongovernment organizations (NGOs) work according to bottom-up strategies (i.e., NGOs work locally trying to solve specific problems). Both approaches to public health are good and should be more intertwined. The former involves professionals who follow rigid work rules. The latter involves volunteers who accept flexible rules. Note that NGO's volunteers are usually very well trained and experienced professionals. Both approaches can be combined. Google, for example, allows its employees to work 20 % of their time on their own projects. Therefore, 80 % of Google's employee time is devoted to top-down requirements and 20 % to their own bottom-up creativity. One strategy nurtures the other and conversely.

The top-down design strategy is based on planning in order to reduce uncertainty and therefore leads to rigidity. On the opposite, the bottom-up design strategy is based on constant problem-solving in order to cope with uncertainty requiring flexibility. From a risk-taking point of view, the former tries to reduce and even avoid risk, as the latter tries to optimize risk. Risk reduction, avoidance and optimization refer to Llewellyn's possible relationship between level of perceived risk, risk orientation and risk acceptability (Boy 2013).

Agile Approach for TIS Development

TIS design and development requires extreme vigilance with respect to the TOP model (i.e., monitor the evolution and emergence of new appropriate technology, practices, and organizational setups). When you start a project, you never know if you will be finished on time, if the product will fit the requirements and fulfill the initial vision, if people will accept it, and so on. You then need to address uncertainty, unpredictability, risk, continuous variability, and socio-technical evolution.

TISs are usually designed and developed as independent entities that need to be integrated into a living environment. Let's take the UBER app. This application was developed in California and is very successful. It enables you to very quickly find a means of transportation (typically a car owned by someone else) at very low cost. It is easy to use and very effective and efficient. The French government had to decide to forbid this app, because taxis were very upset. Taxis were very upset because their prices were very high compared to what UBER offered; the reason is that they have very high license fees (e.g., 250 K euros) to start their business and need to compensate. Consequently, UBER app—a pure product of contemporary information technology—created a huge societal breakdown, even if the concept is very much in line with the evolution of our information society. You can see on this example that context and culture are extremely important to consider at design time and incrementally during the life cycle of the product. By designing a new TIS, you should understand the various impacts of the use of this TIS. Again, the TOP model is always very useful in this rationalization process.

"Tell me and I forget. Teach me and I remember. Involve me and I learn." This Benjamin Franklin statement is very relevant in HCD. Stakeholders should be involved and even engaged in the HCD process. HCD requires quick development of prototypes that can be tested by appropriate people and repeats this process as many times as possible. This is called an "agile" approach.

Let's take SCRUM as an example of the agile approach in the software engineering domain. SCRUM is both a support for the development of a product and a collaborative environment that is supposed to handle design team issues. Each piece, let's say a TIS, is built upon previously created pieces. Building TISs as small pieces "encourages creativity and enables teams to respond to feedback and change, to build exactly and only what is needed… An agile method provides a small set of rules that create just enough structure for teams to be able to focus their innovation on solving what might otherwise be an insurmountable challenge." (SCRUM 2015). In the same way SCRUM supports creativity and active collaborative work in software engineering, TIS-based agile HCD promotes creativity and active collaborative work in systems engineering. People at work should belong to the group and interact with other people, constantly learn and grow, do effective things, actively contribute to the creation of appropriate features, and incrementally improve existing designs (Fig. 4.4).

Fig. 4.4 Agile TIS-based agile HCD team member attributes

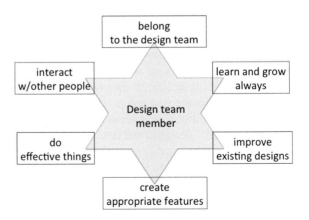

Standardization and Technology Evolution

Standards provide normalized objects and methods that can be assembled to make something new, which, in turn, needs to satisfy standard requirements. In other words, a standard provides a homeostatic syntactic-semantic framework that keeps cultural homogeneity of a community of practice (e.g., ATA standard very precisely provides definition, properties, and methods in aeronautics). A useful and usable standard is not set up immediately; it takes years to create and refine it. Taking the Orchestra model as a metaphor, a standard can be considered as a crucial part of the music theory (e.g., classic, jazz, rock'n' roll, rap). This book presents a series of concepts that are useful for standardization of TISs. By any means, they do not have a standard per se, but I believe that they can contribute to the creation and refinement of a future standard (e.g., tangibility, SFAC model, NAIR model, complexity, flexibility, stability, maturity, and sustainability).

If we look at the way smartphone apps evolved to "stabilize" as they are today, they appear as rounded rectangles with a picture on it and a string of characters underneath (i.e., a name). You just tap on the visible picture, and the related app opens on the screen of your smartphone. If you deal with time, it could be a calendar, a watch, or a scheduling application. Standardization is based on successfully imposed designs that persist over time in this case. A fashion that lasts! However, this is not the way conventional standardization is carried out in industry. There are committees of experts meeting regularly to fix a framework of good practice first, then socially accepted emerging norms, and finally incremental refinement of these resulting standards. Standardization processes are typically tedious and long. For example, international consortiums, such as the Object Management Group (OMG), develop standards on open memberships. OMG works on enterprise integration standards (OMG 2015). Problems come when the resulting community of practice has to follow standards out of definitional context. People have to solve problems instead of following procedures, which is an entirely different cognitive process. Indeed, designers framed into a very strict standardization sometimes have difficulty to innovate. From that point of view, innovation and standardization are almost contradictory.

Let's explore various kinds of time provider TISs, usually called watches! One of the first automata was the clock. Clocks have been designed in many ways. The most persistent design is a circular quadrant graduated in second, with mention of hours and minutes. We learned how to read time using such an interface. As a matter of fact, the position of the needles is the salient information; we often do not read the exact time, but we immediately know what time it is. We have adapted to clocks, to the point that we instantly know when it does not work. The problem comes when there is a serious issue. Let's take a watch as an example to support the use of the AUTOS pyramid and an outside-in approach. First, what is the best user interface for a watch? The first option is what I call "the conventional watch" (Fig. 4.5).

It has two needles (one for the hours and one for the minutes). It is interesting to notice that we have learned how to read time on such watches when we were young and we rarely make mistakes even if the graduations on the watch are from 1 to 12 (for the hours) and often none for the minutes (that should be graduated from 1 to 60).

Fig. 4.5 Option 1:
conventional watch

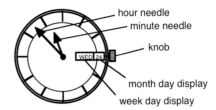

Fig. 4.6 Option 2: the
four-knob needle watch

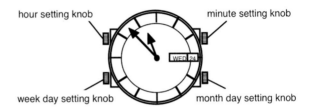

We have developed an embodied situation awareness cognitive function that is very robust and trustable. We also have the weekday and the month day displayed on two separate windows. The watch is also equipped with a knob that has its own functions. If you pull the knob fully, you can adjust the two needles to a desired time. This knob has also two other intermediary positions that enable you to fix the weekday and the month day. In my experience, I always have difficulty fixing these two parameters because the right intermediary positions are difficult to find (i.e., an issue of physical tangibility). You can see that this watch option requires learning several things.

An alternative option is what I call the "four-knob needle watch" that eliminates the difficulty in finding the right position of the single knob to fix the weekday and the month day (Fig. 4.6). You just have to know what knob is for what parameter. This option replaces a mechanical maneuver by a memorization cognitive function. You need to remember which knob is for which function (i.e., minute or hour setting and week or month day setting).

We can go a step further and propose another option, the "four-knob digital watch" that eliminates the memorization cognitive function because each knob faces its corresponding parameter to fix (Fig. 4.7). There is no ambiguity, and affordances are great, in Gibson's sense (Gibson 1979).

These three watch options illustrate a human-centered approach to define design rationale. The first two options could work for mechanical watches. The third one only works for digital watches. But let's go a step further again, and propose the "speech recognition watch" that enables its user to fix all parameters by voice, telling the watch what time it is and what day it is (Fig. 4.8). This option requires more sophisticated technology. It also could be disturbed by external signals.

Making progress on watch technology, the next step is automated setup of time using Wi-Fi and global positioning system (GPS). Let's call the resulting appliance "automatic datalink watch" (Fig. 4.9).

Fig. 4.7 Option 3: the four-knob digital watch

hour setting knob

minute setting knob

week day setting knob

month day setting knob

Fig. 4.8 Option 4: the "speech recognition watch"

speech recognition button

microphone

Fig. 4.9 Option 5: the "automatic datalink watch"

automatic datalink

In this case, you do not need to adjust the time when you travel from a time zone to another. The system does it all for you. This involves external systems such as radio transmitters and receivers, as well as satellites. The complexity of the watch becomes then tremendous. You do not see this complexity. What you get is a very useful and convenient device when everything works, but you will never be able to fix anything if it fails. Therefore, Option 5 is a tangible interactive system when it works (Fig. 4.9). Design of the automatic datalink watch requires definition of the various interactions among the various agents (e.g., people using the watch, satellite GPS technology, and Wi-Fi).

You can see that these various time provider TISs are based on different types of autonomy. Option 1, the conventional watch, requires skills from its user to fix the four basic time parameters. It does not have any dependency on anything outside, except the user him/herself. Options 2 and 3 improve affordances and therefore watch usability. Option 4 definitely improves usability, taking into account that the environment is not too noisy. Option 5 is totally dependent on an external computing and transmission network (e.g., the cloud), but it works fine; it is the ultimate time provider TIS. You also can see the usefulness of the AUTOS pyramid to rationalize related evolution of time provider TISs.

Collaborative Human-Centered Design

Several people asked me why HCD is different from human factors and engineering (HFE). I already developed this issue by saying that HFE happens after engineers have developed a system in order to evaluate human-system interaction. For a long time, HFE had very little or no input at design time. The main problem is HFE corrective approach has very little impact on structures and functions of the system and necessarily leads to the definition of user interfaces and operational procedures, sometimes attempting to compensate design flaws, in the human-centered sense. HCD takes into account human issues from the beginning of design and has a strong impact on system structures and functions. Obviously, HCD requires a deep redefinition of organization structures and functions. What does this mean?

First, designing a complex system requires several kinds of knowledge and knowhow. Consequently, several disciplines should be working together within the design team. Resulting organization should be able to support participatory design where collaboration is key. What does "collaboration" mean? It is the ability to work jointly with and contribute to a multidisciplinary team. The organization should enable collaborative creativity, especially when we are interested in nontypical problems (i.e., where there is no standard). In particular, the organization should support creative generation of ideas. In addition, the organization should provide the ability to iteratively develop innovative solutions insuring that systems being designed and developed are desirable, viable, and feasible. Virtual engineering is certainly a crucial support for iterative prototyping (see Chap. 3).

In any organization, authority is a key factor where the way leadership is set up is crucial. In space missions, for example, astronauts alternatively swap from situations of leadership to situations of followship. This swapping process is not trivial. First, people involved need to know each other and recognized other's knowledge and skills. Second, people involved should be able to collaborate tactically and strategically. Obviously, some tools do or don't facilitate creativity, collaboration, and communication. This is why prototypes need to be tested iteratively, using appropriate scenarios, to identify functions and structures to be improved.

> **Collaborative human-centered design breaks with the overnormative approach to systems engineering too much based on reporting and promotes expertise, direct communication, and continuous testing toward human-systems integration.**

However, innovation cannot happen without a favorable climate for creativity. Indeed, people are creative when they are free from constraints. In current organizations where so-called quality processes dominated by ISO 9000 norms rule professional activities, there is no room for creativity. Conversely, these processes are based on reporting that has often become more important than the job it documents. Sometimes, people spend more time reporting than effectively doing real work. In addition, reporting content has to be always positive if people want to get their bonuses. Consequently, unsuitable consequences come out from this kind of framework (e.g., late delivery, constant modifications, and in the end lack of holistic control). Collaborative HCD breaks with this overnormative approach to systems engineering. It promotes articulation work, where people are encouraged to constantly communicate, cooperate, and coordinate among each other, especially in the context of computer-supported cooperative work (Fjuk et al. 1997). Again, empathy is one of the most important emotional and cognitive processes that workers need to use. Quality should naturally emerge from articulation work and empathy, not from cold speculative rigid and preestablished processes. Of course, it requires expertise, accumulated and digested experience, hard work, persistence, and discipline to take this route, but I believe—from my experience—that this is likely the only one that supports creativity toward success.

Obviously, we need standards to simplify work and increase safety, but we also should make sure that people do not use these standards as ultimate solutions applicable anytime anywhere without educated common sense intimately associated with domain knowledge and knowhow. Standards support work activities; they do not replace people's work. They contribute to modify people's jobs however. This is why it is crucial to discover and identify emerging properties and behaviors by observing and analyzing various activities as much as possible (i.e., M&S, human-in-the-loop simulation, and activity analysis need to be carried out). This discovery and identification of HCD work is intrinsically collaborative (i.e., it requires collaboration of people designing, using, evaluating and regulating).

Ethnographical Design: Ideation and Sensemaking

Ethnography,[3] often used in social sciences, particularly in anthropology and sociology, is a qualitative research method used in HCD to elicit viewpoints and concepts from groups of people. Elicitation requires special skills. First and foremost, people want to be polite and helpful and answer questions even from relative strangers (i.e., you as an ethnographer), when you appear to be well informed about our professional specialty (i.e., you are on the same page as people you interview). In many cases, people may be tempted to say more than they should because they feel appreciated and feel that they are doing something important and useful. Consequently, human-centered designers, as ethnographers, need to proceed with empathy and constantly integrate the target community (i.e., be considered as one of them).

Ethnographical design is about divergent thinking (e.g., generation of ideas through brainstorming) and convergent thinking (e.g., analysis, synthesis, evaluation, prioritization). Divergent thinking is a matter of right hemisphere of the human brain, and convergent thinking is a matter of left hemisphere of the brain.

---

[3] Ethnography comes from the Greek *ethnos* (i.e., people) and *graphein* (i.e., writing).

The great pleasure and feeling in my right brain is more than my left brain can find the words to tell you. — Nobel Laureate Roger Sperry.

The distinction between right and left hemisphere of the brain can be represented as follows. The left hemisphere of the human brain enables logical inference, argumentation, fact processing, detail management, scientific reasoning, and rational behavior and tries to be objective. The right hemisphere enables holistic thinking, emotion, intuition, abstraction, artistic, and irrational behavior and is definitely subjective.

Creativity is then supported by both brain hemispheres. It involves:

- Original thinking (i.e., things that were never thought before)
- Synthesis (i.e., combining information from different sources into a new pattern)
- Extension (i.e., extrapolating an idea beyond current constraints and limitations)
- Duplication (i.e., improving or reusing an idea often in a new area or domain)

Creativity is about finding the right problem to solve. In his famous book, *How to Solve It*, George Pólya proposed four steps to solve a mathematical problem: (1) understand the problem, (2) make a plan, (3) carry out the plan, and (4) look back on your work to improve it (Pólya 1957). Most importantly, he advised to change the problem statement when you cannot solve the initial problem (i.e., simplify the problem, find another related problem that will be easier to solve).

Creativity is risk-taking. Being creative is projecting you into the future. Creativity involves intuition, expressivity, least commitment, and cultural blocks:

- According to Hubert Dreyfus, **intuition** is the process that enables someone to do the appropriate thing without rationalization (i.e., without providing any explanation). Talking about the expertise of chess players, Dreyfus claimed that expert performance depends "almost entirely on intuition and hardly at all on analysis and comparison of alternatives" (Dreyfus 1998). They take risks, but they use heuristics to guide their constant abductive inference processes.
- In genetics, **expressivity** refers to variations of a phenotype in individuals carrying a particular genotype.[4] The notion of phenotype is interesting in HCD because it expresses what you can observe, meaning activity, performance, and behavior. Phenotypes result from the "genes" of the multi-agent organization that generates them. In HCD, these genes are the cognitive functions involved in the various interactions among agents, tasks, and influential factors coming from the organization itself and situations (think about the AUTOS pyramid).
- A problem can be decomposed breath-first or depth-first. This distinction is commonly used in artificial intelligence for the implementation of search algorithms based on graphs and trees. Assuming that you can represent the problem to be solved by a tree structure, a breadth-first search is implemented by level of

---

[4] Wilhelm Johannsen proposed the distinction between phenotype and genotype to denote the difference between the heredity of an organism and what it produces (Johannsen 1911).

decomposition from the root to the first level of decomposition, to the second level and so on. In contrast, a depth-first search is implemented from the root and follows one of the branches of the tree as far as possible until either the node you are looking for is found or you hit a leaf node (i.e., a node with no children). Human beings proceed with a combination of breadth-first and depth-first strategies; they are opportunistic in that regard. Most interestingly, smart behavior is not to commit in the generation of the search trees until you know more about the situation. Consequently, a **least commitment** approach to problem-solving keeps undecided breadth-first and depth-first searches until situation clarifies. This approach involves both boldness and prudence.

- Do not forget that there are **cultural blocks**. Analytical engineering culture may block storytelling. Constant search for objectivity (i.e., look for normalization) may block subjective thinking (i.e., look for meaning). Consequently, creativity will improve if these cultural blocks are removed.

The Group Elicitation Method

The group elicitation method (GEM) was developed during the 1990s to help knowledge managers to collect articulated information from groups of experts (Boy 1996, 1997). In this book, GEM is considered as a method to be used to state a design problem. GEM has five sequential steps.

Step 1. First, you need to **formulate a question** (problem statement) to be answered (possible solutions) by a group of people, which has to be well selected with respect to the design topic to be explored. Problem-solving is hard when not well stated. The following questions help in stating the problem. What is the goal of the system that we plan to analyze, design, or evaluate? How is the system or its equivalent being (or planned to be) used (e.g., provide current practice, observed human errors)? How would you use this system (i.e., users' requirements)? What do you expect will happen if the corresponding design is implemented (e.g., productivity, aesthetics, and safety)? What constraints do you foresee (e.g., pragmatic investigation of the work environment)? You can also provide naive and/or provocative suggestions (i.e., how about doing the work this way!)

Step 2. **Brainwriting** usually involves a set of subject matter experts who write viewpoints (ideas) on sheets. Optimal number of participants is typically seven. They write viewpoints contributing to answer the question established in step 1. Brainwriting starts by a first viewpoint generation of around 10 min. Then, each participant gives his/her sheets to his/her immediate neighbor who reacts to all viewpoints written on the sheet. Reactions could be threefold: (1) agreement, (2) disagreement, and (3) new viewpoint. The circular permutation of sheets is continued until all participants reviewed all sheets. When each participant receives his/her initial sheet, he/she reviews all reactions and comments. For seven participants, it usually takes 1 h to achieve the brainwriting. One of the main advantages of brainwriting is viewpoint generation in a quiet atmosphere where everybody can express himself/herself without any influence from the others (i.e., personalities do not enter into play). Another advantage is parallel viewpoint generation, which contributes to improve performance time. Finally, all viewpoints are written and constitute a compiled database for subsequently information processing.

Step 3. **Concept construction** is based on this compiled viewpoint database. It is carried out orally. Each participant reads his/her viewpoints together with agreements and disagreements from other participants. The facilitator uses the following categorization technique for the generation of a concept list. In the beginning, the concept list is empty. (1) The currently read viewpoint suggests a concept that is not already listed; then the facilitator generates a new concept in the list. (2) The currently read viewpoint belongs to a concept that is already listed; then either it is added to this concept as an additional element or the concept is rewritten. (3) The currently read viewpoint suggests that two or more already listed concepts should be merged; then a new concept synthesizing these concepts is generated and these previously generated concepts are deleted. (4) The currently read viewpoint suggests that an already listed concept is too large and should be split into two or more new concepts. This categorization process is carried out until all viewpoints are processed. This step is usually performed in about 2 h.

Step 4. Each participant ranks each concept in the generated list using a 1-to-10 subjective scale. When this **ranking process** is finished, an average rank is calculated together with a standard deviation. This step is usually performed in 10–15 min.

Step 5. The whole group of participants then reviews the list of ranked concepts. The facilitator starts stating that the top ranked concepts reflect a strong consensus among the participants and verifies that everybody agrees. Then lower ranked concepts are reviewed, checking if some of them should be kept or eliminated. Interesting discussions typically start when checking intermediate concepts. Two cases are usually discovered: (1) concepts that are not well defined and people rated them "in the middle" and need to be rewritten and (2) concepts that are well defined but participants disagree on their levels of importance. Once this **debriefing** is done, concepts can be reformulated one more time, and top concepts constitute excellent starting points for HCD problem stating.

Prototyping

Better understanding the complexity of a concept by becoming more familiar with the complexity of its prototype.

GEM results can then be used to develop the first mock-up or prototype of the product being designed. It is crucial to get visual accounts of the product as soon as possible. Using the SFAC model (Fig. 3.8 in Chap. 3), visualization of structures (i.e., objects) and functions (i.e., processes) provides concrete account of the product being designed. Of course, everything that is being visualized should also be described both declaratively and procedurally (i.e., defining the abstract mirror of concrete visualization). Summarizing, a prototype should capture, describe, and visualize structures and functions of the product being designed.

Innovation cannot be achieved without prototyping. A prototype provides similar properties of the product being designed. It should be tested in a variety of contexts using various kinds of relevant scenarios. The more it is tested, the more it provides opportunities for exploring activities produced by the execution of corresponding tasks. Prototyping materializes viewpoints and concepts generated in GEM sessions.

Prototypes are also mediating representations enabling design team members to communicate, cooperate, and coordinate their design activities.

More than anything else, prototypes enable to test various kinds of complexity. First, we should focus on the complexity of the algorithms implemented in the system being designed. Usually, we observe that users adapt to such complexity by becoming familiar with it. The problem is for the human-centered designers to determine if this familiarity can be true for a large variety of situations or if it is restricted to a small subset of test situations. The design of appropriate scenarios is the key issue here. Second, we should focus on the complexity of the visualization of observable variables and effectiveness of available controls. This type of complexity is also a question of familiarity. In the case of the Onboard Weather Situation Awareness System (OWSAS) designed at FIT Human-Centered Design Institute (HCDi), during the first iterations, several pilots had difficulty using OWSAS because they were using a different type of tablet (Laurain et al. 2015). Since these tablets had different capabilities in terms of visualization, these pilots were expecting a certain kind of behavior that was provided by OWSAS, because of the limitations caused by its tablet support. We changed to a different tablet and experimental results were much better. This very simple human-systems integration example is one among several others that contributed to incrementally improve OWSAS prototypes.

Formative Evaluations

More generally, formative evaluations contribute to iteratively improve prototypes, as opposed to summative evaluations that contribute to product certification. These formative evaluations should be conducted in simulation environments that are as much realistic as possible (e.g., OWSAS was evaluated in HCDi Boeing 737 simulator), with end users as realistic as possible (e.g., OWSAS formative evaluations were conducted with professional airline and military pilots). As already advocated, HITLS enables testing activity (i.e., what people really do) and not task (i.e., what people should do). HITLS are much superior to traditional approaches that are based on task analysis.

TIS formative evaluation requires principles and criteria. Here is a first non-exhaustive list of principles that can be upgraded with respect to the domain (e.g., medicine, automobile, entertainment): integration, interconnectivity, complexity, homogeneity, distraction, workload, elegance (i.e., ability not to induce complicated situations in case of abnormal contexts), flexibility, maturity, stability, and sustainability. Of course, these principles should be further developed, and I encourage you to do it. However over the years, I figured out that human-systems integration can be assessed using the following criteria:

- Consolidation or fragility (e.g., number of human errors and system failures due to the use of the TIS)
- Homogeneity or heterogeneity (e.g., syntax, color, shape, size, weight, height, distribution, texture, language, architectural design)
- Consistency (i.e., lexical consistency that deals with terms and symbols attached to concepts, syntactic consistency that deals with rules used to combine terms and symbols and organize interaction, semantic consistency that deals with concepts, and pragmatic consistency that deals with the way concepts are understood in a given culture)
- Assimilation (i.e., ease of learning, ease of retention, ease of association with existing concepts)
- Inclusion (i.e., ease of integration in the set of other TISs—e.g., integration of a new TIS, such as a traffic awareness system, in a car)
- Distraction (i.e., excessive use and focus of attention on the TIS that diverts attention from other important processes)

Actual evaluations may be held either as standalone processes or integrated in regular use of the TIS being delivered as a beta version. The former type of evaluation can be done in an evaluation lab using classical usefulness and usability protocols, methods, and criteria. The latter requires integrated recording systems of user's activity, which can be downloaded for further analysis.

Of course, formative evaluations produce recommendations that should be taken into account for incremental design improvement (i.e., in an agile way).

References

Agile Manifesto (2015) http://www.agilemanifesto.org. Retrieved on 26 Jan 2015)

Boy GA (1996) The group elicitation method: an introduction. In: Proceedings of EKAW'96, Lecture notes in Computer Science Series, Springer, Berlin

Boy GA (1997) The group elicitation method for participatory design and usability testing. Interactions Magazine, March 1997 issue, Published by ACM Press, New York; also in Proceedings of CHI'96, the ACM conference on human factors in computing systems, Held in Vancouver, Canada

Boy GA (ed) (2011) Handbook of human-machine interaction: a human-centered design approach. Ashgate

Boy GA (2013) Orchestrating human-centered design. Springer, London. ISBN 978-1-4471-4338-3

Boy GA, Brachet G (2010) Risk taking. Dossier of the Air and Space Academy. Toulouse, France. ISBN 2-913331-47-5

Dreyfus HL (1998) Merleau-Ponty's critique of mental representation: the relevance of phenomenology to scientific explanation intelligence without representation. http://www.class.uh.edu/cogsci/dreyfus.html. Retrieved on 11 Jul 2015

Fjuk A, Nurminen MI, Smørdal O (1997) Taking articulation work seriously – an activity theoreti-cal approach. Turku Centre for Computer Science TUCS technical report No 120, August. ISBN 952-12-0036-7; ISSN 1239-1891

Gibson JJ (1979). The ecological approach to visual perception. Boston, MA: Houghton Mifflin

Johannsen W (1911) The genotype conception of heredity. Am Nat 45(531):129–159. doi:10.1086/279202

Kramer U (2010) Coping and defence mechanisms: what's the difference? – Second act. Psychol Psychother 83(Pt 2):207–221. doi:10.1348/147608309X475989

Krznaric R (2014) Empathy: why it matters, and how to get it. Perigee Books. ISBN-13: 978-0399171390

Laurain T, Boy GA, Stephane AL (2015) Design of an on-board 3D weather situation awareness system. In: Proceedings 19th Triennial Congress of the IEA, Melbourne, 9–14

OMG (2015) Object Modeling Group. http://www.omg.org/gettingstarted/gettingstartedindex.htm. Retrieved on 26 Jan 2015

Pereira B, Carlos L, Maravall JM, Przeworski A (1993) Economic reforms in new democracies. Cambridge University Press, Cambridge

Piaget J (1985) Equilibration of cognitive structures. University of Chicago Press, Chicago

Plutchik R (2002) Nature of emotions. Am Sci 89:349

Pólya G (1957) How to solve it. Doubleday, Garden City

SCRUM (2015) https://www.scrum.org. Retrieved on 26 Jan 2015

Chapter 5
Complexity

Exploring the complexity of our universe is certainly a topic of interest for millennia. People always tried to develop models to explain where we live, where we come from, who we are, and so on. These models were matched to observable cues, until they were challenged by creativity and/or contradictions. Ancient Greeks, such as Aristotle and Ptolemy, described the cosmos in a geocentric way (i.e., planets like the Sun and the Moon were turning around the Earth on circular trajectories). During the mid-sixteenth century, Copernicus challenged the geocentric model by introducing the heliocentric hypothesis that the Earth was turning around the Sun. The invention of the telescope enabled astrophysicists, such as Galileo, to discover more planets and moons, as well as more precise properties of the solar system (e.g., Jupiter has moons; Venus is between the Earth and the Sun). Kepler discovered that planets trajectories around the Sun are elliptical. This model shift from geocentric to heliocentric caused huge resistance. People and institutions like stability and continuity in their beliefs. Changes cause instability that needs to be managed. In the light of this short preliminary astrophysics story, this chapter focuses on three human needs: world complexity exploration, solution discovery, and change management.

Mastering Complexity by Modeling

World complexity exploration is strongly based on observation and creating means for enabling observation to be possible. It is also about studying the various relationships among the elements that we can observe. In other words, it takes us many views of the real world, whether it is the sky and the stars or two flocks of birds converging to make a single flock, to make abstractions and build a model of what we can observe (Fig. 5.1). The first instance of the model is usually called a hypothesis, which needs to be validated. When the model is validated and recognized by a

© Springer International Publishing Switzerland 2016
G.A. Boy, *Tangible Interactive Systems*, Human–Computer Interaction Series,
DOI 10.1007/978-3-319-30270-6_5

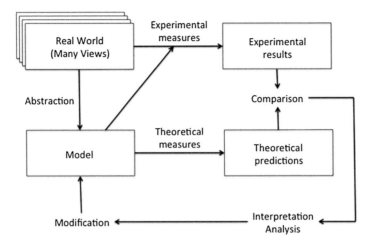

Fig. 5.1 Modeling process

large community of established experts, it becomes a socially recognized theory. This is the basic framework of scientific research.

> **A model is a useful abstraction of the real world. The more it is used, the more it can be challenged, improved and sometimes totally changed.**

A flock of birds is a multi-agent complex system. Each agent is autonomous (i.e., there is no central control), but must obey three simple coordination rules (Reynolds 1987): (1) separation (i.e., avoid crowding neighbors—short-range repulsion), (2) alignment (i.e., steer toward average heading of neighbors), and (3) cohesion (i.e., steer toward average position of neighbors—long-range attraction). This means that each agent needs to look for the closest agents and apply the separation-alignment-cohesion rules to coordinate with its neighbor agents. Each rule can be modeled mathematically by an algorithm, whose complexity is $O(n^2)$.[1] If each bird adjusts its velocity and position to the other birds within a fixed distance in a steady state, the time it takes to converge to a steady state is an iterated exponential of height logarithmic in the number of birds (Chazelle 2014). Birds react to each other dynamics. When one changes speed or direction, surrounding others adapt immediately to keep harmonious collective flight, no matter the size of the flock.

As a complex system, the generic flock of birds has **emergent properties** such as an apparent robust orchestration that is independent of its size. Several analogs have been tried to model flocks of birds, considering birds as fluid particles and/or

---

[1] Let's take an algorithm such as a multiplication of two numbers of n digits which requires a number of steps at the most proportional to $n(n+1) \approx n^2$. In this case, we then say that algorithm complexity is n^2.

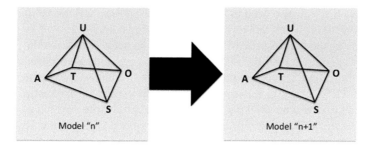

Fig. 5.2 Evolution of AUTOS pyramid models during the design process

flock phenomena as convection and diffusion. More generally, modeling is done to make sense of observed phenomena (i.e., descriptive models whose syntax and semantics have to be specifically defined) and enable us to predict them (i.e., predictive models whose behavior is already known and resembles the one of the observed phenomenon to be modeled).

Current growing air traffic complexity (i.e., constant growth of the number of aircraft, limited capacity of certain airports, and high safety requirements) requires more accurate modeling of the airspace multi-agent system and, by analogy with the flocks of birds, the definition of new tangible interactive systems (TISs) to guaranty safety, efficiency, and comfort of flying aircraft.

Models are incrementally upgraded as we get more knowledge from the comparisons between experimental results and theoretical predictions (such as presented in Fig. 5.1). In TIS design, it is highly recommended to maintain AUTOS pyramid models from step "n" to step "n + 1" (Fig. 5.2).

Complexity and Familiarity

Anytime you move to a new region to live, you suddenly find everything complex. You find the roads and streets bizarrely organized. You take the wrong direction, especially when you are in a hurry. After a few months, everything becomes easier. Your situation awareness cognitive function is now more effective. Nothing has changed externally. You have built a mental model of the region. You are now familiar with this extrinsic complexity. You have a set of indices that enable you to navigate efficiently.

Familiarity usually increases when you use a map of the region. The map is a model of the region that includes meaningful elements such as roads, main buildings, woods, lakes, and so on. You use a map by mapping what you observe outside with what corresponds on the map. This requires concentration (i.e., you often need to stop and identify correctly the geography of both external landscape and map, taking into account that the map is an abstraction—a model). This method involves the use of a static object that requires appropriate cognitive functions from its user.

This means that you also need to learn how to use the map and get familiar with it (i.e., various signs, icons, and representations of the landscape).

Another method consists in asking someone who is likely to know the region. If he or she is familiar with the region, you will be provided with meaningful and effective directions. This is a multi-agent approach to situation awareness.

Today, GPS[2] helps in navigation tasks. It is a tangible interactive system. Consequently, if you are walking, you will use your favorite smartphone application; if you are driving, you will use your car-integrated GPS system. This kind of device will give you both visual and auditory directions in real time. Familiarity is in the device. You are dependent of a device, based on data that may not be always accurate. Consequently, you need to use critical thinking (e.g., GPS database may not be up to date).

These three navigation methods involve a static object, a human agent, or an interactive system using some kind of artificial intelligence. The first kind of support involves complexity of the various representations used on the map. The second kind of support involves complexity of explanations given by a supposedly knowledgeable third party. The third kind of support involves TIS complexity. It is tangible when information provided by the system matches what its user identifies in his or her perceivable environment. If what the system provides requires too much concentration in real time, then its user will quickly have difficulty in his or her navigation task. Again, the user will have to become familiar to his or her navigation system (assuming that the user interface is well done).

Dealing with Complexity in Systems Engineering

I recently attended a series of presentations that advocated formal systems of systems models at a model-based systems engineering (MBSE) conference. These models were very well thoughts, but I wondered how they could be implemented in the real life, and even if they would be implemented, how could they be used in real operations? I felt that these very complicated models would rigidify systems engineer's work when design tasks actually would require flexibility. In addition, these models were very much based on a reductionist approach, even if the speakers repeatedly mentioned the fashionable concept of "emergence." The main question I had was the following: how can we use emergent properties obtained at operations time to modify these models? Of course, talking about operations time could be thought in terms of simulations and effectively done at design time, fostering human-centered design (HCD).

This brings back the concept of atomic system (constituent or component) functions that influence a system of systems (SoS) and create emergent properties. For example, today we never stop developing small applications (apps) that incrementally modify the way we work and, more generally, the way we live. These apps

---

[2] Global positioning system for navigation purposes.

should be designed in the same spirit of the coordination rules used by birds to make emerge dynamically stable and sustainable flocks.

Complexity of engineered systems is increasing along with the evolution of our societies, which are becoming more complex themselves. Interconnectivity is mainly responsible for this complexity increase. Systems that we develop include both technology and people, which we call agents, interacting among each other. For that matter, the nature of the underlying organization needs to be clearly identified to attempt mastering local and global complexity. This is the exact opposite of the formal rigid models that are often currently used in systems engineering.

Indeed, there may be both collaboration and competition among the various agents. Each agent has a level of authority. **Authority** may be assigned, but it may also emerge from interactions. In any case, authority can be analyzed using the "cognitive function" representation in terms of **control and accountability**. First, somebody has the authority when he or she is in control of the situation. This meaning emphasizes capability, capacity, competence, skills, and knowledge, which enable somebody to act correctly. Second, somebody has the authority when he or she is accountable to somebody else. This meaning emphasizes rule following, goal reaching, and reporting, which enable somebody to be responsible.

Complexity of an agent network, which will be called an organization, can be investigated and assessed using cognitive function analysis (CFA) (Boy 1998). Relevant cognitive functions of each agent in the organization are typically described by expressing their roles, context of validity, and resources, in terms of control and accountability. The role attribute is typically described in terms of level of authority, expressing control capabilities and accountability relationships. Context of validity defines the boundaries of this authority. Resources are described in terms of means serving the authority (i.e., internal and external means, such as physical and cognitive capabilities). For example, the current air traffic management (ATM) system, as a multi-agent system, should be described and investigated using clearly defined cognitive functions in terms of authority (i.e., control and accountability).

From a general standpoint, CFA enables us to support investigation of the discrepancy between what various agents of a domain (e.g., ATM) have to do (i.e., the task space) and what they really do (i.e., the activity space). I remind here that, by definition, a cognitive function transforms a task into an activity. I also would like to extend CFA to cognitive and physical function analysis. At the control level, cognitive and physical functions can be linked among each other with respect to two dimensions: context and resources (i.e., a resource can also be considered as a physical or cognitive function). At the accountability level, cognitive and physical functions can be linked among each other with respect to their roles. Analysis of resulting accountability networks provides support to examine leadership and followership. We then can develop two kinds of cognitive and physical function networks: control and accountability networks. The difficulty always consists in finding the right level of granularity of cognitive and physical functions. In addition, such complex organizations constantly evolve and self-adapt.

Natural Versus Artificial Complexity: The Affordance Issue

Even if you build a very simple object, when a human being uses it, the whole thing becomes complex and sometimes extremely complex. This is due to the nonlinear nature of natural systems. Of course, in this book, the human is a complex system. For example, assume that you want to build a chair. The function of a chair (i.e., the purpose of a chair) is usually to seat on it. The structure of the chair usually includes a horizontal surface where you can seat, a backrest vertical surface, and four legs. Chairs have many affordances, in Gibson's sense, including one that consists in using the chair as a static elevator. You may climb and stand on a chair to reach an object on a shelf, which was too high for you to reach standing on the floor. We may say that this is common sense (i.e., people know that they usually do not climb on chairs, but chairs afford to do it). If an affordance is present, then somebody will use it (no statistics, just a question of possibility).

Getting a Wrong Affordance Is a Risk   In safety science, risk is typically assessed using the following formula, R(E) = P(E) × CS(E), where "P(E)" is the probability of the occurrence of an event "E," "CS(E)" the severity of its consequence, and "R(E)" the calculated risk. A main problem arises when the probability is very small (i.e., tends to zero) and the severity is very high (i.e., tends to infinity compared to most serious cases). We learn in mathematics that zero multiplied by infinity is undetermined. This was precisely the case of the Fukushima Daiichi nuclear power plant disaster in Japan. The problem is intrinsic to the probabilistic risk model. It would be much better to choose a "possibilistic" approach to risk. Using possibility theory (Dubois and Prade 2012), we learn that probability is a single number that does not take into account ignorance (or degrees of ignorance). Instead of representing uncertainty of an event "E" by a probability "P(E)" (i.e., a number between 0 and 1), it is much better to choose an interval, with an upper value, called "possibility" (i.e., a number between 0 and 1 and noted "Pos(E)"), and a lower value, called "necessity" (i.e., a number between 0 and 1 and noted "Nec(E)"). Formally, we have the following relationships:

$$\mathrm{Nec}(E) \le P(E) \le \mathrm{Pos}(E).$$

The ignorance "Ign(E)" that we have on event "E" is given by the difference:

$$\mathrm{Ign}(E) = \mathrm{Pos}(E) - \mathrm{Nec}(E).$$

Total ignorance is Ign(E) = 1. This means that Pos(E) = 1 and Nec(E) = 0. Therefore, instead of having a single formula [R(E) = P(E) × CS(E)], we will have two. First, we will assess the possible risk using the following formula: $R_{\mathrm{Pos}}(E) = \mathrm{Pos}(E) \times$ CS(E). Second, the necessary risk will be $R_{\mathrm{Nec}}(E) = \mathrm{Nec}(E) \times$ CS(E). Of course, in the case of the Fukushima Daiichi disaster, since Pos(E) = 1, what only counts is CS(E) and necessity, which could be calculated using factors and data provided by civil engineering and nuclear engineering in particular. We will not enter into any calculation, but we can say that Nec(E) is bigger than zero.

Designing a TIS involves taking into account the possibility of having people take action using the wrong affordance (when there are several possible affordances,[3] of course!). Affordances are not built per se. They emerge from interaction. We then need to test human-system interaction and discover them. Remember that if a wrong affordance is possible, then somebody in the world is likely to take action on it at least once. You can see now why the concept of affordance is important. It enables design teams to look for them by analyzing the way people interact with incrementally refined prototypes. Note that a task analysis will never support affordance discovery. **It is only by observing activity** (i.e., actual human-system interaction) **that affordances are identifiable**.

> **Affordance discovery requires observing activity.**

Anytime we add a TIS into another, whether natural or artificial, the resulting system is a new entity on its own. When the Japanese added several nuclear power plants on the Fukushima Daiichi landscape, they modified this region forever. First, nuclear power plants (NPPs) are TISs in the sense that they require interactions between human operators and sophisticated machines. NPP's tangibility can be tested with respect to:

1. **Safety**. We know the risks involved in the use of such systems, which become tangible when the calculated risk is acceptable (e.g., lower than an acceptability threshold, if the risk model is also acceptable of course).
2. **Efficiency**. We build and use such systems because they are highly efficient and effective for energy production (they are therefore tangible by purpose, i.e., this is why they are built).
3. **Comfort**. We know that they do not pollute in normal conditions compared to other energy sources such as oil and coal, but they are extremely dangerous when there are major failures or disruptions.

The overall tangibility of an NPP can increase by using various kinds of appropriate TISs such as the context-sensitive mobile operations support system (COSMOSS) prototype designed at HCDi. COSMOSS is currently being designed to provide context-sensitive appropriate visualization to field workers anytime anywhere in the NPP. Consequently, COSMOSS should contribute to enhance situation awareness and decision-making of the entire NPP personnel, which has direct repercussions on safety, efficiency and comfort, and therefore tangibility of NPP technology.

---

[3] When a TIS has only one affordance, it is a simple TIS. Conversely, when it has several affordances, it is a complex TIS.

Combining TISs Into a Meaningful Whole

Architects have learned how to combine bricks, beams, and walls to make a house. These building blocks can be basically considered as static objects. Now, if these building blocks become dynamic, and more interestingly have autonomous behavior making them capable of interacting among each other, how would we think about the resulting whole? People building bridges, for example, have already thought and build such interactive structure as a system of systems (SoS). They are aware of the **interactions among the components** (e.g., when the bridge is "at work" with many cars and trucks moving on top of it). I propose to take this analogy of conventional architects combining bricks, beams, and walls to make a house, to define the job of human-systems integration architects combining TISs to make a complex life-critical system.

> **Designing a new TIS requires that we know about people who will use it as well as organizations where it will be used**.

A main problem today is this tendency to accumulate TISs for good individual reasons, but without any care of the whole. For example, cars are invaded by a set of TISs such as GPS, collision avoidance systems, line tracking systems, telephone hand-free kits, and so on. Individually, each of these TISs is great and is useful for the purpose that it was designed and developed for. However, when they are all available in the car, they need to be all monitored, and therefore driver's workload is likely to go up. They are not integrated enough to provide safe, efficient, and comfortable driving experience. Of course, this kind of integration can be done by the driver himself/herself through training and experience, but this may take an extended amount of time when there is no incident or accident induced during the period. This is a typical **human-systems integration** (HSI) issue that needs to be addressed as early as possible during design (i.e., taking an outside-in approach), instead of after systems are developed (i.e., taking an inside-out approach). From this example, we can see that it is the overall integrated assistance system that needs to be tangible.

We can see this integration in two possible ways: (1) integration from scratch or (2) integration of a new TIS into an existing system. In both cases, structures and functions have to be taken into account correctly (refer to Chap. 3). We need to understand connectivity among the various TISs and be able to play the interactions among the underlying agents in order to incrementally discover emergent properties of the whole system (e.g., driver, passengers, car, and road environment). Both **cognitive and physical functions**, and their structural counterparts, have to be identified and properly modeled in order to assess the complexity of the TIS network. We then need to be able to simulate this network. Human-in-the-loop simulations are often required. The degree of realism of such simulations is crucial to identify credible emergent properties.

Designing a new life-critical system (e.g., aircraft, car, or hospital operating room), as a multi-TIS system, requires us to understand the relative importance of each TIS constituent. How can we define this relative importance of TISs? I will use the metaphor of human body organs, taken as natural TISs. First, there are TISs that are crucial (i.e., if they fail, the whole system fails). For example, our heart is a crucial organ because if it fails we may die. There are TISs that may work even if they have important failures. We may lose half of our lung, for example, and live a normal life under certain conditions. There are TISs that are nice to have because they enable us to improve performance, safety, and comfort. For example, peripheral audition enables us to hear specific noises that can alert us of possible danger. If we lose it, we can still live in certain conditions and contexts. This kind of consideration should be studied and taken into account seriously anytime we design an artificial TIS.

Heart transplant has become a common medical operation. Since the 1950s, heart surgeons have taken many risks in order to lift surgery to its current level. Heart transplant is a very complex task. Surgeons are incrementally dealing with underlying complexity by developing categories of risk factors. Again, complexity was mastered through increasing familiarity and rationalization. Thanks to systematic and regular feedback, they have built up knowledge that enables them to prepare, anticipate, and operate properly. They have learned to recognize risk factors in patients and operational situations. They have perfected their actions, skills, and know-how: surgeon's hand is critical (as Dr. Loisance advocated in Boy and Brachet 2010). New TISs such as extracorporeal blood circulation have facilitated heart operations. They also make different demands on the surgeons in terms of skills. In other words, the integration of extracorporeal blood circulation created the emergence of new cognitive functions that surgeons had to learn. Technology matured over the years. Medical practice changed and also matured.[4] For example, surgeons no longer act on last-minute symptoms but on prior causes. The issue then becomes persuading the patient to accept an operation even though they feel perfectly healthy. Anticipatory surgery is much simpler, easier, and more successful than post-crisis operations. This is the same for technology (i.e., it is much simpler, easier, and more successful to use a HCD approach than a corrective human factors and ergonomics [HFE] approach). We then need to persuade decision-makers that HCD is more effective and globally cheaper than correcting technology-centered engineering using conventional HFE.

The user interface is a concept of the twentieth century. It results from the need of conciliating technology-centered engineering and human factors principles. It is less important in HCD, since it is necessarily taken into account and tested from the beginning of the design process.

---

[4] Technology maturity and maturity of practice will be further developed in Chap. 7.

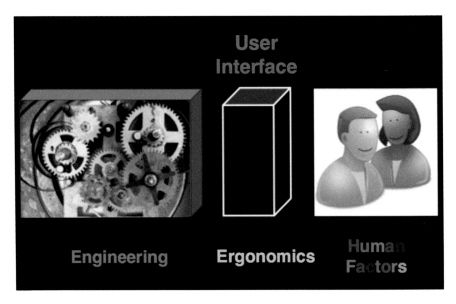

Fig. 5.3 Technology-centered engineering leads to corrective human factors and ergonomics evaluations and user interface design. HCD makes this approach obsolete since HSI is done from the beginning of the design process

Combining TISs into a meaningful whole is a difficult process. As already said, engineering common practice was for a long time testing technology first and human-systems integration second. End users were effectively considered when machines (i.e., systems) were fully developed. This approach led to the concept of user interface (Fig. 5.3). The big issue of this approach is the reconciliation of the "now-classical" analytical engineering methods with the necessary **holistic synthesis** of HSI. Classical engineering cannot bridge this gap without being led by human-centered designers. We then need to change current philosophy that still put this synthesis at the end of the development process.

Such synthesis and integration should be done as early as possible. As a matter of fact, HCD promotes creativity as synthesis and integration from the beginning of the design process, where design thinking and formative evaluations have to be combined. This creativity process could not be validated for a long time for complex systems design because these systems could not be tested with people in the loop before everything was developed. As already said, today this process is possible using contemporary modeling and simulation methods and tools, thanks to information technology. It is possible to incrementally assemble TIS prototypes and test them in an agile approach, which is human centered because end users can test and provide useful feedback very early during the design process, as many times as necessary. Function and structure can be created and tested concurrently at any time during the design process.

The Number Effect

More generally, the world population never stops to increase exponentially (Fig. 5.4). In 60 years, our world population grew from 2.5 billion in 1950 to 6.9 billion in 2010, which is more than from 10,000 years ago (1 million people) to 1950, in terms of number (i.e., 2.5 billion in 10,000 years versus 4.4 billion in 60 years). Numbers matter. From a complexity science point of view, this incremental growth inevitably creates emergent behaviors and properties that were not known before.

We, as human beings, tried to control our lives since the beginning of humanity because we have a cortex that enables us to design things, which in turn enable us to expand our lifetime expectancy. Agriculture, science, and technology extensive developments enabled our species to develop even more. This would be fine if we did not exploit energy sources (e.g., coal, oil, and gas) that started to degrade our planet in terms of pollution. For example, "CO_2 concentration has increased from 280 parts per million (ppm) at the start of industrial revolution to 400 ppm in 2013" (Emmott 2013). Emmott, a British scientist working on complex systems, claims, "We had started to change our climate." In particular, CO_2 increase has a tremendous impact on the global temperature of our planet's climate (i.e., our atmosphere, hydrosphere, cryosphere, and biosphere).

Since the 1990s, we started to see a crucial emergent issue, freshwater availability. Since forecast is nine billion people in 2015, we will need more water, food, land, transportation, and energy. From a homeostasis point of view extended to social and environmental issues, we are installed into a "neurotic" loop (Cannon 1932; Menninger et al. 1963). How can we come back to a regulated system that restabilizes life on Earth? Human evolution created this divergent instability. We then need to first understand our evolution and its repercussions on our living environment in order to control this instability and recreate something sustainable.

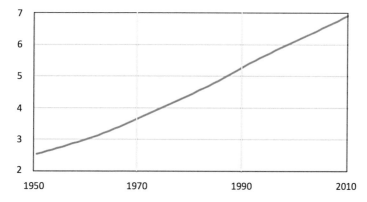

Fig. 5.4 Total population, both sexes combined, as of July 1 (billion of people). Data from the United Nations, Department of Economic and Social Affairs, Population Division, Population Estimates and Projection Section (http://esa.un.org/wpp/Excel-Data/population.htm)

Since the first industrial revolution, people built a tremendous amount of technology in the wild. We will not stop designing, developing, and using technology. I consider that technology is concrete realization of human intelligence. However, it is time to take into account human and social sciences during the design of artifacts in order to measure possible repercussions on our environment and us directly. Our market economy is based on a single axiom, i.e., increase personal interest of individuals. It is time to change this axiom into a more sustainable one, such as optimize the basic imbalance between technology, organizations, people, and environment. The concept of tangibility needs to include these factors. In addition, the notion of individual has very little sense because each individual is immediately connected to a network of relations (Cyrulnik 2001).

Technology is concrete realization of human intelligence.

The number effect is therefore an important factor that we need to take into account in the design of new technology. Up to now, we were more or less capable of modeling human-machine systems using classical mathematics (e.g., cybernetics and subsequent control theories). The number effect requires new kinds of mathematical means that include formal models of integrated systems that involve intertwined transfer of energy and information, autonomy and coordination of agents, and nonlinear interactions among these agents that produce emergent properties as attractors (to be discovered). Examples of complex systems are the human brain, natural language, and social systems (Cilliers 1998). Current developments of TISs, such as smartphones, highly automated aircraft, and more generally automotive systems and the Internet, open new interaction spaces where humans and systems constitute highly interconnected networks. These new human-systems networks are complex systems, with their own emergent properties that need to be clearly understood for the sake of safety, efficiency, and comfort of each individual and the whole.

The number effect requires new kinds of mathematical means. Complexity science can contribute to the provision of these means.

From Air Traffic Control to Air Traffic Management

Consciousness emerges from the interaction among about 100 billion of neurons. These neurons interact with other neurons, creating millions of billions of connections in the brain. This interactivity among a huge number of neurons makes

RPKs (billions)

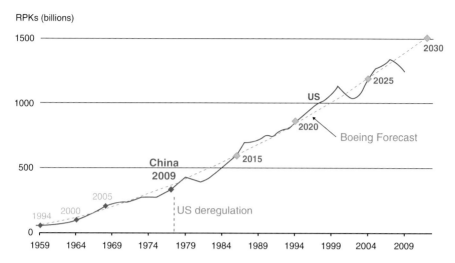

Fig. 5.5 Compared evolutions of passenger air traffic growth between China and the USA (US DOT Form 41 CAAC Boeing CMO 2010)

possible several human cognitive functions such as language, logic, emotion, cognition, memory, learning, motor control, and so on. This phenomenon of emergence characterizes biological systems, but also social systems such as ants or termite colonies. Termites, for example, construct habitats that have thermoregulation, defense, agriculture, climate control, and so on. These creatures are supposed to be very simple entities, but their collaborative work creates emergent behaviors that are extremely sophisticated and intelligent, by human standards.

It is interesting to look at the history of aviation. In the beginning of the twentieth century, few airplanes flew and did not have any problem navigating because the sky was almost empty! In particular, approach and landing was not a big issue, except finding a good runway to land, just because existing runways were not numerous and not necessarily well indicated and equipped. Then, radars were built and massively used. Air traffic controllers (ATCOs) had a tool to locate airplanes. Traffic increased but remained very manageable until recently. It is generally admitted that air traffic increased by a factor of 4.5 % every year for the last 30 years, which is an exponential growth that will not stop increasing if we take into account the strong growth of Asian air traffic. Indeed, the growth in passenger traffic in China mirrors that of the USA but at an accelerated rate (Fig. 5.5).[5] The number effect makes a big difference. There is a threshold above which "linear" control becomes "nonlinear" management. Above a number of aircraft, ATCOs need to become air traffic managers (i.e., they cannot control aircraft point by point but airflows taking into account that pilots take care of their trajectories).

---

[5] http://www.boeingblogs.com/randy/archives/2010/11/

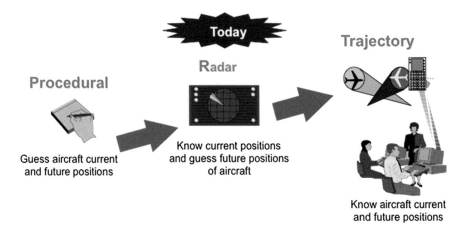

Fig. 5.6 ATM evolution from procedural control to trajectory management

There were three periods in the evolution of air traffic (Fig. 5.6):

1. The early stages of aviation when there were very few airplanes in the sky and air traffic control (ATC) was an occasional activity (i.e., procedural control)
2. The use of the radars that supported ATCOs until today (i.e., problem-solving control using radar systems)
3. The starting oversaturation period that requires mastering complexity using new kinds of models (i.e., trajectory management)

Below airspace saturation, ATCOs could control aircraft trajectories point by point, solving conflicts incrementally. Above airspace saturation, they cannot control aircraft individually any longer. They need to manage them. This is why we are currently moving from ATC to air traffic management (ATM), where aircraft will have contracts that they need to follow, and eventually negotiate with air traffic managers. This is called trajectory-based operations (TBO) where trajectories are in space and time (4D trajectories).

Human factors studies on ATCO's activity, conducted by Jean-Claude Sperandio and his team, have shown that task cost is a function of the quantity of information to execute a task and task execution success leads to the choice of less costly strategies that include the most important (primary) information and remove information that is considered secondary (Sperandio 1972, 1980). Of course, the distinction between primary and secondary information may depend on experience and expertise. Hartsfield-Jackson Atlanta International Airport, the busiest airport in the world, currently accommodates 2,500 flight arrivals and departures daily,[6] which around 120 airplanes per hour flying in and out during busy periods. Taking into account the growth indicated in Fig. 5.5, it is important to develop new systems supporting ATCOs. These systems should take into account explicitly the complex-

---

[6] http://atlanta-airport.com/Airport/ATL/ATL_FactSheet.aspx

ity of the airspace relative to the number of aircraft and their interconnections. ATCOs currently take care of this complexity in a centralized way (i.e., authority is on the ground). Decentralized ATM will transfer authority to cockpits conditionally to the implementation of new kinds of TISs (e.g., creating integrated and distributed flight envelopes very probably based on a flock-of-birds analogy).

The main problem in such very dense environments (i.e., airspace with many aircraft) is becoming the decentralized nature of the phenomenon. ATCOs were centralized authorities providing orders to aircraft. In the ATM context, pilots will have to follow a plan. In a normal situation where all aircraft will not have any failure of any kind, planning will be the best solution because air traffic managers will know where all aircraft will be and where they will go. However, when a failure will occur, pilots will have to replan their trajectory, and this act could have a tremendous impact on the overall traffic (e.g., domino effect). How can we solve this complexity problem?

Up to now, ATCOs had developed skills from a long collective experience to solve conflicts based on aircraft flow patterns. They used this incrementally refined know-how and knowledge in real time. In high-density situations like today on top of some airports, ATCOs cannot manage the whole traffic and need to put several aircraft on hold. With the overall traffic growing, each aircraft will need to handle separation from other aircraft automatically (this is called self-separation). This cannot be done without an explicit model of various "flocks of aircraft." Like for the birds, aircraft will need to be equipped with appropriate sensors (e.g., the ADS-B[7] is the first attempt in this direction) and algorithms that constantly guaranty safety, efficiency, and comfort. HCD advocates modeling and simulation of such potential solutions. This is crucial to discover emergent properties as early as possible in order to fine-tune coordination rules that aircraft will need to have. These rules will necessarily lead to tangible interactive systems that should be clearly understandable by the various actors in the airspace and on the ground.

Moving to ATM, air traffic managers will oversee the good execution of flight contracts passed with airlines. In the near future, aircrews will handle these trajectory-based operations (TBO) contracts. They are trajectory plans established before departure. If planning reduces aircraft trajectory uncertainties, it also rigidifies operations. In case of serious incident or failure, airspace actors need flexibility. This is why TBO planning will need to be better understood and mastered. Without new interactive technology, this kind of dynamic planning and plan execution will not be possible. Such interactive technology should also be tangible to people involved. New kinds of TIS will need to be created, developed, and tested. Some work has been started at HCDi and other research labs to investigate biologically inspired technology. In this case, we are interested in flocks of birds, which have specific functions that keep them flying together without any collision. On aircraft, resulting TISs will need to be created, implemented, and tested to verify emerging safety and efficiency.

---

[7] Automatic Dependent Surveillance – Broadcast: a technology that broadcast aircraft position from a satellite to both aircraft and ground.

Complexity and Diversity

Scott Page (2010) proposed an excellent account on the role of diversity in complex adaptive systems. Diversity is very relevant for the integration of TISs into a system of systems (SoS). TISs can be considered as adaptive (or not) entities interacting among each other and producing emergent properties that need to be studied if we want to understand the overall SoS performance. Page explains how diversity underpins system-level robustness, allowing for multiple responses to external shocks and internal adaptations, and how it drives novelty and innovation. Page looks at the different kinds of diversity, such as variations within and across types, distinct community compositions, and interaction structures. Note that Page's explanations apply to both HCD process and product.

Great discoveries and inventions come from the blend of several disciplines. We have already discussed in Chap. 2 that modern control engineering comes from cybernetics, developed in the 1940s by Norbert Wiener, a brilliant and famous mathematician, who worked with Arturo Rosenblueth Stearns, a physician and physiologist, who was Walter Cannon's student at Harvard University. Cannon coined in the 1930s the term homeostasis, a concept that was already discovered as "internal environment preservation" at the end of the nineteenth century by Claude Bernard, a physiologist. This example shows cross-fertilization of various disciplines (i.e., diversity) contributing to form useful concepts. This cross-fertilization was sequential. Today, researchers work in interdisciplinary teams, which facilitate faster participatory cross-fertilization.

Let's take an example of how people design complex systems today. Back to the design of a nuclear reactor (refer to Chap. 3), several kinds of expertise need to be integrated. The I2S-LWR project involved a team of about 30 smart people who provided their expertise and knowledge for the design of the nuclear reactor. It was interesting to watch this diversity of people interacting among each other to create a new kind of nuclear reactor. Each of them knew deep concepts and how to use them in his/her specific domain of expertise. Each of them also knew what were the links between his/her expertise and others' expertise. Complex systems design requires large expertise diversity as well as articulation among the various stakeholders involved. I also experienced the same kind of observation in the aeronautical domain, where aircraft design requires aerodynamicists, mechanical and electrical engineers, information technologists and computer scientists, and human-centered designers (not an exhaustive list).

Designing a complex life-critical system requires appropriate criteria for the assessment of human-systems integration (HSI). The TOP (technology, organizations, and people) model provides a categorization of various possible criteria. There are many aspects that need to be taken into account such as:

- (T) Robustness, reliability, resilience, efficiency, technology maturity, modeling and simulation, and advanced interaction media
- (O) Communication, cooperation, coordination, orchestration, social issues, environment, organizational complexity, organization design and management, and function allocation

- (P) Safety, training, occupational health, skills, knowledge, performance support, and life criticality

These lists are far from being exhaustive. The reason I give them is because I wanted to show the difficulty of establishing appropriate concepts that could be used to assess HSI. You could continue to add useful concepts having your own problem in mind. More generally, the main issue is that concept elicitation depends on your background, expertise, and understanding of the problem you have to solve. This is why you need to create a group of people who represent the diversity of the attributes that make sense using to solve your problem. Involving the appropriate expert group is key. Once you have this group formed, the next issue is to have an effective method that supports group knowledge elicitation (e.g., group elicitation method; Boy 1997). Experience-/expertise-based assessment during the design process is often more effective and efficient than any statistical method, in terms of resources, budget, and reactivity for formative evaluation.

Antoine Lavoisier, a French chemist, stated, "Nothing is lost, nothing is created, everything is transformed." This statement is known in France as Lavoisier's law. However, humans have tried to transform nature to satisfy their needs and desires, and we observe today that nature is changing rapidly losing many species and creating new ways of living. This transformation has exponentially increased since the beginning of the first industrial revolution. In other words, there are some basic laws of nature that we, humans, should know to start building systems that conform to them, instead of conforming to our needs by using nature only. It is clear that we should find a balance that does not create irreversible evolutions that ruins our quality of life.

Future TISs should take into account laws of nature, which should be integrated into design principles. For example, TISs could be developed to enhance house comfort and efficiency in terms of energy (e.g., TIS design principles could be based on nature circadian rhythms—such as using warm temperature during the day and cool temperature during the night or interseasonal thermal storage). Energy efficiency is therefore a matter of technology adaptation in terms of impact on nature and smart use of appropriate materials and their integration. No matter what technology humans develop, there are always waste. A design principle should be waste reduction in terms of human awareness, adaptation, and accountability.

Consequently, when you design a new system, take into account people who will be likely to use this system as soon as possible during the design process. One of the main reasons is adaptation. People adapt to almost anything, even to things that are badly designed. It is therefore important to observe and understand how people adapt to the new system being designed. Design is a process in time. Therefore, we should take time to observe and understand the various affordances that emerge from the various usability and usefulness tests to appropriately modify the system and in turn adapt it to people. Affordance diversity is a matter of putting HSI at work. More generally, the HFE community already introduced the term "ecological interface design" (Rasmussen and Vicente 1989; Vicente 2001), itself developed on the basis of ecological psychology (Gibson 1966). This ecological approach is a matter of functional diversity.

Let's end this diversity issue analysis by a story. When I was a kid, my father was making coffee very early in the morning. Smell of fresh coffee was always the trigger of my waking up, a wonderful feeling for me to start a new day! Today, we start to have home automation TISs that automatically brew coffee at a given time in the morning, providing you with the similar feeling. This kind of TISs uses the diversity of our senses, and smell in particular. I find it much better than an aggressive ring from an alarm clock. This is a great example of a pleasurable human-made ecosystem.

Internet, Apps, and Trust

Is the Internet tangible? I remember the time when I needed to go to the community library to search for books that were supposed to help me in my homework for school. I had to walk for more than half hour to reach the library. I knew the librarians who were always very helpful to me. The big library room was a huge space with tables and people working in quiet atmosphere. I have a vivid memory of this time, when I was a teenager. Today, I use the Internet that provides instant gratification to any kind of information search. From this viewpoint, the Internet is tangible. When I write a paper and need a reference, for example, I get it immediately. The same search took much longer time in the past. For this reason, I find the Internet extremely effective and useful.

Today, French TV reported that high school student unions, principals, and even the French government worry about a smartphone application, called "Gossip." This application proposes reading anonymous gossips that are transferred via phone numbers or Facebook. It displays harassment video or photo once and during ten seconds only. It quickly became very popular and caused many psychological problems. For this reason, this kind of app can be very disturbing. In the same way, the Internet is being used to internationally recruit young people by terrorist organizations. Consequently, Internet technology, which can be very useful for good causes, can also be used for terrible and violent purposes.

Fast-developed life-critical apps are TISs that require more maturity of practice than we allow today. In particular, people need to use critical thinking to better understand the various consequences of using them. Impersonal connectivity with people you do not know could be a danger. The issue of **trust** is at stake. People using apps or Web sites tend to trust them until they have a major problem with them, and they do not use them any longer. It seems that it is easier for some people to interact with a computer, even with other people through a computing application, than have face-to-face discussions. They are able to express things that would be difficult to say in a face-to-face discussion. It is interesting to observe that an app can provide tangible interaction in the figurative sense, but not at all in the physical sense. For example, you may interact with a terrorist on the Internet without knowing it and feeling some tangible empathy in the figurative sense (i.e., you will believe what this person says). However, you will not be able to establish a tangible relationship in the physical sense (i.e., you will not understand the real motivation of your utterer). Terrorists are using figurative tangibility through the Web to create empathy—something that would not be possible in a face-to-face relationship using physical tangibility, because most people would see propaganda almost immediately.

Back to the interactive cockpit concept, layers of software tend to increase the distance between pilots and mechanical things. The more software systems are efficient and effective, the more pilots trust them. An important question is: what should pilots know about these software systems? This is the same kind of question a manager of large organization would have. We could say that physical tangibility is about control and figurative tangibility is about management. However, great managers, from a human-centered viewpoint, are those who know about their employees' work, which is mainly related to physical tangibility. This is a reason why managers should start their careers doing physically tangible jobs.

> **Physical tangibility is about control and figurative tangibility is about management.**

There is a major difference between systems that open an activity that people cannot do and those that support an existing activity. This distinction brings the controversial issue of prostheses versus tools. Sometimes, we prefer to use the term "tool" instead of **prosthesis** because we do not design systems for handicapped people. However, lots of systems are prostheses because they open an activity that people cannot naturally do. For example, we do not naturally fly like birds and are somehow handicapped. Therefore, aircraft are prostheses that enable us to fly. Computers enable to calculate complex operations for us. I remember the time when I was tediously using mathematical methods to operate numbers with ten decimals (additions, subtractions, and multiplications). Today computers do that for us "without effort." The main problem is that most of us forgot how to do these calculations and, from that viewpoint, computers have become prostheses. In the same way, pilots need to know what flying physics is about; users of app prostheses need to know what they really address from both physical and figurative tangibility viewpoints. The "prosthesis" issue is therefore crucial in TIS design because we may build things that will enable us to do more things (e.g., fly), but also help us to lose our skills and experience (e.g., reading). On the one hand, we removed large amounts of concrete complexity, and therefore physical tangibility. On the other hand, we created new kinds of abstract complexity and therefore figurative tangibility. TIS design should take these issues seriously and balance physical and figurative tangibility.

References

Boy GA (1997) The group elicitation method for participatory design and usability testing. Interactions. ACM, New York, pp 27–33

Boy GA (1998) Cognitive function analysis. Greenwood/Ablex, Stamford. ISBN 9781567503777

Boy GA, Brachet G (2010) Risk taking. Dossier of the Air and Space Academy. Toulouse, France. ISBN 2-913331-47-5

Cannon WB (1932) The wisdom of the body. Rev. and Enl. Ed edition (17 Apr 1963). W.W. Norton & Company, New York. ISBN-13: 978-0393002058

Chazelle B (2014) The convergence of bird flocking. J ACM 61(4), Article 21 (July 2014), 35 pages. doi:http://dx.doi.org/10.1145/2629613

Cilliers P (1998) Complexity and postmodernism. Understanding complex systems. Routledge, London

Cyrulnik B (2001) L'ensorcellement du monde. Odile Jacob, Paris

Dubois D, Prade H (2012) Possibility theory. In: Meyers RA (ed) Computational complexity: theory, techniques, and applications. Springer, New York, pp 2240–2252. ISBN 978-1-4614-1799-6

Emmott S (2013) Ten billion. Vintage Books, New York

Gibson JJ (1966) The senses considered as perceptual systems. Hughton Mifflin, Boston

Menninger K, Mayman M, Pruyser P (1963) The vital balance: the life processes in mental health and illness. Viking, New York

Page SE (2010) Diversity and complexity. Princeton University Press, Princeton. ISBN 9780691137674

Rasmussen J, Vicente KJ (1989) Coping with human errors through system design: implications for ecological interface design. Int J Man Mach Stud 31:517–534

Reynolds CW (1987) Flocks, herds and schools: a distributed behavioral model. ACM SIGGRAPH Comput Graph 21(4):25–34

Sperandio JC (1972) Charge de travail et régulation des processus opératoires. Travail Humain Journal. Presses Universitaires de France, Paris, 35:85–98

Sperandio JC (1980) La psychologie en ergonomie (psychology in ergonomics). PUF, Paris

Vicente KJ (2001) Cognitive engineering research at Risø from 1962–1979. In: Salas E (ed) Advances in human performance and cognitive engineering research, vol 1. Elsevier, New York, pp 1–57. ISBN 0-7623-0748-X

Chapter 6
Flexibility

The concept of flexibility can be interpreted in various ways. First, flexibility can be synonymous to **autonomy**. We can say that an individual is autonomous, and then flexible, when he or she is able to act without external guidance. Second, flexibility can be related to **openness**. When an individual has an open mind, he or she can think and use several possible solutions without preconceived constraints. Third, flexibility can be intimately related to **change**. An individual who is able to easily change his or her way of living is said to be flexible.

Technology can free people by providing degrees of freedom that they did not have before. For example, aviation enables people to quickly go from a place to another located far away (by previous standards). On the other end, business developed taking into account this kind of flexibility and generated new kinds of rigidity because you now need to go to faraway places where people never thought going before. Very often, we do things because they are possible, but not because they are necessary except in urgency. We then create new illusions of necessity. Flexibility of the possible is transformed into rigidity of an artificial necessity. Therefore, we need to be careful when we look for flexibility. For example, it is now possible to use smartphones, and most of us do. At the same time, if this kind of tool offers lots of flexibility because we can be reached at anytime anywhere, we mostly become dependent of it, which creates an artificial necessity (e.g., if for some reasons we do not have our smartphone, we may miss important connections or information).

In this chapter, I will uncover the need for flexibility in design and development, subsequent use, and evolutionary redesign of tangible interactive systems (TISs). Anytime an artifact is developed, it introduces some kind of rigidity because it fixes some life activities that were only handled by people before, but it also creates new possibilities that are discovered incrementally. Once these possibilities become useful and are effectively used, they are transformed into artificial necessities.

© Springer International Publishing Switzerland 2016
G.A. Boy, *Tangible Interactive Systems*, Human–Computer Interaction Series,
DOI 10.1007/978-3-319-30270-6_6

Flexibility in Human-Centered Design

Describing the AUTOS pyramid, we have seen in Chap. 3 that the distinction between **task** (i.e., what is prescribed) and **activity** (i.e., what is effectively done) needs to be taken into account in human-centered design (HCD). More specifically, designers and developers need to learn and practice the art of task analysis and activity analysis. Indeed, technical managers tend to give tasks to designers and developers without checking what they are capable of doing. Instead, the first thing to do is to check what these people are doing when they are given an initial talk to do. This is the only way to observe their activity. In SCRUM, for example (Schwaber 2004; SCRUM 2015), it is usual to give a small period of time to designers and developers to produce a version of the product to be designed and developed. This period is typically called a "sprint" cycle (i.e., we represented such cycle as multiple small-Vs in Chap. 3 Fig. 3.6 and called it MVM). After a first cycle is carried out, you can see what can be done. The trick here is not to discuss what designers and developers did effectively, but how they did it. They then need to address collaborative work and reshape participation in order to improve their production. This is what Ohno suggested for Toyota's production system a long time ago (Ohno 1988). The only way to anticipate the length of a project is to know how design and development teams work in the first place.

Of course, end users should be part of the game. Participatory design is powerful not only because end users can influence design and human-systems integration during each cycle of the **agile** process but also because they are involved, end users automatically guaranty acceptability at delivery time. I had very interesting discussions with Gerry Griffin, former Director of NASA Johnson Space Center and Flight Director of lunar landing missions Apollos 12, 15, and 17, among many other prestigious responsibilities. He told me insightful stories about the qualities of Apollo's teams on the ground and in space. All actors were young, always considered themselves as extensions of the others (ground and crews), absorbed training like sponges, and trusted and respected each other. Their greatest strength was situation awareness, which he described at three levels:

1. Perceiving critical factors in the environment
2. Understanding what those factors mean, particularly when integrated together
3. Understanding of what will happen with the system in the near future (Griffin 2010)

Another thing that Gerry Griffin insisted on was the "fear of screwing up!" During the Apollo program, situational awareness, teamwork, trust, and disciplined execution were key. These people were concentrated, constantly checking results, available, and flexible to solve problems when they occurred. I promote this experience and take it as a basis and driving force for HCD.

In a motivated team, it is interesting to observe that when people do not have enough resources, they tend to cooperate to achieve their goals. I remember the farmers, during my childhood, who did not have any other choice than cooperating to get their harvesting done before bad weather came. In a couple of days, harvesting was finished, leading to satisfactory achievements. Today, people do not have to cooperate anymore since they have "super-robots" that do most of their jobs for them. When tasks are simple and well established, there are almost no problems. However, when tasks become complex, robots (or what is commonly called automation) tend to rigidify things that, on the contrary, require flexibility. This is the case of quality processes that require scoring and explaining key performance indicators (KPIs), for example, because people currently spend more time reporting than doing their jobs. As a matter of fact, for some of them, their jobs almost became reporting! Design, and engineering design in particular, requires flexibility instead of rigidity. Consequently, new performing companies have established simple rules that people have to follow naturally, instead of complicated processes, which force them to stay in an artificial world that they do not understand most of the time.

Summarizing, HCD promotes leadership based on the following rules:

- Understand what stakeholders do (i.e., designers, developers, end users, certifiers, maintainers, trainers, and so on).
- Carry out integration from the beginning of the design process; understand and respect authorities in the design and development process (i.e., sometimes stakeholders are leaders, and some other times they are followers—leadership and followship should be accepted by everyone).
- Share a same vision of the enterprise; increase and reward cooperation in problem-solving.

One of the key assets of human beings is **adaptation**. No matter what happens, people will try to adapt to survive, to a certain extent. If people do not have enough flexibility, they will never be able to adapt. When you are too rigid, you are stuck! This is the same in design. Design teams that are constrained by rigid rules will never be able to create new things. There is no creativity and innovation without flexibility.

Managing Uncertainty in a Semi-Open World

Flexibility could not be an issue in a close world where boundaries are very well defined and internal rules taken into account rigorously with discipline. This assumes that we are in a totally rational world. However, people are not only rational thinkers and doers. They can be irrational, express emotions, and act by instinct (Plutchik 2002). In the ancient Greek mythology, Zeus had two sons, Apollo and Dionysus. The former was the god of the rational and the latter the god of irrational. This distinction between logical and creative is interrelated within each of us, as well as in societies where we belong. Logicians need to close their study space (typically called "world") to be able to use and develop rational thinking. Artists and creators work in an open world. This is a major difference. However, anytime we design a new artifact, we combine logical thinking and creative thinking. We try to define a semi-open world that enables us to design and develop artifacts. This is also true for the new world that we create by continuously integrating new artifacts into it. It depends where we put the cursor. If the cursor is close to the Apollonian limit, then we need to assume that the close world model that we have is close enough to the real world to make sure that integration of the new artifact will lead to a new stable world. If the cursor is close to the Dionysian limit, then we need to make sure that interactions among agents will be contained to avoid overflow. The Apollonian model works as long as everything is well defined, and there is no unknown or unexpected situation occurring. The Dionysian model requires constant attention and problem-solving to avoid explosion. With air traffic growth expanding, we are facing this kind of dilemma: "should we go Apollonian or Dionysian?" Trajectory-based operations (TBO), also called 4D trajectories, close the airspace and somehow contribute to rigidify the sky; problems will come when unanticipated events will occur. This solution is Apollonian (i.e., rigid, planned, and procedural). Another solution is to explicitly consider the real-time electronically connected network of aircraft (i.e., taking the metaphor of the flock of birds). This solution is reactive, compared to TBO that is planned. It is Dionysian (i.e., flexible, reactive, and creative). The real solution is certainly between these two extreme solutions and still needs to be found.

> **Authority is a matter of both control (minimizing uncertainty) and accountability (coping with uncertainty).**

Grote produced a remarkable piece of work on how an organization handles intrinsic and extrinsic uncertainties (Grote 2004). She made a major distinction between organizations that minimize uncertainties and those that cope with uncertainties. Based on Grote's initial findings, I proposed an organizational model that I called the Orchestra to capture current evolution of our socio-technical systems, such as the evolution of the airspace (Boy 2009, 2013; Boy and Grote 2009).

One of the most important concepts for the study of organizational uncertainty is **authority**, which can be analyzed in terms of **control** and **accountability** (Fig. 6.1). It is interesting to observe that we develop technology to improve control. Technology incorporates procedures that were previously handled by people. In other words, it provides external automation of procedures, which:

1. Minimizes uncertainty
2. Tends to rigidify related activities (which are already planned and incorporated into the system)

On the accountability side of authority, people:

1. Cope with uncertainty.
2. Provide flexibility using knowledge and skills that are not programmed into the system.

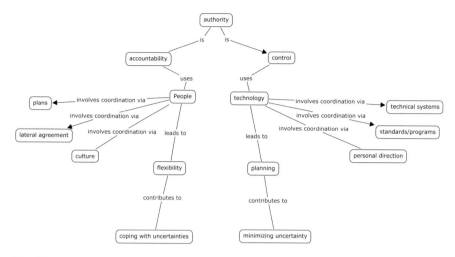

Fig. 6.1 Authority, as control and accountability, concept map

Consequently, TIS designers should think in terms of authority (i.e., who is in charge and who is accountable). Of course, anytime a system is designed, it involves control issues, but also accountability issues. We will see in the next chapter that maturity of the technology and maturity of practice are crucial to minimize and cope with uncertainty. Highly automated systems tend to minimize uncertainty in very specific contexts that people need to know, because outside these contexts, they will have to cope with uncertainty. Consequently, life-critical systems require knowledgeable users, unlike what is commonly thought (i.e., highly automated systems can be handled by "cheap idiots").

Today, we can develop prototypes that can be tested very quickly during the design process. Prototypes enable design teams to progressively reduce uncertainty. Reducing uncertainty in the design of complex systems consists in continuously adjusting the balance between stability and flexibility in order to secure successful performance (Grote 2009).

TISs are designed and developed with the TOP model in mind (i.e., taking into account technology, organizations, and people). Indeed, a TIS is typically designed as a component of a bigger system (i.e., the concept of system of systems is relevant here). At this point, I will take the example of a system that we are developing at FIT, the Onboard Weather Situation Awareness System (OWSAS).

Managing Weather Uncertainty in Aviation: OWSAS

Weather certainly provides one of the most important extrinsic uncertainties in aviation. It is very difficult to predict weather correctly with current technological means. Commercial aircraft are equipped with weather radar (located in the nose of

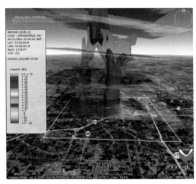

Fig. 6.2 NOAA radar data visualization and Honeywell's IntuVue

the aircraft). This is good information for pilots, but it is also short-term information (i.e., you need to be close to the weather to get information).

Weather is a natural system that causes 70 % of flight delays in the USA and 23 % of airplane accidents. Therefore, not anticipating weather conditions correctly leads to disastrous consequences for human lives, economy (e.g., airlines lost around 2 billions of dollars per year due to weather issues (Weber et al. 2006)), and environment (e.g., delays lead to increasing fuel consumptions and pollution). This is taken into account in the FAA NextGen program.[1] In addition, this unpredictability of weather needs to be combined with increasing saturation of air traffic.

Situation awareness (SA) is commonly modeled as pilot's ability to perceive, comprehend, and project a given situation (Endsley 1995). Getting the right SA is difficult when we deal with life-critical systems in unpredictable situations. Weather SA that aircrew can form can be supported by appropriate onboard 3D visualizations (Laurain et al. 2015). We use several sources of data, including the National Climatic Data Center (NCDC) that hosts all National Oceanic and Atmospheric Administration (NOAA) meteorological data and the National Weather Service (NWS). Radar technology evolved from basic radars, WSR-57 (Weather Surveillance Radar—1957) built with the WWII technology, to most recent radars, the WSR-88D (Weather Surveillance Radar—1988), which are Doppler radars (88D) also called NEXRAD (Next-Generation Radars). The radar data are refreshed and updated every 10 min. In addition, huge amounts of software applications (i.e., TISs) are currently available to create and visualize 3D weather models. Google Earth (GE) is the most famous. It was used in several projects related to weather, such as Butler's NASA project that enables visualization of weather data using Google Earth interactivity (Butler 2006). Another Google Earth-based system was proposed for the localization of climate in the UK (Strangeways 2009). Finally, but the list is not exhaustive, NOAA's display of a 3D radar data representation can be very useful (Fig. 6.2).

---

[1] NextGen purpose is to redesign the US air traffic system entirely as a socio-technical system, using new technologies of both aircraft and air traffic control, as well as changing the role of each actor.

Fig. 6.3 Testing OWSAS on the FIT HCDi Boeing 373 simulator flight deck

OWSAS is currently implemented as a TIS on a tablet (iPad), which enables easy manipulation in the cockpit. This tablet could be used as either a mobile device or a fixed instrument in the cockpit. In 1 year, we designed and developed three versions of OWSAS, which we tested with professional pilots on our flight deck simulators, Boeing 737 and Airbus 320, using an agile approach (Fig. 6.3). Indeed, after a period of 2 months of software development, we defined scenarios and test criteria and use them with pilots. Simulation-based flight tests quickly showed what aspects of the current OWSAS TIS should be modified or improved.

For example, main parameters were identified as being the angle of the layers, the shapes of the 3D geometric forms (i.e., cylinders), forms' colors, and opacity. Indeed, verticality on the planet Earth is always very small compared to horizontal distances, and the various layer angles were exaggerated by a factor 3. Geographers commonly use two different factors depending on the maps: a factor of 1.5 for a mountain relief map (e.g., San Francisco) and a factor of 7 for deep water relief variations (Rumsey and Williams 2002). Coastal environment experts prefer a factor of 3 (Milson and Alibrandi 2008). Other authors directly integrate a cursor to modify these exaggeration factors depending on the needs (Kienberger and Tiede 2008). In order to simplify prototypes and pilots' interpretation, storm shapes were represented as cylinders, which are called critical storm constraints. We used bright colors for the cylinders consistent with NEXRAD data colors (e.g., red and orange).

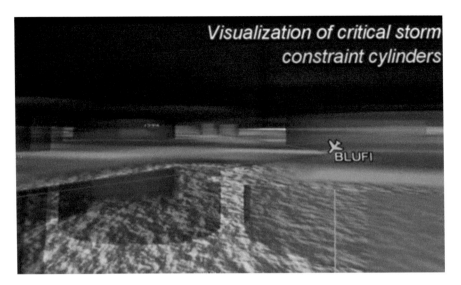

Fig. 6.4 OWSAS weather visualization as a set of cylinders

This two-color coding enables distinguishing two zones: dangerous zones (i.e., red), where the storm is currently striking, and unadvised zones (i.e., orange)—where it could be dangerous to go in the near future. Cylinder opacity depends on the color, because the red cylinders needed to be well seen but not too much, otherwise they would hide the relief. The opacity of the data layers has also been changed, allowing seeing the relief across the first three layers (common altitude in flight). This transparency enables the pilots to see radar data (i.e., enough opacity to be seen and understood without effort) and orient themselves by looking at the relief, cities, and waypoints. Finally, the flight management system (FMS) flight path was added to the 3D model (Fig. 6.4).

When I started writing this book, OWSAS was still a work in progress using an agile design, development, and evaluation process. At each step of this iterative process, OWSAS has been proven to improve situation awareness. The next iteration always involves decision-making, either to stop or modify OWSAS for the test of an improve version. Improvements are not only software based, they can also be hardware based (e.g., we needed to choose a different tablet after the first iteration). We also tested maturity (e.g., a new kind of authority sharing between flight deck and ground was discovered after the second iteration). Of course, OWSAS was modified to take into account these activity-based discoveries. We typically talk about emergent properties (see Chap. 5 on complexity). Based on several scenarios tested with human-in-the-loop simulations (HITLS), we also confirmed incrementally that OWSAS was a strategic TIS, in contrast with current tactical information provided by the aircraft nose radar. OWSAS incremental design, using modeling and simulation (M&S) and professional pilots, showed the great flexibility of the TIS-based approach (Boulnois and Boy 2016).

In addition, OWSAS was designed using the AUTOS pyramid. From the beginning, OWSAS artifact was conceived for pilots by pilots (using human-in-the-loop simulations) considering weather situation awareness process as a task to be executed within the aircraft/airspace environment, including organizational and situational issues. Having personally experienced the use of the AUTOS pyramid designing OWSAS with my students, I can say that it provides guidance and enables not forgetting mandatory aspects (see Chap. 3). Of course, design is an open-ended process. You cannot certify that all possible events can be taken into account, but the AUTOS pyramid is a good framework for completeness checking and elicitation of generic tasks/activities useful and usable in various organizations and situations, which actually provides flexible use of the TIS being designed.

Dealing with the Unexpected

Twentieth century's engineering was strongly based on *a linear* approach of human-machine systems (HMSs), where linearity was understood in three ways: proportionality, single causality, or chronological order such as reading a paper-based book or document (Boy 2014). Nonlinearity does not satisfy these conditions; it can be understood as non-proportionality, multiple causality, or out of chronological order such as browsing the Web. The use of procedures and standards leads to often-rigid linear processes and behaviors. Managing unexpected situation and problem-solving requires flexible nonlinear processes and behaviors.

Twentieth century's technology-centered engineering led to the birth of two intertwined concepts that human factors and ergonomics specialists developed: **user interfaces and operational procedures** (UIOP). UIOP contributed to linearize the use of the system (i.e., a prescribed task leads to an effective activity). Of course, the intention behind this approach was to close the initial open world. Unfortunately, closing the world leads to the removal of several possibilities, such as human operators deviating from the (linear) norm (created by the engineering design team), and rare external events occurring at operations time. These possibilities are commonly called unexpected events or exception. Engineers learned to simplify complex problems in order to solve them. Such simplification supports the definition of a specific operational context, often implicitly. Consequently, when human operators get out of this context, UIOP do not work any longer.

Today, UIOP are superseded by the concept of TIS. Since design of a TIS is thought as incremental integration of a TIS of TISs into a TIS, the original purpose of the TIS should be preserved and overtaken. Preservation and overtaking are the two components of sublation (*aufhebung*), a central Hegelian concept (Palm 2009). We then need to look for safety, efficiency, and comfort when we introduce or modify a TIS in a given environment (e.g., OWSAS introduction and modification in a cockpit). We typically use the TOP model to make sure that:

1. Technology provides both tolerant and resistant constraints with respect to situations.
2. Organization enables collaborative support.
3. People need to know these context limitations and follow prescribed rules or have knowledge and skills to handle out-of-context situations.

Of course, other criteria can be given. For example, the Air and Space Academy held a conference on "Dealing with the Unexpected" (ASA 2011), where the following factors were identified, such as accurate and effective situation awareness, synthetic mind, decision-making capability, self-control, multitasking, stress management, and cooperation (team spirit).

Autonomy Versus Automation

Automation Leads to Rigidity Current automation is software based. Therefore, it is a computerized procedure. Indeed, even a paper procedure automates people when they strictly follow it (Boy and Schmitt 2013). Automation is a software procedure implemented into a system (a machine). Consequently, the major difference between following a paper procedure and using automation is **delegation**. Following a paper procedure is controlled; using automation is managed. When they are strictly used, both functions involve rigidity. Problem happens when the procedure, whether on paper or executed by a computer program, is used out of context. In both cases, people using automation or operational procedures should know their contexts of validity. They should also know how to solve problems when procedures (paper based or software based) are no longer valid. As already said, in life-critical systems, people using automation (or operational procedures) should be knowledgeable about how systems work and how to work without automation or operational procedures when the situation is out of their context of validity[2] (e.g., pilots flying on highly automated aircraft should know about embedded systems and how to fly at the same time).

So, **why do we automate**? It is usually because we try to simplify work or any kind of activity. Automation and operational procedures support your activity (i.e., they do a specific job for you), making sure that you do not forget to do something important, using the right sequence, execute complex algorithms of actions, and so on. Why can automation generate issues? There are many answers to this question. It is usually because they execute complex procedures that may not be appropriate in the context of the actual activity (sometimes unanticipated). This may be due to maturity of the technology and maturity of practice (we will examine this aspect in Chap. 7). Today, we observe that many automated systems are produced and not fully integrated among each other. Indeed, a system that is extremely useful independently of the others can be difficult to use when it is used with other systems,

---

[2] Using iBlocks representing procedures is highly recommended to figure out and improve their situated logic (Boy 1998b).

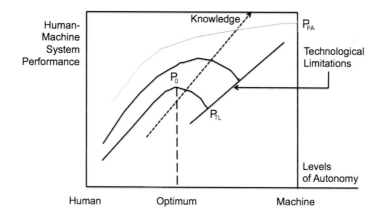

Fig. 6.5 Human-machine system performance versus levels of autonomy (Adaptation of Boy's NASA technical document, 1985)

generating additional multitasking activities. This observation leads to the concept of TIS autonomy of use, which needs to be examined in more depth.

We need to come back on the controversy between tool and prosthesis. Automation can be seen as a cognitive prosthesis that enables us to do things that we usually cannot do otherwise or we can do with much difficulty. Whenever people extend their capabilities with appropriate cognitive prostheses (Hamilton 2001), they increase their performance. However, if these cognitive prostheses use automation to a point that is not clearly understood from an operational standpoint, performance may decrease and, in some cases, cause serious problems. This is what Earl Wiener called "clumsy automation" (Wiener 1989).

When I was working on the Orbital Refueling System of the Space Shuttle in the mid-1980s (Boy 1987), I found out that there is an optimum P_0 in terms of autonomy level and performance of the overall human-machine system (Fig. 6.5). Technology-centered engineering typically automates at the point P_{TL} (i.e., on the technological limitations limit). It takes experimental tests and efforts to go back to P_0. HCD takes into account the existence of P_0 and incrementally tries to find out this optimum through creative design and formative evaluation using HITLS. Interestingly, the more we know about autonomy of the various human and machine agents, the more the optimum P_0 moves to the right and goes up on Fig. 6.5. Of course, if we knew everything about the environment and the various agents involved in the various interactions, the optimum P_{FA} would be on the full autonomy of the machine (e.g., in the case of an aircraft, P_{FA} would correspond to a drone).

This shift of optimum P_0 to the right is strongly related to maturity. In HCD, we distinguish between technology maturity and maturity of practice. The former deals with reliability, availability, and robustness of the technology being designed and developed. The latter deals with people's adaptation to and resilience of the technology; often new practices emerge from technology use. We then need to observe usages as early as possible to anticipate surprises before it is too late. HCD proposes methods and tools that enable HCD teams to detect these emergent properties at design time (e.g., using HITLS). In any case, there is a maturity period required to assess if a product can be delivered or not. When a product is delivered before it is mature enough, people can reject it. For example, the Newton personal digital assistant (PDA) was discontinued despite Apple's $100M investment[2]. Newton PDA was a great concept, but it did not match expectations at that time. Designers, and people in general, were not ready for this kind of tool. Even if Newton technology was discontinued, underlying knowledge did not get lost. Indeed, two ex-Apple Newton developers founded a company "Pixo," which created the operating system for the original iPod.[3] They learned from the immaturity of the Newton, and Steve Jobs created a vision (i.e., the iPod as starting point of a series of appliances that include iPhone and iPad). iPod's technological maturity was insured from the beginning because it was reliable, easy to use, always available, and robust. iPod immediately demonstrated a strong maturity of practice. It was extremely easy to use. Its functionalities were easy to learn and it was resilient to almost any human error. It was also fun to use! The immediate development of the iPhone and iPad, and their clones smartphones and tablets, created a new culture. These systems became life critical in the sense that most people cannot live without them today.

Autonomy Should Lead to Flexibility Now, we know that applications (apps or TISs) are massively developed. They cannot be considered as regular automation as we did so far. They need to be coordinated. Indeed, the more an agent becomes autonomous, the more coordination rules are required, whether agents are people or systems. For example, it is now common to use our smartphone as a GPS to guide our journey, whether walking or driving. This TIS is a very flexible appliance because it is multifunctional and can be used anytime anywhere. More generally, a TIS should be designed to be flexible in the environment where it will be used.

Autonomy in design deals with collaborative problem-solving, workflow management, and organizational models. When designing a TIS, it is important to think in terms of human-system collaboration. Back on the smartphone GPS application, the fact that it remembers previous routes increases flexibility because you can manage mundane navigation tasks at the last minutes, for example. You do not need to remember things; the corresponding TIS does it for you. You also can call the person you planned on visiting to ask for some more directions while the GPS is still working; this is another feature providing flexibility.

Flexibility emerges from appropriate association of functions. Designing for flexibility requires rigorous definitions of the various functions and their coordination. Designer's role is like the role of a composer making a symphony. It takes deep knowledge of activity at stake (i.e., music as a metaphor), creativity as synthesis and integration, and constant refinement of the various functions being designed (i.e., scores). Flexibility is then defined as a property around a well-defined coordinated corpus of functions. For example, musicians may perform some variations around the

---

[3] http://en.wikipedia.org/wiki/Newton_%28platform%29

prescribed scores with respect to the overall mood or inflections given by the conductor. In case of failure or human error, flexibility can also provide recovery means.

If there is no question on smartphone efficiency and comfort, it should also be used safely and securely. Let me tell you a story. Every morning when I go to work, after I arrive close to my car in the garage, I take my phone out of my jacket and put it on the roof of my car, put my jacket on the back seat, close the door, take my phone, sit on the driver's seat, and put my phone on its slot (to get an onboard hand-free communication device). That morning, I forgot the phone on the roof of the car. Since it was protected by a rubber case, it stayed on the roof while I drove to the freeway. When I accelerated on the freeway, I heard a noise and had this horrible experience to see my phone in the rear mirror. I had all kinds of thoughts including a persistent one, "I hope that the car behind me will crash it!" I suddenly realize that I had very sensitive information in this TIS and did not want anybody else to see. This is an emergent property of smartphones. You do not know how life critical such a system is until you lose it! A smartphone increases your autonomy, but it also increases your dependence to it. Unlike the aircraft that provides prosthesis to people because they cannot fly by themselves, the smartphone creates new kinds of people who become handicapped when they cannot use it. The notion of prosthesis has a different meaning and implication in this case because people could communicate before the smartphone.

Are Single-Pilot Operations Tangible?

Will we still have a pilot in an aircraft cockpit? If we look back at the flight decks of commercial aircraft of the 1930s, the Boeing 314 had five technical crewmembers on board. In addition to the captain and the first officer were a flight engineer, a radio operator, and a navigator (Fig. 6.6).

These five actors or agents had five high-level functions: the captain was in charge of the entire aircraft and mission; the first officer assisted the captain in flying the aircraft; the flight engineer supported the captain and copilot (the flying crew) in making sure that all systems were working fine and provided solutions in case of failures; the radio operator was dedicated to voice communication equipment; and the navigator supported the flying crew with navigation tasks.

The number of aircrew members in cockpits was reduced over the years during the last 60 years or so, going from five until the 1950s when the radio navigator was removed (the radio navigator was dedicated to voice communication equipment) to four until the 1970s when the navigator was removed (when inertial navigation systems were introduced), to three until the 1980s when the flight engineer was removed (new monitoring equipment for engines and aircraft systems were introduced), to two until now.

For the last three decades, commercial aircraft flight decks have two crewmembers, a pilot flying (PF) and a pilot not flying (PNF)—also called pilot monitoring (PM). Typically, the PF is in charge of the control of the aircraft, and the PNF is in

Fig. 6.6 The flight deck of a Boeing 314 (http://www.thisdayinaviation.com/24-june-1939/)

charge of system monitoring, communication with the ground, and safety monitoring of flight progress. This progressive elimination of technical crewmembers in commercial aircraft cockpits results from the replacement of human functions by systems functions. These functions are both cognitive and physical. The reason we only talk about cognitive functions is because electronics and software progressively dominated the development of systems. Today, it is clear that many onboard systems have their own cognitive functions in terms of role, context of validity, and resources used (Boy 1998a, b).

Motivated by cost reduction, the shift from two-pilot operations to single-pilot operations (SPO) requires us to investigate how cognitive functions will be redistributed among humans and systems. How can we assess tangibility of such new aircraft? First, if the objective is to have a single pilot in the cockpit, there will be other human agents on the ground or on board (e.g., flight planners, flight followers, and flight attendants) who could be involved. In this section, I would like to show that operational flexibility requires redundancy.

The major advantage of two crewmen cockpits is redundancy (i.e., it is better to have two pairs of eyes and two brains than only one of each). Safety deals with stability, resilience, and therefore cognitive redundancy. This is something that will need to be challenged and tested in the SPO framework. In particular, a comparison of the current two crewmen cockpit operations with SPO should also be conducted. When we shifted from three to two crewmen cockpits, we first developed a time line analysis (TLA), which consists in developing scenarios of events as well as interactions among the various agents involved (e.g., captain, first officer, ATC, aircraft). Since then we made lots of progress in usability engineering and TLA could be combined with cognitive function analyses. We also ran simulations that enabled to play these scenarios and observe activities of the various agents.

Again, the best way to better understand the underlying function allocation is to carry out a cognitive function analysis (CFA), design prototypes, and prepare HITLS to observe possible activities (Boy 2011). This investigation typically enables the discovery of **emerging cognitive functions** (ECF), which cannot be deliberately defined in the first place. ECF can only be discovered at use time. Risks in the choice of configurations (i.e., cognitive functions of the agents involved) and scenarios (i.e., tasks and chronologies of events) are mitigated by subject matter experts (SMEs). This approach enables us to eliminate unsatisfactory solutions from the very beginning of the life cycle of a product. We are not working on short-term predictions but on tests of possible longer-term solutions. Creativity is the main challenge for the generation of these possible solutions. Creativity in human-systems integration is typically the product of experienced design thinking and incremental expertise-based syntheses.

When agent roles and number change within an organization (i.e., when the cognitive function network changes), there is a redistribution of the various authorities. As already presented, authority is about control (i.e., being in charge of something) and accountability (i.e., you need to report to someone else). CFA enables us to study authority redistribution by making explicit the various roles, contexts, and resources and the links among them. When we moved from three to two crewmembers in cockpits, we needed to study the redistribution of cognitive functions between the two crewmembers and the new systems (highly automated) that were executing tasks that the previous third crewmember was executing in the past. The main problem was to identify the emerging cognitive functions induced by the new human-systems integration (Boy and Narkevicius 2013). Pilots were moving from classical control tasks to systems management tasks. For that matter they had to create and learn new cognitive functions to accomplish the overall flying task.

As a general standpoint, commercial airline pilots are typically involved as SMEs. The various variables and processes that we typically study are the following: pilot's goals, workload (or task load during the TLA), human errors (i.e., possible error commissions and recovery processes), situation awareness, decision-making, and action taking. Scenario data are chronologically displayed on a classical spreadsheet, which can be upgraded as needed when the analysis progresses. An example of such an approach is provided in Boy and Ferro (2003).

Current technology indicates that we can move to SPO. Two institutions support this new shift: NASA in the USA and ACROSS[4] in Europe. It is clear that the main goal of moving from two crewmen cockpit operations to SPO is the reduction of costs. We now need to investigate how safety would be impacted by this shift. It is true that SPO is already well experienced in general aviation (GA); in this case, we know its advantages and drawbacks. In particular, ATC is already familiar with

---

[4] ACROSS: Advanced Cockpit for Reduction Of Stress Consortium.

interaction with single pilots. In addition, military fighters are operated with only one pilot in the cockpit.

We foresee two main approaches to SPO. The former is an **evolutionary** approach that continues the move from five to four to three to two to one where automation is incrementally added as the aircrew number is reduced. The main issue is pilot incapacitation. We always certify an aircraft entirely safe for (n-1) capacitated flying pilot(s). When $n = 1$, there is a discontinuity, and the piloted aircraft becomes a drone. We then need to define ground support and/or flight attendant support. The latter is a **revolutionary** approach that breaks automation continuity and goes to the design of a fully automatic flying machine (commonly called a drone or a flying robot). The problem becomes defining human operator's role. Consequently, human-robot interaction activity needs to be entirely defined from the start within a multi-agent environment and not only when the pilot is incapacitated, having a single-agent approach in mind.

In both approaches, function allocation is a major mandatory endeavor. In the evolutionary aircrew-reduction approach, it is purposeful to compare the differences and commonalities between general aviation (GA) single-pilot resource management (SRM) and commercial aviation SPO SRM (to be defined). The FAA has identified six tenets of SRM in GA[5]: task management, risk management, automation management, aeronautical decision-making, control flight into terrain awareness, and situation awareness. Another important question is the definition of the role (job) of the single pilot in SPO and related operations support (i.e., procedures, automation, and problem-solving skills). It is also crucial to find out risks involved in SPO as early as possible before delivery. This is why fast-time simulations and HITLS are planned and carried out from the beginning of the design process. Finally, it is important to identify and design a new cockpit configuration for SPO integrated into a global infrastructure covering the entire air traffic management (ATM).

In the revolutionary approach, instead of looking for what we lose when we remove the first officer (a negative approach where "overload" is studied and cumulative assistance is searched), it is urgent to understand what function allocation should be developed between the SPO aircrew and systems that will need to be developed (a positive approach where situation awareness, decision-making, and human-machine cooperation are studied and developed from the start). What will be the role of an aircrew flying a drone? There is a major difference between controlling and managing a transport drone from the ground and inside it. The latter is likely to be more socially accepted by passengers. Therefore, the primary question is the definition of the role/job of this new type of aircrew; the use of socio-cognitive models and complexity analyses will be necessary. In addition, we need to find out emerging human factors issues such as situation awareness, decision-making (who is in charge and when), fatigue, and incapacitation. This should be studied in nominal and off-nominal situations.

---

[5] FAA Order 8900.2, General Aviation Airman Designee Handbook, (retrieved on June 13, 2015), http://fsims.faa.gov/wdocs/orders/8900_2.htm

The major distinction between RPAS (Remotely Piloted Aircraft Systems[6]) and SPO of drones is crucial. When the person responsible for safety, success, and wealth of a mission (a flight) is himself/herself directly involved (life-critical embodiment instead of remote control), he/she will have totally different relationships with the machine being controlled and managed. This approach does not remove the need for ground assistance. There will be decisions to be made whether or not we want to make pilot's manual reversion possible and/or have RPAS as an emergency/recovery possibility. In any case, board and ground personnel, organizations, and technology roles should be defined in concert (i.e., consider complex and nonlinear systems and design/test global solutions) and not in isolation as it is done today (i.e., simplify problems, linearize and find local solutions). Tests will be performed using various human factors metrics and methods including workload, skills, knowledge, and performance assessments. Other metrics can be used such as simplicity, observability, controllability, redundancy, socio-cognitive stability, and cognitive support (Boy 2002).

Using CFA to define SPO leads to the identification of cognitive functions for the various agents including the pilot (or another qualifier in the SPO revolutionary context), ground operators, and systems. Each of these agents has a set of cognitive functions providing him, her, or it with some degree of authority. Authority can be viewed as control (i.e., the agent is in charge of doing something and control the situation) and accountability (i.e., the agent is accountable to someone else). Control can be either handled directly or delegated to other agents who have authority to execute well-defined tasks. In this latter case, these other agents (should) have appropriate and effective cognitive functions and are accountable to the agent delegating. CFA enables us to rationalize the allocation of cognitive functions among agents.

Technical crews (i.e., pilots) have the role and authority of bringing a set of passengers from a location A to another location B. They have the primary responsibility for safety, efficiency, and comfort of the passengers. In SPO, current cognitive functions of current PF and PNF are distributed among technical/commercial crews, ground operators, and new systems. In particular, technical/commercial crew cognitive functions have a set of resources distributed among ground operators and aircraft/ground systems. Ground operators have different cognitive functions that can be named dispatching, ATC coordination, crew scheduling, maintenance triggering, customer service, and weather forecast. All these cognitive functions can be supported by systems when they are well understood and mature. Dispatching and piloting are currently associated to develop a flight plan, find out what fuel quantity pilots should take, meet weight and balance requirements, ensure compliance with the minimum equipment list (MEL), de-conflict with other aircraft, help in case of equipment failure, and, more generally, guide the flight from gate to gate.

Normal piloting cognitive functions consist in reading checklists, cross-checking life-critical information, troubleshooting and recovering from failures, fuel monitoring, and so on. Abnormal and emergency cognitive functions are triggered by specific conditions such as engine failure, cabin depressurization, fuel imbalance, and so on. Current air traffic controllers have specific dispatch cognitive functions. Their

---

[6] http://ec.europa.eu/enterprise/sectors/aerospace/uas/index_en.htm

job will change with SPO and will need piloting cognitive functions in the case of malfunctions in the airspace, including pilot incapacitation and its duality, total system failure. Consequently, they will need tools such as in aircraft cockpits. The whole ATC workstation will evolve toward an ATM/piloting workstation for SPO. In addition, they will not have to control only one aircraft but, in some cases, several.

A first cognitive function analysis shows that there are functions that can be allocated to systems such as checklist-based verifications and cross-checking of life-critical information. As always, allocating functions to systems requires maturity verification. Whenever technology maturity is not guaranteed, people should be in charge and have capabilities guarantying good situation awareness. In any case, tests are mandatory. In the above-defined revolutionary approach to SPO, we typically think about lower levels of control being entirely automated (i.e., trajectory control and management); human agents only act on set points, for example. We need to be careful however that the SPO pilot will be aware of the crucial internal and external states of his/her aircraft environment. He/she will also need to be knowledgeable and skilled in aviation to perceive and understand what is going on during the flight as well as act on the right controls if necessary. Full automation does not remove domain knowledge and skills in life-critical systems.

Symmetrically, some aircraft systems (or artificial agents) should be able to monitor pilot's activity and health. This induces the definition, implementation, and test of new kinds of system cognitive functions based on physiological and psychological variables. Obviously, this will require sensors that could be physiologically invasive (e.g., electroencephalograms) or noninvasive (e.g., cameras). In any case, pilots will have to accept to be monitored. Pilot's activity and health monitoring can be done by aircraft systems and also by ground operators.

Other processes and technology that need to be human-centered designed and developed are related to collaborative work. In this new multi-agent world, agents have to collaborate and be supported for this collaboration. Computer-supported cooperative work (CSCW) technology and techniques need to be developed to this end. When an agent fails, for example, whether a human or a system, recovery means and strategies should be in place to continue the flight safely. It is also important, in this increasingly automated multi-agent world, to keep enough flexibility. HITLS could be used to find out the effectiveness of possible solutions.

Trust, Precision, and Flexibility

Even if a drone can be considered as a flying autonomous system, it has to be controlled or managed by people remotely. How do we trust that a drone will behave appropriately? Can we trust its performance? A drone is a robot that is programmed to execute certain types of tasks (e.g., fly over a set of buildings, take pictures, and in a not-too-distant future carrying passengers). Managing this kind of robot involves sufficient data feedback that provides meaningful information to human operators who will be able to decide with respect to appropriate criteria. In some situations, orders have to be sent to the drone to insure safety and efficiency, for example. Trust can be seen at different levels, such as what the drone is capable of doing, quality of information feedback provided to human operators, and human operators' competence to make appropriate decisions.

Technology provides precision. Organization should support trust and communication. People provide flexibility… the TOP model again! When "all" contextual conditions are satisfied, systems can do a better job than people. Let's take the example of rendezvous and docking in space. US Astronaut Buzz Aldrin's Ph.D. dissertation at MIT in 1963 on "Manned Orbital Rendezvous" proposed the technique for piloted rendezvous of two spacecraft in orbit.

> *Flying a spacecraft is very different than flying a plane. There is no true up or down and the dynamics of orbital flight make maneuvering to dock, or rendezvous, two spaceships very complex. I focused my research on solving the problems of speed and centrifugal energy which lead to an 'orbital paradox' – a situation in which a pilot who speeds up to catch another craft in a higher orbit will end up in an even higher orbit, traveling at a slower speed and watching the second craft fly off into the distance. The solution to this paradox is counter intuitive, and required new orbital mechanics and procedures. Later, after joining the NASA astronaut corps, I spent time translating complex orbital mechanics into relatively simple flight plans for my colleagues – they thanked me (with a mixture of respect and sarcasm) with the nickname Dr. Rendezvous.*
> Buzz Aldrin – Waterkeeper, Fall 2005[7]

Since the beginning of the space era, there were failure and successes regarding rendezvous, docking, and berthing. Main objective was the transfer of space crew from one vehicle to another. Related operations are very complex because orbital mechanics is very complex. Therefore, either space crew learns to master orbital mechanics for rendezvous, docking, and/or berthing or robotic systems are developed to handle related tasks. People may have depth perception problems to adjust relative velocity (velocity vector) and axes (radial vector). This requires sophisticated knowledge and skills. Today, advanced robotics enables high-precision rendezvous, docking, and berthing.

However, depending on the maturity of technology, people can be superior resources in terms of success when they have enough expertise and experience. In July 1969, Apollo 11's Lunar Module was descending toward the Moon. Descent was entirely automatic until suddenly the crew got a mission abort alarm. Neil Armstrong immediately decided to turn off automation and fly the spacecraft manually. His piloting proficiency and space knowledge turned out this radical decision into a magnificent success (Mindell 2008).

However, when context changes suddenly and systems are not programmed for handling this change, people are unique problem identifiers and problem-solvers. Therefore, one of the main issues in HCD is complementary human-systems function allocation. Fitts (1951) provided a very insightful list of human and system assets, known as MABA-MABA (i.e., men are best at-machines are best at). Since then no other better proposal came out. However, Fitts's list is an a priori static guideline. It does not take into account effective interactions among human and machine agents and therefore possible emergent properties that result from this

---

[7] http://buzzaldrin.com/space-vision/rocket_science/orbital-rendezvous/

interaction. This is another reason to promote HITLS involving evolving human and system roles being designed to discover these emergent properties.

The concept of single-pilot operations has been discussed in this chapter. If this solution is considered seriously, we need to find out what it involves to allocate appropriate functions in the case of pilot incapacitation. Technology could handle the aircraft as a drone. Organization will involve ground services that will need to cooperate with aircraft systems. People will include the single-pilot and ground operators, whose cognitive functions will need to be further defined. We do not know yet what is the set of emergent properties resulting from such interactions. This is still a topic of research. In particular, flexibility and trust will be the main issues. In the case of pilot incapacitation, ground operators will need to remotely fly the aircraft and manage its systems, on very short notice. New jobs will then need to be created. Since the SPO concept is dictated by economy, more financial studies are still required, but common sense tells me that keeping two pilots on board will remain the best solution for a while. This gives us time to human-centered design and develop and test transportation drones correctly (i.e., using the TOP model and HITLS).

Human-Centered Systems Engineering

Model-based systems engineering (MBSE) and more specifically SysML[8] (Systems Modeling Language) were developed to move from document-centered to model-centered systems engineering (Friedenthal et al. 2009). MBSE benefits are multiple. It enables sharing understanding (intersubjectivity) of system requirements and design among design team members. It is a common frame of reference for analysis, design, validation, and risk management. This common frame of reference supports progressive and shared complexity analysis of systems being developed from several perspectives, including system integration, traceability of design history, flexibility of design and development changes, design quality and refinement, ambiguity and human errors reduction, holistic view of the overall design as well as design details (i.e., systems of systems awareness and visualization), verification and validation, risk reduction, knowledge capture, and life cycle product management.

MBSE is great when we focus on systems engineering from a technology perspective (i.e., technology-centered engineering), but it can become extremely complex when people are in the loop. No matter the simplicity of a system, people will also introduce complexity, nonlinearity, and unexpected events. People are not deterministic. Even if we have behavioral patterns for many categories of people (e.g., developers, integrators, project managers, testers, regulators, vendors, and

---

[8] SysML was adopted in 2006. The Object Management Group (OMG) of the International Council on Systems Engineering (INCOSE) sponsored its development with broad industry and vendor participation. It is a Systems Modeling Language that supports specification, analysis, design, and verification of complex systems. SysML enables modeling of requirements, functions (behavior), structures, and parameters.

finally customers), activities they will produce are far from being predictable. Therefore, HITLS are precious tools to elicit emerging patterns that were not anticipated at design time. Human-centered systems engineering requires human and organization modeling, as well as HITLS.

MBSE leads to the design and development of diagrams with systems represented by input-output boxes. On this kind of diagram, boxes also always represent people. Problem is that people generate emerging behaviors and properties of the resulting human-systems integration. MBSE does not take this factor into account, yet! In fact, it is important to understand that design and development are a small part compared to human-centered evaluation and validation. Therefore, MBSE is a good approach for increasing flexibility of systems being designed, but even more important is human-centered evaluation and validation of incrementally developed prototypes using HITLS (i.e., the agile approach). This is the price to pay for effective human-systems integration. Why? MBSE is mostly interested in deliberative design of structures and functions based on task analyses and configuration design. In contrast, HCD focuses on discovering emerging properties of structures and functions based on activity analyses and configuration management. Combination of MBSE and HCD is about human-systems integration design and management.

At this point, we need make a distinction between human activity and system activity. In systems engineering, system activity diagrams specify controlled sequences of actions. In HCD, human activity is what people do when they interact with their environment and includes both controlled and automatic actions, in Shiffrin and Schneider's sense (1977). Human controlled actions can be compared to system controlled actions in the cognitive sense, but human automatic actions typically result from training and experience involving integration of emergent operational properties in the human-systems integration sense. Consequently, HCD recommends that dual human-systems automatic actions, resulting from human-in-the-loop tests, should be taken into account in systems engineering.

References

ASA (2011) Dossier on air transport pilot facing the unexpected. Retrieved on June 13, 2015, http://www.academie-air-espace.com/event/newdetail.php?varCat=14&varId=216. Air and Space Academy. Paris, France

Boulnois S, Boy GA (2016) Onboard weather situation awareness system: a human-systems integration approach. FIT Technical Report, Melbourne

Boy GA (1985) Fault diagnosis in orbital refueling operations. NASA document presented at the space station human factors research review, NASA Ames Research Center, CA, 3 December

Boy GA (1987) Operator assistant systems. Int J Man Mach Stud 27:541–554, and Mancini G, Woods DD, Hollnagel E (eds) Cognitive engineering in dynamic worlds. Academic Press, London

Boy GA (1998a) Cognitive function analysis for human-centered automation of safety-critical systems. In: Proceedings of CHI'98, the ACM conference on human factors in computing systems, Los Angeles, USA. Published by ACM Press, New York, pp 265–272. ISBN:0-201-30987-4

Boy GA (1998b) Cognitive function analysis. Greenwood/Ablex, Stamford. ISBN 9781567503777

Boy GA (2002) Procedural interfaces (in French: Interfaces procedurals). In: Proceeding of the french conference on human-computer interaction. AFIHM, ACM-Press, New York

Boy GA (2009) The Orchestra: a conceptual model for function allocation and scenario-based engineering in multi-agent safety-critical systems. In: Proceedings of the European conference on cognitive ergonomics, Otaniemi, Helsinki/Finland, 30 Sept–2 Oct

Boy GA (2011) Cognitive function analysis in the design of human and machine multi-agent systems. In: Boy GA (ed) Handbook of human-machine interaction. Ashgate, Surrey

Boy GA (2013) Dealing with the unexpected in our complex socio-technical world. In: Proceedings of the 12th IFAC/IFIP/IFORS/IEA symposium on analysis, design, and evaluation of human-machine systems. Las Vegas, NV, USA

Boy GA (2014) Dealing with the unexpected. In: Millot P (ed) Risk management in life critical systems. Wiley ISTE, London. ISBN 978-1-84821-480-4

Boy GA, Ferro D (2003) Using cognitive function analysis to prevent controlled flight into terrain. In: Harris D (ed) Human factors and flight deck design. Ashgate, Aldershot

Boy GA, Grote G (2009) Authority in increasingly complex human and machine collaborative systems: application to the future air traffic management construction. In the Proceedings of the 2009 International Ergonomics Association World Congress, Beijing, China

Boy GA, Narkevicius J (2013) Unifying human centered design and systems engineering for human systems integration. In: Aiguier M, Boulanger F, Krob D, Marchal C (eds) Complex systems design and management. Springer, London, 2014. ISBN-13: 978-3-319-02811-8

Boy GA, Schmitt KA (2013) Design for safety: a cognitive engineering approach to the control and management of nuclear power plants. Ann Nucl Energy 52:125–136, Elsevier. doi:10.1016/j.anucene.2012.08.027

Butler D (2006) Virtual globes: the web-wide world. Nature 439:776–778

Endsley MR (1995) Toward a theory of situation awareness in dynamic systems. Hum Factors: Hum Factors Ergon Soc J 37:32–64

Fitts PM (ed) (1951) Human engineering for an effective air navigation and traffic control system. National Research Council, Washington, DC

Friedenthal S, Moore A, Steiner R (2009) OMG Systems Modeling Language (OMG SysML™) Tutorial. Object Management Group INCOSE (International Council on Systems Engineering). Retrieved on Aug 19, 2015, http://www.omgsysml.org/INCOSE-OMGSysML-Tutorial-Final-090901.pdf

Griffin G (2010) Crew-ground integration in piloted space programs. Keynote speech at the International Conference on Human-Computer Interaction in Aerospace (HCI-Aero 2010). Cape Canaveral, Florida, USA

Grote G (2004) Uncertainty management at the core of system design. Annu Rev Control Elsevier 28:267–274

Grote G (2009) Management of uncertainty. Springer, London. ASIN: B004A16LG2.

Hamilton S (2001) Thinking outside the box at IHMC. IEEE Comput 34:61–71

Kienberger S, Tiede D (2008) ArcGIS explorer review. GEO Inform 11:42–47

Laurain T, Boy GA, Stephane AL (2015) Design of an on-board 3D weather situation awareness system. In: Proceedings 19th Triennial Congress of the International Ergonomics Association, Melbourne, 9–14 Aug

Milson AJ, Alibrandi M (2008) Digital geography: geospatial technologies in the social studies classroom. International social studies forum: the series. In: Diem RA (ed) University of Texas – San Antonio, The College of New Jersey, Jeff Passe, Ewing, NJ

Mindell DA (2008) Digital Apollo – human and machine in spaceflight. MIT Press, Cambridge, MA. ISBN 9780262134972

Ohno T (1988) Toyota production system: beyond large-scale production. Productivity, Cambridge, MA

Palm R (2009) Hegel's concept of sublation – a critical interpretation. Ph.D. dissertation in philosophy. Retrieved on June 13, 2015, https://lirias.kuleuven.be/bitstream/123456789/234670/1/. Katholieke Universiteit Leuven, Institute of Philosophy

Plutchik R (2002) Nature of emotions. Am Sci 89:349

Rumsey D, Williams M (2002) Historical maps in GIS. In: Knowels A (ed) Past time, past place. GIS for history. ESRI Press, Redlands, CA, pp 1–18

Schwaber K (2004) Agile project management with scrum. Microsoft Press, Redmond, WA. ISBN 978-0-7356-1993-7

SCRUM (2015) Retrieved on Jan 26, 2015, https://www.scrum.org

Shiffrin RM, Schneider W (1977) Controlled and automatic human information processing: II. Perceptual learning, automatic attending, and a general theory. Psychol Rev 84(2):127–190

Strangeways I (2009) Using Google Earth to evaluate GCOS weather station sites. Weather 64:4–8

Weber M, Evans J, Wolfson M, DeLaura R, Moser B, Martin B, Welch J, Andrews J, Bertsimas D (2006) Improving air traffic management during thunderstorm. In: 12th conference on Aviation, Range, and Aerospace Meteorology, 29 Jan–2 Feb 2006, Atlanta. Retrieved on June 13, 2015, http://www.ll.mit.edu/mission/aviation/publications/publication-files/WW-12668.pdf. American Meteorological Society, Boston

Wiener E (1989) Human factors of advanced technology ("Glass Cockpit") transport aircraft. NASA Contractor Rep. 177528. See also Cooketal RI et al., The natural history of introducing new information technology into a dynamic high-risk environment, 1990 Proceedings of the Human Factors Society, 429

Chapter 7
Maturity

This chapter presents an approach of **product maturity** that takes into account user experience. Socio-technical systems evolve concomitantly with the emergence of new practices. This point is analyzed for tangible interactive systems (TISs) and extended to everyday contemporary appliances. A product is judged sufficiently mature by its users, when it is sustainably accepted for safe, efficient, and comfortable use.

Defining Maturity

What does it mean that a product is mature for use? Answering this question is highly contextual. It depends on the type of user, environment, and organizational context, for example. There are people who adopt a product when it is not yet mature, that is, not efficient, safe, nor comfortable to use. They even can pay a substantial price. These people are techno-fanatics, early adopters, and beta testers. The rest of us wait until the product, or more generally technology, is mature enough to be used efficiently, safely, and comfortably. Maturity is intimately related to user's experience and awareness of technological benefits and stability. This is **technology maturity**. It is also important to better understand how the new product will modify practices to find out about its social acceptance or rejection. This is **maturity of practice**. Product maturity is a mix of technology maturity and maturity of practice. Reaching product maturity is a complex process. This chapter presents an approach supporting the anticipation of product maturity based on user experience.

> **Product maturity is about technology maturity and maturity of practice.**

© Springer International Publishing Switzerland 2016
G.A. Boy, *Tangible Interactive Systems*, Human–Computer Interaction Series,
DOI 10.1007/978-3-319-30270-6_7

The field of commercial aircraft design and certification has a long tradition based on flight tests and quasi-permanent connection with the pilot community. The formalization of experience feedback is gradually refined through training, maintenance, test pilot involvement, and development of databases from airline pilot inputs. Advanced computerization of interactive cockpits fostered such formalization. Pilots have become managers of highly automated systems (i.e., artificial agents). When fly-by-wire technology and glass cockpits had to be certified during the 1980s, classical approaches, methods, and tools of human factors and ergonomics (HFE) were not appropriate to understand the acceptability of this technological revolution. We needed to develop new approaches based on cognitive science and psychology applied to engineering. Human-centered design (HCD) is now a methodological support to the analysis, design, and evaluation of life-critical systems (Boy 2012). More specifically, this chapter presents concepts and models for testing the maturity of human-systems integration.

HCD takes into account the life cycle of a product by eliciting and analyzing human factors during the genesis of the product (design and development process issues) and its use (usability, acceptability, utility, and maintainability). We can thus say that a product is mature when a community of target users accepts it (i.e., the product is easy to develop, use, and maintain on a permanent basis). We then talk about socio-technical maturity.

Technology Readiness Levels

Maturity is currently "measured" in terms of industry processes that are categorized with respect to nine levels. The US Department of Defense (DoD) and National Aeronautics and Space Administration (NASA) provided definitions for Technology Readiness Levels (TRLs). NASA TRLs[1] can be summarized as follows:

- TRL 1: Basic principles observed and reported (i.e., scientific research is beginning and those results are being translated into future research and development)
- TRL 2: Technology concept and/or application formulated (i.e., technology is very speculative, as there is little to no experimental proof of concept for the technology)
- TRL 3: Analytical and experimental critical function and/or characteristic proof of concept (i.e., both analytical and laboratory studies are required at this level to see if a technology is viable and ready to proceed further through the development process)
- TRL 4: Component and/or breadboard validation in laboratory environment (i.e., multiple component pieces are tested with one another)

---

[1] https://www.nasa.gov/directorates/heo/scan/engineering/technology/txt_accordion1.html (retrieved on June 14, 2015).

- TRL 5: Component and/or breadboard validation in relevant environment (i.e., a more rigorous continuation of TRL 4 by running simulations in environments that are as close to realistic as possible)
- TRL 6: System/subsystem model or prototype demonstration in a relevant environment (ground and space)
- TRL 7: System prototype demonstration in a space environment
- TRL 8: Actual system completed and "flight qualified" through test and demonstration (ground and space)
- TRL 9: Actual system "flight proven" through successful mission operations

This categorization of maturity by TRLs enables design and management of an organization that is in charge of large programs. These programs require the orchestration of thousands, even tens of thousands, of processes. From a pure systems engineering perspective, processes can be modeled by graphs of black boxes, which can themselves be modeled by graphs of black boxes. We often refer to systems of systems. The main problem with this approach comes from the fact that people cannot be modeled by black boxes. Why? People, as highly nonlinear systems, can and do generate emergent properties that are not predictable analytically. These emergent properties can only be observed until we know underlying appropriate models that take time to elaborate. This is crucial! Consequently, the only way to discover human-systems emergent properties is to run human-in-the-loop simulations (HITLSs), observe human activities, deduce emerging cognitive functions, and simulate the resulting cognitive function network. Again, please note the need for HCD that requires activity analysis, in contrast with the classical approach in engineering and traditional human factors that only are focused on task analysis.

People cannot be modeled by black boxes in systems engineering diagrams.

Technological Life Cycle and Maturity

The life cycle of a technology can be divided into two periods where criteria of choice differ fundamentally: (period 1) technology and performance and (period 2) ease, reliability, and price. User's behavior changes. For example, until the early 1980s, only highly skilled engineers were capable of using large computers. The use of computers was based on technical prowess. The advent of the microcomputer has democratized the use of computers to such an extent that almost everyone acquired a personal computer. I remember changing practices during the first half of the 1980s when the Macintosh was introduced, and a lot of my fellow engineers at the time did not want to commit to use such gadget that even a child could use! We were in the transition from period 1 to period 2. Then at the turn of the twentieth century, the computer became increasingly invisible (Norman 1999), embedded within familiar tools such as telephone, automobile, or microwave oven. We are currently transiting to another technological period that includes the cloud, data analytics and visualization, and digital life.

At each transition point, the problem of maturity arises. A more sophisticated approach than the previous leads to the definition of four stages of the life cycle of a product: design, development, exploitation, and obsolescence. What characterizes current socio-technical evolution is the short duration of the life cycle of many products. Indeed, information-intensive products rapidly become obsolete; it often takes 6 months to a software product to be replaced by a more efficient and less expensive one. Therefore, can we really speak of product maturity? Or are we entering a new era in which we must accept a permanent evolution of technology, instead of traditional stability? The second half of the twentieth century saw the emergence of a significant amount of automation that has greatly contributed to change our lifestyle both professionally and privately. In order to better analyze issues related to maturity evolution, let's make a quick point on the automation concept.

The Misleading Issue of Automation Surprises

The shift from electromechanical cockpits to glass cockpits in commercial aircraft motivated HFE studies during the 1980s and 1990s (Boy and Hollnagel 1993; Sarter et al. 1997). These studies focused on human factors based on continuity of work and not on **change management**. They argued that problems were workload pattern changes, new attention and knowledge demands, breakdowns in mode awareness, new coordination demands, the need for new approaches to training, new opportunities for new kinds of human errors, complacency, and trust in automation. They proposed human-centered automation solutions that were not possible to implement at that time. Today, however, HCD is possible because information technology provides great capabilities for testing systems very early on during the design process. Therefore, the automation surprise issue, which was mainly due to the technology-centered engineering approach, is misleading today when we use a HCD approach because we are looking for human-systems integration (HSI) from the beginning of the design process. This process is typically implemented using an agile approach based on incremental formative evaluations.

> **Automation surprises should be discovered as HSI emerging properties during the maturity period as much as possible**.

Indeed, crucial concepts were not emphasized. The first concept that automation introduced is **rigidity**. Automation was developed on the basis of availability of automatic control technology and not enough on the optimization of function allocation with respect to authority sharing (already discussed in Chap. 6). Automation is freezing a set of operational procedures into a system. As a matter of fact, paper-based operational procedures and checklists used by pilots, and more generally human operators of complex systems, are **automation of people** (Boy and Schmitt 2013). Whenever people are forced to use procedures, whether they are on paper or embedded in a machine, if they are reduced to be executants only, they will be likely to face unexpected events (ASA 2011). For this reason, they need to be knowledgeable of how the system they are managing works and what operations are about; otherwise, they will have surprises, of course! The problem becomes determining the right level of granularity they need to know about the system they are managing and operations they need to accomplish. This is a major issue today. The good news is that we now have complexity analysis and HITLS methods and tools to analyze, design, and test this kind of knowledge requirements. Obviously, discovering **emergent behaviors and properties** is never finished and will continue at operations time. Unlike in the recent past, we can do this much before product delivery and discover many of these emergent factors before it is too late.

> **Automation "automates" systems behavior.**
>
> **Operational procedures automate people's behavior.**

The second concept is **maturity**. Indeed, automation was incrementally adapted using experience feedback from pilots using it. It took us a fair amount of time understanding the shift from control to management on aircraft flight decks. Pilots used to control all crucial flight parameters. A new agent, called automation, was suddenly handling most of these parameters. Consequently, pilots had to supervise this new agent instead of controlling individual parameters, as they were doing in the immediate past. The shift was similar to a promotion in an organization. That is when somebody moves from a basic job to a management position, where he or she has to manage a group of people (i.e., human agents). Some of these agents are doing the job that the promoted person was doing before. It is sometimes tempting to micromanage when an employee performs a job that we used to do before (i.e., pilots were micromanaging automated systems that were doing the job pilots used to do before). It is essential to understand this practice shift (i.e., control to management). This is a maturity of practice issue, which can be tested much earlier than during the 1980s and 1990s because HITLS capabilities and complexity analysis methods have made tremendous progress. They provide useful means to this end. Today, we can observe pilot's activity using HITLS and incrementally discover emergent behaviors and properties, which we could not afford doing 20 years ago. The difference is that automation is no longer an add-on, but software that is created and incrementally refined and tested during the design process to satisfy a purpose.

Summing up this discussion, automation surprises are a matter of technology maturity and/or maturity of practice. In other words, automation should be incrementally modified in a human-centered way (i.e., adapted to current users' practices), and users should be better trained to adapt to automation (i.e., user needs to learn a new way of using highly automated aircraft). In addition, automation design should not be an issue now since we can fully develop the overall function of a system since the beginning in an agile manner by incrementally testing HSI of a selected solution. I propose that automation should be renamed **embedded system functions**.

From Single Agent to Multi-Agent Approaches

Automation and computer technology have contributed to shape our increasingly software-based world. We get banknotes from an automated teller machine, and another interacting machine enables us to fill in our car tank with gas. Similarly, a pilot relies on automata taking care of handling qualities, navigation and collision avoidance, and so on. Forty years ago, automation was essentially supported by analog computers based on control theory. Aircraft autopilots, for example, are used since the 1930s. Automata progressively became software-based machines, which are typically called systems. The level of complexity of these new systems grew up to the point that we no longer try to understand their internal mechanisms during operations. Some of these systems can even detect their own possible malfunctions. For example, current cars include so much electronics and software that mechanics require specific and sophisticated test benches to find out causes of troubles, and in some cases they need to refer to a specialized repair company equipped with appropriate software. We have evolved into a multi-agent environment where agents are no longer solely human beings but also specialized systems.

Marvin Minsky stated that an agent is a society of agents, by introducing the concept of cognitive or mental process as a specific type of agent (Minsky 1986). We say that all agents, whether human or machine, have several cognitive functions. A cognitive function is typically represented by its role, context of its validity, and necessary resources to implement the function. The automation process can be modeled as a transfer of one or more cognitive functions of a human being to a machine. Maturity issues related to this transfer are not easy to formalize, and consequently the responses in terms of usability are far from obvious. Indeed, it is not a simple transfer but creating one or more new cognitive functions of the generated controller, which induces the emergence of new human cognitive functions. It is therefore important to identify and describe the relevant network of both human and machine cognitive functions. For this reason, prototypes must be developed and tested as early as possible in order to discover emerging cognitive functions.

Maturity of Practice and Automatic Information Processing

People learn when they use systems. They learn about many facets of these systems, such as shape, color, economic values, and more generally affordances. They learn about syntax and semantics that support the use of systems they are using. For example, when you go to another country that you do not know, you use banknotes that are very different from the ones that you are currently using in your country. You then need to control your activity whenever you execute a very simple task such as buying a loaf of bread. You do not have such a very attentive control using banknotes of your country because you have various kinds of attributes that enter into play (e.g., color, shape, and various kinds of signs on the banknotes). You have embodied these attributes, and you have become extremely conscious of the value of all banknotes automatically.

The distinction between automatic detection and controlled search in human information processing has been described a long time ago (Schneider and Shiffrin 1977; Shiffrin and Schneider 1977). Shiffrin and Schneider showed "the dependence of automatic detection on attending responses and demonstrate how such responses interrupt controlled processing and interfere with the focusing of attention." People learn about categories (e.g., attributes of banknotes).

Information processing, whether automatic or controlled, is crucial in systems design. Designers need to identify the capacity of a system being designed of inducing user's automatic information processing. For example, I was driving in Australia last summer, a country where people drive on the left-hand side of the road. Even if I cognitively know that everything has to be reversed, I made many mistakes driving. Several times, I stroke windscreen wipers instead of turn signals. Usually driving in the USA, cars are equipped with turn signal levers on the left-hand side of the steering wheel. I automated this process of striking the turn signal lever using my left hand for a long time. Of course, standardization of these attributes of cars would simplify activity and improve safety, efficiency, and comfort, when people are traveling from country to country. In other words, situation awareness and decision-making is context sensitive, very much influenced by learning and therefore familiarity.

Therefore, maturity of practice can be very positive because it increases safety, efficiency, and comfort by being supported by highly compiled automatic information processing functions (i.e., functions that can be cognitive or physical). But, maturity of practice can also be negative when these functions are used out of context of validity.

The more individual maturity of practice is reinforced and spread out, the more it becomes common for groups (i.e., teams, communities, and organizations). In other words, there are a psychological individual time and a sociological collective time, which are intimately interrelated. For example, all cars have now standardized systems such as classical driving instruments, GPS, collision avoidance systems, and air conditioning. The way they are implemented depends on local culture and policies (e.g., driving on the right or left side of the road).

Maturity and Situation Awareness

Now, how do we test human-systems integration maturity? Let's provide an HCD approach. When we start to design a new system, it is because we have a purpose to fulfill. Then we design and develop a first prototype. We test it in a HITLS environment. We observe users' activity and try to discover emergent properties. Among the various possible observations, one is specifically important, situation awareness (SA). Can users figure out what is going on when they use the prototype?

For more than two decades, situation awareness (SA) has been a recurrent topic in the HFE community, and Endsley's SA model was, and still is, very influential (Endsley 1995a, b, 1998; Endsley and Garland 2000). This model typically claims that SA is "the perception of elements in the environment within a volume of time and space, the comprehension of their meaning, and the projection of their status in the near future" (Endsley 1995b). Several other authors worked on variations of this model such as Smith and Hancock (1995), Vidulich (2000), Stanton et al. (2001), and Dekker et al. (2010). SA is thought as knowledge we have about the environment, which can guide our actions. However, the perceived environment (i.e., what we usually call the situation) constantly evolves, and people need to constantly update knowledge they have on this environment. People have several limitations, one of them being their working memory saturation. In addition, their level of familiarity with various types of situation makes the situation awareness process more or less easy to perform. This depends on the mental model that they have developed (e.g., expert, occasional, or novice human operators do not have the same operative mental model and therefore will not derive the same meaning or interpretation of a same situation). These factors need to be addressed in more depth and details than they have been addressed until now. For example, as already said, humans do not naturally fly; they need to "wear" a prosthesis, called an aircraft, to be able to fly. It takes some time to become a pilot; and it takes even more time to become a proficient pilot. Proficiency is expressed in number of flight hours. The main reason for this proficiency acquisition is the need for flight embodiment. In the aviation community, we say that pilots need to acquire the "sense of air."

SA deserves a deeper definition. I propose an experience-based[2] critical analysis of the concepts of "situation" and "awareness." First, what do we mean by a "situation"? Is it what we perceive in the environment or what the environment really is? Is it what we expect to happen or what really happens? Is it a snapshot or a dynamic evolution of the environment where we are? How do we model a situation? Is it a set of environment variables or sophisticated model of the environment? What do we mean by environment? Is it what surrounds us? Are we part of it? About awareness: is awareness an intentional cognitive (i.e., conscious) process, a reactive (i.e., subconscious) process, or both? In other words, we need to address the distinction between conscious process and subconscious process. This discussion leads to a

---

[2] Thirty-five years of continuous experience (practice and research) in the field of aircraft cockpit design and more generally HCD of life-critical systems.

more philosophical analysis of awareness, consciousness,[3] and embodiment. These concepts will be analyzed breaking with the Cartesian approach that separates mind and body and shifting to a **phenomenological** approach that puts forward experience (Derrida 1954). Edmund Husserl broke with positivist philosophy (Comte[4] 1865; Zahavi 2003). He studied the structure of consciousness, making a distinction "between the act of consciousness and the phenomena at which it is directed (the objects as intended)." He also developed the concept of intersubjectivity (i.e., the psychological relation between people—which I extend to relations among humans and/through interactive systems), which today makes a lot of sense when we study multi-agent systems, emergent properties of multifunctional tasks, and collective SA (Salmon et al. 2009). For example, automation, as it is implemented and used up to now, is often considered as an agent (i.e., a third crewmember in current commercial aircraft cockpits) and should be analyzed as such.

Extrinsic Versus Intrinsic Situation Models

Since the "situation awareness" concept is twofold (i.e., "situation" and "awareness"), let's analyze the concept of situation first. I looked at several dictionaries and encyclopedia, and the most frequent definitions (or most related concepts) for the concept of situation are the followings: location, set or combination of circumstances, state of affairs, condition, case, position, post of employment, and job. It can be also defined as a set of fact, events, and conditions that affect somebody or something at a particular time and in a particular place.

Situation may refer to a dynamic set of states including multiple derivatives, in the mathematical sense. Let's try to construct a model of the various kinds of situations (Fig. 7.1).

Ideally, the real world is characterized by an infinite number of highly interconnected states. This is what we call the "real situation." It may happen that some of these states are not available to us. For example, many states describing aircraft engine health are not directly available to pilots. States available to a human observer define the "available situation" (e.g., aircraft engine health states available to pilots). Note that the "available situation" is theoretically part of the "real situation." In other words, the "available situation" may not be totally or clearly perceived by the observer. What he/she perceives is called the "perceived situation." Of course, the "perceived situation" is part of the "available situation," but is also directed by what is being expected. The "desired" situation typically expresses a goal-driven behavior (e.g., we want to get to this point). The "expected" situation expresses an event-driven behavior (i.e., we anticipate a set of states to happen).

---

[3] In this paper, consciousness is taken in the sense of a compilation of "experiences" that results in combined mental and physical skills.

[4] Auguste Comte (1798–1857) founded positivist philosophy and is the first philosopher of science in the modern sense.

Fig. 7.1 Various kinds of situations

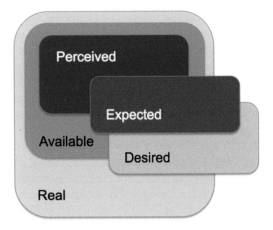

When people very strongly expect something to happen, they may be confused and mix the "perceived situation" with the "expected situation" (i.e., this is usually related to cultural context, distraction, and focus of attention). There is a huge difference between monitoring activities and control activities. People involved in a control activity are goal driven. Their SA process is directed by the task they need to perform. Conversely, to people who only have to monitor a process (and who do not have to act on it) they need to use, they typically construct in real time an artificial monitoring process that may be difficult, boring, and sometimes meaningless. In this second case, the situation awareness process has many chances not to be accomplished correctly.

Finally, the "perceived situation" is not necessarily a vector of some available states, but a model or image that emerges from a specific combination of these states, incrementally modified over time. This is called experience acquisition. Human operators build their own mental models or mental images of the real situation. This mental image depends on people, cultural context, current people's activity, and other factors that are specific to the domain being studied.

Consequently, human operator subjects, who are not familiar with situations in laboratory setups, may lead to false interpretations in the long term. For this reason, HCD formative evaluations dealing with complex systems require training, minimal experience acquisition, and longer involvement of human operator subjects. At FIT, for example, we choose to design new systems using realistic aircraft simulators and professional pilots. We systematically use the AUTOS pyramid to incrementally check technology maturity and maturity of practice.

Real and available situations are categorized under the concept of extrinsic situations. Expected and desired situations characterize the concept of intrinsic situation. Perceived situations belong to both concepts of extrinsic and intrinsic situations. Extrinsic situations are related to the complexity of human operator's environment. Intrinsic situations are related to the complexity of human operators' capabilities. Both types of complexity could be expressed in terms of number of states and interconnections among these states. In both cases, appropriate models need to be developed.

Awareness and Consciousness

Many SA models forget to mention what mental processes they are referring to. As already introduced above, SA could take place at a subconscious level (e.g., the skill-based behavior level of Rasmussen's model) because human operators tend to compile their knowledge to become expert, proficient, and effective in their activities (Rasmussen 1986). This compilation results from training and experience. The concept of compilation should be understood as an analog of software program compilation (i.e., once compiled it is very difficult and most of the time impossible to decompile). This compilation leads to a set of skills (i.e., executable routines). We will say that resulting situation awareness is embodied (Fig. 7.2). Of course, SA could also take place at the conscious level (e.g., the rule-based or knowledge-based behavior levels of Rasmussen's model). In this case, situation awareness is purely cognitive (i.e., interpreted following the software engineering analogy of the compilation concept) and corresponds to HFE classical definitions.

In a recent article, Dekker started a debate on the circularity of complacency, intentional bias, and loss of situation awareness, where he stated that complacency causes losing situation awareness and losing situation awareness causes complacency (Dekker 2015). This debate can be quickly ended if we consider the distinction between awareness and consciousness seriously. Of course, consciousness includes awareness (i.e., the awareness of something by a person), but it also includes the fact of being awake (Farthing 1992). In human-systems interaction, being awake means

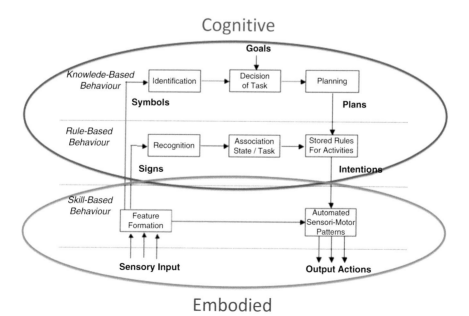

Fig. 7.2 Embodied versus cognitive awareness, using Rasmussen's model

not being complacent. For this reason and referring to Dekker's article, I much prefer to use the term "consciousness" instead of "awareness" to denote this overall SA concept that the HFE community is using for more than two decades. You could object that if you are not awake, you cannot be aware. But there are degrees of awakeness that modulate awareness, depending on intrinsic factors (i.e., level of experience and proficiency) and extrinsic factors (i.e., level of availability of the situation).

Sometimes you need to have a good story that triggers your own experience to really understand things both cognitively and physically. For example, I spent my childhood and teenage time skiing in the Pyrénées Mountains, which provides me with very accurate meaning of what sliding in powder snow means both cognitively and physically. Long time after, I worked on various aerospace programs, and in particular on the NASA Lunar Electric Rover, I felt very privileged to hear Harrison "Jack" Schmitt's stories of his Apollo 17 experience. He explained that running on the surface of the Moon was like skiing. The reason was one sixth gravity (compared to Earth gravity) and the regolith in suspension—this was the cognitive awareness. But my own skiing experience provided me with a physical awareness of how it is like running on the Moon!

Tangible situation awareness requires appropriate skills and knowledge based on deeper experience and expertise.

Consciousness could be seen as an emergent phenomena resulting from interactivity among million of billion of synapses and 50–100 billion of neurons in the brain and the whole nervous system of a human being. No computer system can simulate this phenomenon yet. Therefore, it is difficult to formally validate any model of consciousness at this point. However, artifacts (our objects of studies in HCD) are concrete representations of human intelligence, whether they are physical or figurative. According to Changeux,[5] complexity of brain connectivity increased dramatically in the course of human evolution. He claims that Darwinian epigenetic human brain evolution, combined with social evolution, is translated into art production evolution (i.e., art productions are interpreted as extra-cerebral memories). He also claims that the human brain is not a sponge, but constantly projecting, testing hypotheses, exploring, self-organizing, and engaging in social communication (Changeux 2008). Consequently, consciousness should be considered as a highly nonlinear dynamic process that produces and constantly refreshes our operative image (in Ochanine's sense; Paris I Seminar 1981) of the world that surrounds us in both physical and figurative meanings.

---

[5] Jean-Pierre Changeux is a French neuroscientist known for his research in biology, from the structure and function of proteins to the early development of the nervous system up to cognitive functions.

Cognition, Embodiment, and Familiarity

Situational complexity needs to be analyzed both extrinsically and intrinsically. In aeronautics, for example, pilot's mental models are incrementally formed by training and incremental construction of experience and skills. Consequently, human operator's expertise plays an important role when we want to analyze and assess situation awareness (i.e., the intrinsic account). In addition, aeronautical operational situations, for example, need to be modeled to better understand interactions among the various agents involved including automation (i.e., the extrinsic account). Therefore, multi-agent models and expert users (e.g., experimental test pilots in aeronautics) are required.

At this point, it is important to explain what we mean by complexity. First, the opposite concept of complexity cannot be limited to simplicity, but should be thought in terms of familiarity. Familiarity incrementally decreases the perceived complexity of a new place. In other words, the emergent mental model increasingly provides a more familiar image of the situation to the observer. We will see later that once this "familiar" mental image of the situation is acquired, it depends on the way people use it (i.e., it could be located at the subconscious level or the conscious level of the brain and sometimes embodied in our senses). Professional dancers, for example, learned through intensive training to embody jumps, spins, and pirouettes, so they do not think about at a conscious level to execute these kinds of movements. They concentrate on more complex endeavors.

> **The opposite concept of complexity cannot be limited to simplicity, but should be thought in terms of familiarity.**

Expertise and familiarity (i.e., the intrinsic account) are not sufficient to characterize complexity of the way situations are perceived. Another type of complexity needs to be understood and handled. Complexity of the available situation needs to be analyzed and understood also (i.e., the extrinsic account). A pilot cannot fly if he/she does not understand flight physics and meteorology. He/she should have a tangible perception and comprehension of the extrinsic situation of his/her environment. This account is consistent with current HFE mainstream SA definition in terms of perception, comprehension, and projection of the available situation. Note that this does not remove the need for usability engineering tests at design time in order to improve the available situation (Nielsen 1993).

Let's take a real-world example in commercial aviation. When air traffic control asks the aircrew to offset 3 NM on the right from their trajectory, on classical commercial aircraft, the pilot typically manually turns the heading knob to the right until the 3 NM offset is reached and reestablishes the original heading. This is an embodied gesture (Fig. 7.3).

Fig. 7.3 Classical
commercial aircraft's
navigation display. The *left
vertical line* is the initial
trajectory. The right one is
the offset. The pilot
estimates the distance
between these two lines,
here about 3 NM

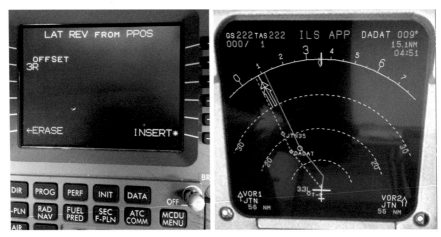

Fig. 7.4 (*Left* picture) The pilot enters "3R" on the user interface of the FMS under the prompt
"OFFSET" and selects "INSERT"; and (*right* picture) the navigation display shows the initial
trajectory (*dotted line*) and the offset trajectory (*plain line*)

Conversely, in modern automated cockpits, the same maneuver is performed
using the flight management system (FMS). The pilot enters "3R" (i.e., 3 NM offset
on the right) on the flight plan page (Fig. 7.4).

The FMS computer (considered as an artificial agent) automatically takes the
requested offset and reestablishes the original heading. In this case, the pilot dele-
gates the offset task to the FMS agent. This is a cognitive act. In these two cases, SA
is not managed in the same way. In the former case, the pilot has to estimate that the
offset is reached by monitoring the evolution of the aircraft on the navigation display
(ND). This monitoring is not a difficult task, but it is not as accurate as what an
automated system can do. The SA process should take into account aircraft inertia

for the estimation of the offset on the ND. In the latter case, the pilot does not have to worry about this estimation because it is entirely done by the system, including inertia management. We see that in modern cockpits SA has to be thought as a human-systems multi-agent activity.

Human Activity and Tangibility

The distinction between body and mind, proposed by René Descartes (Mattern 1978),[6] leads to a definition of consciousness, and then awareness, that is purely cognitive. This approach directly leads to the conception the HFE community currently has of situation awareness (Endsley 1995a, b). However, there is another approach, which privileges **embodiment**, where body and mind are interconnected. This corresponds to the phenomenological thought (Heidegger 1927). This philosophical approach is both anthropological and tangible. On the anthropological side, Lucy Suchman's work introduced the concept of situated actions (Suchman 1987). Suchman introduced a novel reactive approach to HCI (i.e., event driven), contrasting with the classical cognitive approach (i.e., goal driven). She used ethnomethodology to better understand social actions (Garfinkel 1967). Ethnomethodology focuses on people's activity (i.e., what people actually do) and not on tasks (i.e., what people are prescribed to do). This distinction between task and activity was already described to define the cognitive function representation for the implementation of cognitive function analysis (Boy 1998, 2013), as well as activity theory (Leont'ev 1981; Kaptelinin 1995). The concept of activity is related to Ochanine's concept of operative image (Paris I Seminar on D. Ochanine's Operative Image 1981). More recently, exploring the social aspects of interactive systems, Paul Dourish proposed the foundations of a new approach on human-computer interaction through embodied interaction (Dourish 2001). The concept of activity has then to be understood as both cognitive and embodied.

Whenever we explore human interaction with the world, whether it is physical or virtual, tangibility is an issue. Situation awareness has to do with tangibility. Tangibility can be understood in a **physical** sense (i.e., an object that you can physically grasp). For example, when you are driving and need to change the volume of your radio, a rotary knob with physical notches enables you to physically feel how much you turn. Tangibility can also be understood in a **figurative** sense (i.e., a concept or idea that you can mentally accept). In a discussion, we sometimes argue, "this is not tangible, I don't buy it!" This is because interaction is not only rationally cognitive (i.e., people often use heuristics and practice abduction instead of rational demonstration using deduction). Human interaction can be embodied (i.e., physical tangibility) and/or involve educated common sense (i.e., figurative tangibility). Educated common sense was already defined in Boy (2013).

---

[6]In this short essay, Ruth Mattern analyzes René Descartes' correspondence with Princess Elizabeth of Bohemia on the mind-body distinction.

In the early 1980s, I was an engineer freshly graduated with a Ph.D. in automatic control and system design and started learning HFE and cognitive science. At that time, my job was to design and develop new methods to help in the certification of commercial aircraft two-crewmen cockpits (Boy 1983). This was the beginning of a new kind of flying, where automation became a new crewmember onboard. We were worrying about workload because we thought that removing one crewmember from the cockpit was going to add more work to the two pilots remaining. In practice, we incrementally discovered that automation created the opposite trend. Instead of creating more stress, automation created problems of vigilance and later on complacency. Situation awareness was put forward during the 1990s because we started to understand the effect of distance between what pilots perceived in the cockpit and the real-world environment (i.e., aircraft systems and mechanical parts, air traffic control, and physical environment). Cognitive ergonomics became dominant and HFE models became almost entirely cognitive. We started to neglect the physical aspect of things.

One of the main reasons for this was that information technology penetrated mechanical parts (i.e., we massively put software into hardware), creating deeper automation issues. Today, things are totally different. We start designing systems in virtual worlds by developing software to the point that we can test human factors issues very early on during the design process. Automation is no longer an issue because we design and test software and interactivity before we develop hardware. The main issue then becomes tangibility because hardware is developed around and from software, to the point that we can now 3D-print hardware from software. In fact, we design and develop tangible interactive objects (Boy 2014a, b), which more generally become TISs. These TISs need to be integrated, as Salmon and his colleagues suggested in a response to Dekker's article, by using their distributed situation awareness approach (Salmon et al. 2016). These authors claimed that systems can be responsible for losing situation awareness. Consequently, the right approach for situation awareness today is to investigate interactivity of multi-agent (humans and systems) consciousness. System consciousness can be defined as both awareness of something by the system and lack of complacency (i.e., the system does not fail while working).

> **20th century automation made us move from doing to thinking and from thinking to complacency. 21st century tangible interactive systems should make us act in an acceptable ecological world.**

In addition, consciousness is also as much embodied as cognitive; this is what Merleau-Ponty calls corporeity, based on the distinction between phenomenology and positivism philosophies (1964). For that matter, it is crucial that investigators and scientists studying situation awareness for human-systems integration clearly understand how cognition and embodiment are interrelated. In other words, investigators and scientists should understand human operator's level of expertise and proficiency, and on the other hand, they should have experienced these cognitive and embodied skills by themselves in order to set up experiments and interpret results correctly. In particular, in life-critical domains such as aerospace, they need to understand that expertise is most of the time more important in experimental setups than usual statistical requirements to produce an "accepted" scientific paper (e.g., instead of taking 30 students to satisfy statistical requirements, it is often much better to take four professional pilots and a few aerospace experts to derive meaningful conclusions). The experience-based approach is often more effective and meaningful than the statistical approach for HCD of complex life-critical systems. Of course, this observation goes beyond the situation awareness issues being discussed, and statistical analyses should be promoted anytime meaningful experimental setups and results are guaranteed.

Situation awareness complexity comes from several causes. First, as already explained, "awareness" does not include the notion of complacency or its opposite concept, "awakeness." For that matter, the term (and concept) "consciousness" is more complete than awareness. Second, complexity of the situation itself matters. We call it extrinsic complexity. Third, complexity of the awareness process is crucial and involves not only conscious and subconscious mental mechanisms but also physical sensing and feelings. We call it intrinsic complexity.

The extrinsic-intrinsic distinction is interesting because it can support our understanding of situation awareness complexity, even if extrinsic and intrinsic complexity could be ultimately merged into a single model. The extrinsic perspective includes situation models that enable analytical interpretation of situations. This type is commonly used in the HFE community to better understand and assess situation awareness in work environments. It is based on a very simple model that involves three cognitive processes: perception, comprehension, and projection. The intrinsic perspective attacks model-based behavior modeling, which considers that people use operative mental models to act. Operative mental models are incrementally learned by people to interact with systems and, more generally, their environment. In addition, these models include a physical part and a mental part. These models are evolving as people learn about their environment (i.e., as they become more familiar with their environment). Consequently, familiarity plays an important role in situation awareness.

Maturity Criteria

Usually, technology maturity comes first and maturity of practice second. However, it is not systematic. Both types of maturity can be tested at any time. In this book, I will focus on the following maturity criteria:

- Syntactic transparency (integration, conciseness, robustness, reliability, trust, resilience)
- Manipulation (the ability to physically interact with a TIS)
- Usefulness (context-sensitive control amplification and information interpretation, content relevance, timely information)
- Usability (ease of learning how to use a TIS, ease of recovering from human error or system failure, pleasure of use, efficiency, flexibility of use)

These four categories provide a structured conceptual framework to test various levels of maturity. These levels are adapted from Piaget's stage theory of cognitive development. Jean Piaget was a Swiss psychologist, who studied cognitive development of children (Piaget 1957). He found four development stages: sensory-motor stage, preoperational stage, stage of concrete operations, and stage of formal operations. Interestingly, since TIS are designed and developed from software to hardware, TIS maturity levels are defined as a kind of mirror image of Piaget's cognitive development stages:

1. The conceptual model level that defines the purpose of the TIS to be developed, including targeted cognitive functions (deliberately chosen to satisfy the purpose of the TIS)
2. The activity elicitation level that enables the discovery of emerging cognitive functions from human-in-the-loop simulations
3. Preoperational level that enables the orchestration of the various elicited cognitive functions into a socio-technical framework model, as well as tangibility development by keeping useful affordances and eliminating distractive and dangerous affordances
4. Cyber-physical level where tangibility is tested and human-systems integration validated

"We cannot manage what we cannot measure." It is clear that explicit measures need to be defined for each concept of Table 7.1. Measurements are domain dependent and context dependent. They are always based on purposes. But, they become normalized through practice. Here is a first account of possible maturity measures.

Close World Versus Open World

Industry tends to protect products by getting patents and registered trademarks. They close the world for the use and potential reproduction of their products. In other words, a trademark protects its owner from other people using their innovation or concepts. Another philosophy consists in opening the world such as open source systems and open data. These data and systems are freely available to everyone to use and republish as they wish without any constraints. With open systems, not only you can use them freely, but you can also access their code and internal mechanisms freely. This philosophical distinction between close and open world is crucial when

Table 7.1 Maturity assessment concepts with respect to maturity criteria categories and maturity levels

Maturity criteria categories/TIS maturity levels	Syntactic transparency	Manipulation	Usefulness	Usability
1. Conceptual model	Integration	Interaction	Observables and controls	Efficiency
2. Activity elicitation	Robustness Reliability	Affordance discovery	Control amplification and information interpretation	Ease of recovering from human error or system failure
3. Preoperational	Conciseness Trust	Cognitive and embodied functions	Context and content relevance	Flexibility of use
4. Cyber-physical	Resilience	Embodied structures	Timely information	Ease of learning how to use a TIS, pleasure of use

you design a system. The close world option requires very mature technology. A good example is the Macintosh operating system, which does not allow much internal modification, but is very reliable and easy to use for specific purposes by anybody. Conversely, open systems, such as Linux, offer immense possibilities of extensions and reprogramming. They are addressed to proficient people.

However, we can also see the close world versus open world issue from the perspective of maturity. For example, knives have evolved since their early invention. We have very specialized knives for several kinds of food (e.g., fish, meat, and cheese). We have knives for cutting cardboard, glass, and iron. They are all different and adapted for the job they are designed for. This is the result of an evolution, where some kinds of knife attributes have been selected and others rejected with respect to the job they were aimed at performing. In this case, maturity is a matter of categorization of knives (i.e., each knife is designed for a specific use closing the world to other potential usages).

Other artifacts have been designed by accumulating attributes that enable them to be used in a large variety of contexts. For example, a sedan car can transport people and any kind of (reasonably small) things and be used for work and leisure. These types of systems are flexible and lead to open usages. They are also the result of an evolution and multiple tests over long periods of time. Some cars, such as the Citroën 2CV,[7] could be deconstructed (like a Lego) and rebuild easily. Consequently, technology maturity can be seen as specialization, closing the world to specific usages, and generalization, opening the world to multiple usages. In both cases, it is a matter of emergence and discovery of usage-centered attributes that could lead to the development of either several products or a single product with several possibilities of usage.

---

[7] The Citroën 2CV was a French car that was manufactured by Citroën from 1948 to 1990.

So, what about tangible interactive systems? In the same way a Citroën 2CV could be deconstructed and reconstructed piece by piece, it should be possible to construct and deconstruct a TIS if we choose the open world approach. Conversely, if we choose the close world approach, TIS's structures and functions should be specialized for specific purposes. This leads to the search for purpose-specific TIS categories in terms of structure and function.

Change Management

Anytime a new TIS is designed and delivered in the real world, it causes a certain change. This change could be small and, in this case, could be absorbed by the society. However, when the change is bigger, a number of actions should be taken. First and foremost, the right communication should be provided to people who could be impacted. I remember the time when we said to people that automation was good because work would be easier. Instead, the right communication should have been "work will be different." With automation, work is actually easier most of the time, but could be harder in specific situations. Therefore, nominal situations are less interesting than off-nominal situations, where people need to solve problems on their own. In this very specific case of automation, it is now clear that rare situations, which are outside of automation context of validity, should be interpreted as nonlinear situations that should deserve immense attention at design time. Otherwise, such situations will be interpreted as unexpected events, which is currently the case. Reason is that current systems are still generally designed as linear systems in specific contexts (i.e., possibilities of nonlinear situations are removed at design time).

Trying to become familiar with human-systems integration complexity is the right attitude instead of systematically trying to oversimplify by linearization. Once familiarized, you will be able to choose appropriate solutions for handling nonlinear situations. Of course, if these solutions lead to undesirable outcome, they should not be kept. Once more, modeling and simulation are key resources for modifying design appropriately. Understanding complexity introduced by the design of a new TIS typically dictates change management communication and procedures.

Change management should not be limited to a one-way direction (i.e., from the design team to potential customers); it should also be thought in the opposite direction (i.e., from potential customers to the design team). Change management should then be used as a usability engineering resource also. Indeed, early adopters and techno-fans can greatly contribute to both change management and new TIS's improvement and adaptation to societal requirements.

References

ASA (2011) Dossier on air transport pilot facing the unexpected. Retrieved on 13 Jun 2015. http://www.academie-air-espace.com/event/newdetail.php?varCat=14&varId=216. Air and Space Academy, Paris

Boy GA (1983) Le Système MESSAGE: Un Premier Pas vers l'Analyse Assistée par Ordinateur des Interactions Homme-Machine (The MESSAGE system: a first step toward computer-supported analysis of human-machine interactions). Le Travail Humain Journal, Tome 46, no. 2, Paris

Boy GA (1998) Cognitive function analysis. Greenwood/Ablex, Stamford. ISBN 9781567503777

Boy GA (2012) What do we mean by human-centered design of life-critical systems? In: Proceedings of the 2012 IEA World Congress on Ergonomics, Recife, Brazil – Work 41 (2012, doi:10.3233/WOR-2012-0029-4503, IOS Press), pp 4503–4513

Boy GA (2013) Orchestrating human-centered design. Springer, London. ISBN 978-1-4471-4338-3

Boy GA (2014a) Dealing with the unexpected. In Millot P (ed) Risk management in life critical systems. Wiley ISTE, Hoboken, London, UK. ISBN: 978-1-84821-480-4

Boy GA (2014b) From automation to tangible interactive objects. Annu Rev Control:1367–5788. doi:10.1016/j.arcontrol.2014.03.001. Elsevier

Boy GA, Hollnagel E (1993) Cockpit evolution and human-machine interaction. EURISCO Report no. T-93-002-GB-VI

Boy GA, Schmitt KA (2013) Design for safety: a cognitive engineering approach to the control and management of nuclear power plants. Ann Nucl Energy 52:125–136. Elsevier

Changeux JP (2008) Du vrai, du beau, du bien: une nouvelle approche neuronale (About truth, beauty and good: a new neuronal approach). Editions Odile Jacob, Paris. Bottom of Form ISBN-13: 978-2738119049

Comte A (1865) A general view of positivism. (Trans by Bridges JH, Trubner and Co., 1865 (reissued by Cambridge University Press, 2009; ISBN 978-1-108-00064-2)

Dekker SWA (2015) The danger of losing situation awareness. Cogn Technol Work. doi:10.1007/s10111-015-0324-4

Dekker SWA, Hummerdal DH, Smith K (2010) Situation awareness: some remaining questions. Theor Issues Ergon Sci 11:131–135

Derrida J (1954 French Edition; 2003 English Edition) The problem of genesis in Husserl's philosophy. University of Chicago Press, Chicago

Dourish P (2001) Where the action is: the foundations of embodied interaction. MIT Press, Cambridge

Endsley MR (1995a) Measurement of situation awareness in dynamic systems. Hum Factors 37(1):65–84

Endsley MR (1995b) Toward a theory of situation awareness in dynamic systems. Hum Factors Hum Factors Ergon Soc J 37(1):32–64

Endsley MR (1998) A comparative analysis of SAGAT and SART for evaluations of situation awareness. In: Proceedings of the human factors and ergonomics society 42nd annual meeting, The Human Factors and Ergonomics Society, Santa Monica, pp 82–86

Endsley MR, Garland DJ (eds) (2000) Situation awareness analysis and measurement. Lawrence Erlbaum Associates, Mahwah

Farthing G (1992) The psychology of consciousness. Prentice Hall, Englewood Cliffs. ISBN 978-0-13-728668-3

Garfinkel H (1967) Studies in ethnomethodology. Prentice Hall, Englewood Cliffs

Heidegger M (1927) Being and time. (Trans. Macquarrie and Robinson (1962)). Harper and Row, New York

Kaptelinin V (1995) Designing learning activity: a cultural-historical perspective in CSCL. In: Proceedings of the computer supported cooperative learning (CSCL'95). Indiana University, Bloomington

Leont'ev (1981) Problems of the development of the mind. Progress, Moscow

Mattern R (1978) Descartes' correspondence with Elizabeth concerning both the union and distinction of mind and body. In: Hooker M (ed) Descartes: critical and interpretive essays. John Hopkins University Press, Baltimore, pp 212–222

Merleau-Ponty M (1964) The primacy of perception. Northwestern University Press, Evanston

Minsky M (1986) The society of mind. Simon and Schuster, New York. ISBN 0-671-60740-5

Nielsen J (1993) Usability engineering. Academic, Boston. ISBN 0-12-518405-0

Norman D (1999) The invisible computer: why good products can fail, the personal computer is so complex, and information appliances are the solution. The MIT Press. Reprint edition. ISBN-13: 978-0262640411

Piaget J (1957) Construction of reality in the child. Routledge & Kegan Paul, London

Rasmussen J (1986) Information processing and human-machine interaction: an approach to cognitive engineering. Elsevier Science, New York. ISBN 0444009876

Salmon PM, Stanton NA, Walker GH, Jenkins DP (2009) Distributed situation awareness: theory, measurement and application to teamwork. Ashgate, Aldershot

Salmon PM, Walker GH, Stanton NA (2016) Pilot error versus sociotechnical systems failure: a distributed situation awareness analysis of Air France 447. Theor Issues Ergon Sci 17:64–79

Sarter NB, Woods DD, Billings CE (1997) Automation surprises. In: Salvendy G (ed) Handbook of human factors and ergonomics, 2nd edn. Wiley, New York

Schneider W, Shiffrin RM (1977) Controlled and automatic human information processing: I. Detection, search, and attention. Psychol Rev 84:1–66

Paris I Seminar (1981) Operative image (in French). Actes d'un séminaire (1–5 juin) et recueil d'articles de D. Ochanine. Université de Paris I (Panthéon-Sorbonne), Centre d'éducation Permanente, Département d'Ergonomie et d'Ecologie Humaine

Shiffrin RM, Schneider W (1977) Controlled and automatic human information processing: II. Perceptual learning, automatic attending, and a general theory. Psychol Rev 84(2):127–190

Smith K, Hancock PA (1995) Situation awareness is adaptive, externally directed consciousness. Hum Factors 37(1):137–148

Stanton NA, Chambers PRG, Piggott J (2001) Situational awareness and safety. Saf Sci 39:189–204

Suchman L (1987) Plans and situated actions: the problem of human-machine communication. Cambridge University Press, New York

Vidulich MA (2000) Testing the sensitivity of situation awareness metrics in interface evaluations. In: Endsley MR, Garland DJ (eds) Situation awareness analysis and measurement. Lawrence Erlbaum Associates, Mahwah, pp 227–246

Zahavi D (2003) Husserl's phenomenology. Stanford University Press, Stanford

Chapter 8
Stability

Design of tangible interactive systems (TISs) involves understanding and taking into account stability issues. What do we mean by TIS stability? Any time a new artifact or system is designed, we need to question impact of its use in our society and environment. We need to question social stability and environmental stability with respect to technological evolution and consequent emergence of new practices. Stability issues naturally follow maturity issues that were presented and discussed in the previous chapter. They include important concepts such as observability, controllability, redundancy, cognitive stability, cognitive support, resilience, safety, and security of life-critical systems. Let's first remind old concepts and define new ones.

Redundancy

Using an interactive system is based on two important properties: observability and controllability (Boy 2001, 2013). System **observability** requires designers to answer the following question: are the available outputs, called observables, necessary and sufficient to figure out what the system does? System **controllability** requires designers to answer the dual question: are the available inputs, called controls, necessary and sufficient to appropriately influence the overall state of the system? Now, the corollary question is: how do we define the right observables and controls? Of course, a series of trials and errors may incrementally lead to a solution, but there are a few more concepts that will help answering the three questions, such as cognitive model, degrees of freedom, dependent and independent variables, and redundancy.

Whenever you use a system, you develop a specific **cognitive model** that associates observable states and controls. Observables and controls can be more or less integrated. If we want to access each individual level of a system, then their number can be very large. This is the option expert maintainers prefer because they can fix

© Springer International Publishing Switzerland 2016
G.A. Boy, *Tangible Interactive Systems*, Human–Computer Interaction Series,
DOI 10.1007/978-3-319-30270-6_8

failing parts easily. In counterpart, we, as designers, need to provide this access. The more the number of degrees of freedom is high, the more the related cognitive model is complex (i.e., for experts). Conversely, if we want to provide an easy-to-use system for casual usage, then we will integrate observables and control as much as possible to increase safety, efficiency, and comfort. In this case, we say that the number of degrees of freedom is low and the related cognitive model will be simple (i.e., for casual users).

> **TIS usage requires making a cognitive model that relates its observable states and control states**.

The space shuttle had five computers, three inertial systems, and two independent systems that computed its position according to the stars. If one of the computer/system failed, the other(s) would still manage to keep the space shuttle working. Human beings have their own redundancy in order to survive. Redundancy could be seen at the structural level or the functional level. For example, public buildings have, or should have, a staircase in addition to elevators just in case of electrical or mechanical failures of elevator systems. This is **structural redundancy** that is useful in abnormal and emergency situations. From a functional point of view, we now see signs on elevator doors saying: "Use stairs, you will improve your heath!" You obviously don't need to use stairs, but it would be useful for your health because you will make physical exercise. This is **functional redundancy** that is most often useful in normal situations for specific purposes.

> **Two distinctions for the redundancy concept: (1) structural versus functional and (2) syntactic versus semantic**.

Therefore, how can we improve TIS's tangibility by increasing its stability through redundancy? Let's make a distinction between syntactic redundancy (i.e., redundancy of observables and controls) and semantic redundancy[1] (i.e., redundancy about meaning).

Syntactic Redundancy A system is typically characterized by a set of n observable states or outputs $\{O_1, O_2, \ldots O_n\}$, and a set of m controllable states or inputs $\{I_1, I_2, \ldots I_m\}$. The system is intrinsically redundant if there are p outputs ($p < n$) and q inputs ($q < m$) that are necessary and sufficient to use it correctly. The remaining (n-q) outputs and (m-q) inputs are redundant states when they are associated with independent subsystems of the overall system. These redundant states need to be chosen

---

[1] These concepts were already elaborated in previous publications (Boy 2001, 2013). In this book, I label them.

in order to assist the user in normal, abnormal, and emergency situations. In aircraft cockpits, for example, several instruments are duplicated, one for the captain and another for the first officer. In addition, some observable states displayed on digital instruments are also available on redundant traditional instruments.

Semantic Redundancy Thus, controlling a system state by state with the appropriate redundant information is quite different from delegating this control activity to an automaton. New kinds of redundancy emerge from the use of highly automated systems. Traditional system observability and controllability usually deal with the **what** system states. The supervision of highly automated systems requires redundant information on the "why," "how," "with what," and "when" in order to increase insight, confidence, and reliability: **Why** the system is doing what it does? **How** to obtain a system state with respect to an action using control devices? **With what** other display or device the current input/output should be associated? **When** should a piece of information be sent or acquired?

Safety and Dealing with the Unexpected

In aeronautics, safety is handled by "good practice" of design, engineering, training, operations, and maintenance. Taking into account the TOP model, technology has to be reliable, available, and safe. Many tests, including flight tests, are incrementally done before delivery. They are based on various kinds of relevant criteria and scenarios. A large variety of situations are anticipated. Organizationally, a safety culture has been developed over the years based on experience feedback, development of regulations, and operational procedures.

Experience feedback is typically negative. First, it reports system failures and/or human errors, not or very rarely positive experience. From a pure system perspective, this mechanism is excellent and incrementally leads to highly reliable technology. However, detection of human errors leads to either more procedures to follow (i.e., automating human behavior) or automation (i.e., automating systems) and blaming people who committed errors that are violations of operational procedures. Both procedures and automation tend to rigidify human activity since it provides mandatory tailored tasks executed by either people or systems. Problems come when either procedures or automation cannot provide appropriate solutions, and people need to find new solutions themselves. In other words, people who are involved need to know how to deal with **unexpected situations** (Boy 2014). In this case, they need flexibility. Solutions depend on the severity of the consequences of these situations. This point will be developed later in the chapter.

In contrast with the negative approach of the classical experience feedback—which has given very good results—I would like to propose a positive one. Instead of seeing people as problems, we need to see them as solutions. Taking that route, people need to be effectively engaged. They need to know what risk taking involves (Boy and Brachet 2010). They need to be competent, constantly aware of what is

Table 8.1 Situation complexity versus expectation

Situation	Simple	Complex
Expected	Procedural activity	Familiarity-based activity
Unexpected	Linear problem-solving	Crisis management based on high-level expertise and experience and sensemaking

going on, proactive, humble, resilient in case of failure, sufficiently prepared to all kinds of situations, creative when necessary, responsible, and so on. This is the opposite of procedure following! They actually need to be both great procedure followers in well-known situations (i.e., including normal and abnormal situations) and great problem solvers in unknown or unexpected situations. This involves a selection process.

What we just described works in a deterministic world. Unfortunately, the real world is not deterministic, or if it is we don't know yet all its intrinsic rules. Our world is constantly moving, transforming, and evolving in an unpredictable manner. We constantly try to put order into this Brownian movement. We try to find patterns and clusters to become more familiar with its complexity. Today, people are both more autonomous (e.g., they can go anywhere on the planet thanks to transportation means and communicate with almost anybody using networked information technology) and constrained (e.g., we need to use this technology to be autonomous; therefore, we fall into this paradox that makes us dependent of technology to be more independent). In this not-deterministic world where we live, we have become extremely reactive, event driven, trying to predict everything. Predicting the future is necessarily short term and therefore keeps us in the short term all the time. Instead, we need to anticipate; we need to have visions and be goal driven, trying to **test possible futures** in a longer term. We need to be creative and invent the future, instead of trying to predict it, which will never work! Designing TISs, we always need to address this point if we want to keep being human centered.

More specifically, TIS design requires taking into account known normal, abnormal, and emergency situations and the possibility of unexpected situations. In known situations, we can use specific cognitive models that integrate both observable and controllable states. Making sense of unexpected situations requires access to lower level states. It also requires great expertise of human operators. All this is a matter of human-systems integration complexity and severity of the consequences of situations (Table 8.1).

When the situation is both simple and expected, procedural activity is usually the rule. When an expected situation becomes complex, because the environment is complex, tasks are complex and/or technology is complex, people involved should be familiar with such a situation or analogs. When the situation is simple but unexpected, people involved require expertise in problem-solving, which is usually linear (i.e., they can decompose a problem into subproblems until they find the solution; this is usually covered by abnormal and emergency procedures—the problem being to use the right procedures). When the situation is both unexpected and complex, we are in a crisis management situation. In this case, high-level expertise and experience and sensemaking are required. People involved need to understand situation seriousness and base their actions on deeper knowledge and knowhow. They usually choose to keep the vital functions, if at all possible, and protect what can be protected.

TIS design should take these concerns into account. In other words, designers should have in mind what crisis managers should have to be able to restabilize to a more acceptable situation when the situation becomes bad. Think about Fukushima. After the tsunami attack, all systems driven by electricity were unavailable (Kawano 2012). No more lights. Human operators were totally blind! Communication tools were not available, except hotline and landline phone. Human operators were wearing full-face masks, which was very exhausting. Many obstacles and fire protection hoses on the ground handicapped recovery work. Initial strategy had to be changed because of the high radiation level. There were only a limited number of tools available such as flashlights, cables, screwdrivers, engine-driven generators, and compressors. In addition, only a few people knew how to operate fire engines. These facts are about preparation, or lack of preparation in this case. From human and organizational standpoints, Fukushima crisis management showed issues in command and control, roles and responsibilities, communications, clear strategy sharing, and appropriate stuffing. This short explanation shows the importance of taking the TOP model as a conceptual framework to design technology (e.g., command and control, communications means), organization (e.g., clear strategy sharing and appropriate stuffing) and people (e.g., roles and responsibilities).

Resilience is a very fashionable concept these days! I would prefer to talk about **risk taking** because we need to be prepared to the unprepared. In a conference on risk taking that I coordinated in 2008 for the Air and Space Academy in France, representatives of very different high-risk professions chosen to speak at the conference—surgeons, experimental test pilots, and mountaineers—all declared that it was crucial to develop the relevant skills to deal with uncertainties and unforeseen circumstances in conditions that could be at once extreme and routine. In his presentation on "Risk-taking in extreme skiing," Manu Gaidet, triple World Free Ride champion, explained how he went about his preparation: "When looking at a slope, I imagine my descent, the 'line' I want to follow. I analyze the paths of possible avalanches or snowfalls... I choose the itinerary according to an estimate of the speed, my physical condition at the time and my level of self-confidence. I identify 'zero risk' areas and dangerous paths. And then I imagine how to go from one zero risk spot to another... My golden rule is: "if I can't picture it, I don't do it!" (Boy and Brachet 2010).

After all precautions have been taken, comes the time to act! When we are in the unexpected-complex situation case, we are facing risks directly without preparation. What should we do? What are the resources that we need to survive? In life-critical systems, this question is in terms of life or death.

Importance of Context

Following up on what I said before on operational procedures onboard aircraft, they are available on paper format for a long time. Pilots have to learn how to use related books. For example, these books are typically organized by chapters corresponding to all aircraft systems. Transferring such information on electronic devices, such as tablets, is not straightforward (e.g., copying pdf files into an iPad). Since electronic media can be fed with flight parameters, information can be reorganized by contextual situations (i.e., moving to new flight phase can automatically trigger a relevant and necessary piece of information). The main problem then becomes defining context patterns that will enable triggering appropriate information for pilots. This is what does the On-board Context-Sensitive Information System (OCSIS) that is being designed and developed at HCDi (Tan 2015, 2014; Boulnois et al. 2015).

Operational information transfer from paper to electronic brings new issues such as certification. Indeed, paper manuals are additional information provided to human operators to use systems, as software-based onboard information systems are TISs, which have a new status. These systems are new tangible parts of the aircraft, not only user guides. Consequently, they must be certified from a safety viewpoint. For this reason, safety requirements lead to testing socio-cognitive stability of the multi-agent (humans and systems) environment in the cockpit, in particular reliability, correctness, and consistency of information provided by a TIS such as OCSIS.

Context is also about connectivity among elements. Being somewhere means being connected with an environment composed of designed systems and other agents. Situated cognition and actions are at the center of multi-agent interactive systems. Cognition and actions are distributed among contributing interacting agents. This interactivity generates emergent contexts that are difficult, and most of time impossible, to predict—we need to discover them through human-in-the-loop simulation (HITLS). People take into account context to act, and generate new contexts by acting. This is why incremental formative evaluations of a new TIS are so important.

Security

Cybersecurity has become one of most crucial concepts from the beginning of the twenty-first century. Software has become prominent and can be hacked by computer experts. Data can be altered seriously and cause potential catastrophes. The main problem is possible access to this data. In aeronautics, safety is the number one priority from the beginning of its existence. Today, security has become as important. We then need to find ways of making impossible this access to non-habilitated people.

In the OCSIS case, for example, besides the fact that the tablet solution is still preliminary and needs further investigation (e.g., integrated screen in the cockpit like electronic libraries today), they can be easily stolen. Data can be accessed easily and altered. This requires new ways of organizing the aviation domain. Give responsibility to pilots for their equipment. We can think about equipping TISs, such as OCSIS, with personalized access systems (e.g., combined finger, eye, and face identification), as well as compatibility of hardware and software with cockpits and nothing else.

The same is true for datalink between aircraft and ground via satellite (e.g., for communication purposes). In the case of major failure onboard, high connectivity with the ground is a tremendous asset. The successful Apollo 13 accident is a good example for such connectivity, where ground crew helped space crew to recover from a major life-critical failure. Datalink, almost by definition, can be hacked. Various kinds of protection can be designed and developed such as redundancy (i.e., keeping radio communication onboard) and transversal datalink connection with other aircraft via different types of pipelines.

Air traffic management (ATM) is facing the difficult problem of the constantly growing number of aircraft. High-density air traffic provides air traffic managers with nonlinear problems to solve (i.e., there are many possible solutions, but potentially leading to chaotic situations). Therefore, instead of controlling aircraft one by one like what is usually done in air traffic control (ATC) today, airspace agents should communicate, cooperate, and coordinate their activities with respect to a set of rules leading to stability. In current ATC, air traffic controllers have implicit models of the traffic, figuring out patterns and solving conflicts constantly. In the ATM, connectivity among aircraft will need to be more explicit. Each aircraft will need to be aware of the presence of other aircraft in the vicinity, with explicit information of position and direction. We already discussed the flock-of-birds analogy, where birds automatically react according to three types of rules: separation, alignment, and cohesion. Similar rules should be investigated for aircraft to face high-density traffic, with the provision of other rules and constraints related to safety, efficiency, and passenger comfort. Doing this is also subject to security issues. I believe that potential solutions should be found in a right mix of hardware and software protections.

Resilience Versus Stability

A big movement raised in the human factors and ergonomics community on resilience engineering during the last decade or so (Hollnagel et al. 2006). I would like to question the concept of "resilience" and advocate the concept of "stability" instead. Resilience is a phenomenon that could follow a crisis toward recovery of an acceptable situation. First, what is a crisis? It is no more than a patent instability, which can be technical, environmental, social, economical, or political, which provokes radical changes in the state of affairs. If we talk about political crises, for example, people involved are always looking for a regulation framework that could overcome tensions. Indeed, where there is a crisis, there is necessarily divergent objectives and therefore tension. In addition, the end of a crisis does not mean tension drop. Any crisis is usually unexpected. It is a disruption in the current state of affairs. It develops very quickly. People involved are overwhelmed and typically may not know what to do. Of course, when a crisis happens frequently, people know how and have means to respond to it. Conversely, when a crisis happens occasionally, people need to improvise because being equipped for appropriate answers is usually too expensive. Finally, when a crisis comes as an unknown event, people have to invent ad hoc solutions based on creativity.

Similarly, Westrum provided three categories of threats: regular threats, irregular threats, and improbable and unexampled events (Westrum 2006). This kind of categorization is interesting but does not provide any clue on how to design future life-critical systems. How should we deal with the unexpected when we design a life-critical system? Just saying that we cannot prepare for unforeseen situations is not enough. In mountaineering, for example, where risk is very high, we think in terms of life and death. Mountaineers train during long periods of time and keep themselves in excellent shape before they start. This is high cost! In other words, when risk is high, you need to pay the price! You also need to investigate in the right direction (i.e., design appropriate technology, setup appropriate organizations, and train the right people the right way). Training people on procedure following only is kind of short when systems involved are highly nonlinear; people should be trained on problem-solving also. The concept of stability needs to be clearly understood and people need to think in terms of possible futures (i.e., what could happen using the technology that we are designing) instead of prediction (i.e., using a causal approach of the immediate short-term future). Again, modeling and simulation is an important support for human-centered design (HCD) of stable integrated human-systems environments.

The financial crisis of 2008 was very probably based on a wrong expectation model, and the "unexpected" happened. Alan Greenspan compared it to a tsunami and recognized that he did not anticipate it despite his long experience. The mix of linear thinking and nonlinear global economy generated very difficult, and even impossible, to understand world financial evolution. It is great to recognize this, but what should we do or not do not to experience this again? Should we continue with our short-term economy? What are the conditions to find sustainable human-centered solutions? Talking about resilience is fine, but what new economical model should we find? Should we continue to tailor our socio-technical systems to serve finance? Or, should we tailor finance and market economy to serve our socio-technical systems? If we want people to live in harmony within a sane and safe socio-technical and organic environment, we should find out how much it costs and work together to make it work. Again, instead of coming back to previous practice after reacting to events, even catastrophic events, we should develop beautiful visions of possible futures.

HCD proposes the following procedure to help analyze stability at design time using HITLS:

1. Describe the relevant aspects of concepts of operations in terms of function allocation among people and technology, with a specific search for possible breakdowns (e.g., system failures and human errors)

2. Identify risks (e.g., humanitarian, financial, legal) by examining possible failure-consequence relationships and the various issues related to them
3. Test and assess acceptability and sustainability of selected solutions for the TIS being designed (i.e., the all stakeholders should be involved for these tests and assessments)
4. Recommend changes until a fully satisfactory solution is found

TIS Stability

Physics says that passive stability is related to degrees of freedom (e.g., an object in a three-dimensional world is usually defined by three degrees of freedom). For example, a chair is stable when it has (at least) three legs. Very early during their childhood, people learnt how to stay erect on two legs. In fact, they learned to dynamically compensate their physical instability. In other words (Fig. 8.1), **passive stability** does not require any action (e.g., the pendulum comes back to its stable position); **active stability** requires continuous action based on a regulation process (e.g., the inverted pendulum requires a regulation process, such as artists maintaining dishes turning on top of sticks or riders on unicycles). Challenging stability of a system is usually caused by an event, which could be an internal (usually a system failure) or external aggression (typically an external physical disturbance or a human error).

When you use an interactive system, you may produce erroneous actions that are tolerated by the system (i.e., the system returns to a stable state by itself or enables you to correct your error—recovery means are available). You also may produce erroneous actions that are not tolerated by the system (i.e., the system returns to a stable state by itself) and require additional actions from you to keep the system stable. What do we mean by stability in this case? To answer this question, we need to better understand what variability means.

Fig. 8.1 Passive stability (classical pendulum on the *left*) and active stability (unicycle on the *right*)

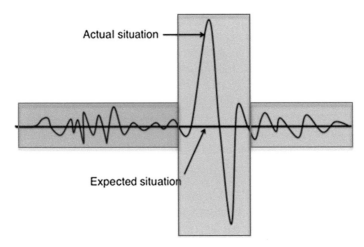

Fig. 8.2 Expected and actual situation showing small variations, in *blue*, typically filtered (and considered as noise), and bigger variations, in *red*, typically considered as unexpected, mainly because they are not taken into account in the conceptual models supporting system design (Adapted from Boy 2014)

Variability of a phenomenon of a complex dynamic system (e.g., climate, physiological functions, genetic evolution) expresses fluctuations that result from the application of internal or external inputs to this phenomenon. Small fluctuations are usually filtered, then eliminated, and most of the time ignored once filtered. Large fluctuations cannot be filtered and are sometimes considered as unexpected events (Fig. 8.2). Complex dynamic systems may have nonlinear behavior and sometimes-chaotic behavior. One of the solutions is to keep people out of these nonlinear or chaotic zones (i.e., defining and implementing safety envelopes). Another complementary solution is to provide people with useful means to handle these nonlinear or chaotic behaviors (i.e., providing automated systems and/or training that enable handling them).

Mastering such variability enables handling TIS stability (i.e., continuously stabilizing small fluctuations, and handling large fluctuations). It is therefore important to know about all possible models (i.e., structures and functions) of the TIS being designed. These models should be about how the system works (i.e., intrinsic model) and also how the system can be used (i.e., extrinsic model). Once these models are identified, formally developed, and potentially simulated, they can be used to check both intrinsic stability (i.e., the proper stability of the TIS or technology stability) and extrinsic stability (i.e., human-system integration stability or practice stability). Of course, practice stability is strongly influenced by redundancy (i.e., both syntactic and semantic consistency).

We will say that a TIS is stable and provides stable interaction when it enables its user to:

- Anticipate possible futures (i.e., enabling preparation of actions or execute actions in advance)

- Interact opportunistically (i.e., enabling execution of actions that can be either reactions to specific events and/or based on user's intentions)
- Recover from system failure or human errors (i.e., enabling easy identification of failing situations and provision of recovery means)

It should be clear that the provision of these functions depends on system complexity and maturity and therefore on the required expertise of TIS's users.

Stability and Complacency

Stability is a matter of constant attention. It may be totally destroyed by complacency. Complacency happens when people become too confident in continuous success of the use of a system. For example, danger in flight tests is much less for the first flight of a new aircraft than after 50 test flights, when experimental test pilots had become familiar with the aircraft as a whole and more specifically its various systems (i.e., when they have become familiar with aircraft complexity). They may become complacent and decrease their vigilance. What are the solutions that enable overcoming human and organizational complacency? Human-systems cooperation is certainly a solution that involves continuous cross-checking and verification of basic safety rules. However, we always need to make sure that competence, critical thinking, and flexibility stay the highest assets.

If life-critical systems require constant attention from their users, it also requires full attention from the entire organization. For example, after the Challenger accident in January 1986, NASA became aware of this necessary need for organizational attention. The same as for people, organizations may become complacent. This is what happened to NASA with the Columbia accident in February 2003, 17 years after the Challenger accident. It is important to say that Space Shuttle operations were extremely sophisticated and dangerous as all space flights. They require lots of attention from various viewpoints, including overall management, engineering, ground control, and crew operations. This is matter of constant distributed and integrated situation awareness.

> **When everything works very well for a while, people and organizations become complacent.**

Therefore, TIS stability should be investigated both as an individual issue and a collective issue. At the individual level, complacency is a matter of engagement, involvement, and constant attention (as already said). At the collective level, complacency is a matter of group cohesion, intersubjectivity, and constant effective collaboration. These properties should be translated in terms of principles and measures, which should be used in evaluation and validation tests. Specific measures depend on the application domain. For example, engagement involves measures of attraction, concentration, minimum distraction, and commitment.

Instead of waiting incidents and accidents to develop human factor methods and techniques to discover what was wrong in design and subsequent operations, it is time to provide concepts, methods, and techniques that design teams could use to anticipate stability issues. The TIS concept enables us to analyze, design, and evaluate systems considered as TISs of TISs. In the next section, instability factors will be provided to guide such analyses, designs, and evaluations.

Instability Factors

Identification of instability factors is useful for TIS designers. Instability factors can be categorized with respect to AUTOS pyramid concepts. Here is a first list.

Artifact-based instability factors: availability of the right equipment at the right time, accountability, information credibility, not enough information and too much information.

User-based instability factors: lack of engagement, team spirit, compliance to rules, control, competence, trust, lack of skills, stress, vigilance, workload, situation awareness, lack or not enough training, and leadership and followership.

Task-based instability factors: availability of the right knowledge at the right time, lack of self-evaluation, lack of change management activity, task allocation, task difficulty, parallel tasks, sequential tasks, not enough procedures, too many procedures, and wrong planning.

Organization-based instability factors: unanticipated liability factors, economical issues, lack of or failing regulatory organization, lack of or failing communication, team structure, human resource management, standards, not enough regulations, too many regulations, and collaborative work.

Situation-based instability factors: routine situations, unexpected situations, complex situations, real versus available situations, perceived situations, expected situations, and desired situations.

Simulation-Based Stability Identification

Stability should then be studied at design time. If stability can be studied a priori for very simple systems, it is practically impossible to study it without a fairly developed system when this system is complex. As already said many times in this book, modeling and simulation are extremely helpful during design to elicit, analyze, and take into account possible emerging properties of the artifact being designed. The first thing to do is setting up a realistic scenario that can be played using a prototype, observe, and detect human-systems integration emerging properties. Of course, as many scenarios as possible should be run; limitations usually come from time and budget constraints. The following procedure is typically used:

- Step 1. A first prototype of the system being designed is developed. It is then tested by a group of experts. Expert judgments are provided, integrated, and analyzed. Experts include expert users, expert designers, and engineers, for example.
- Step 2. Results from the previous test are integrated into the prototype, which is tested in a HITLS environment with real users. For example, if the artifact being designed is a new system for a commercial aircraft, the prototype is tested in a cockpit simulator with airline pilots. Observations could be done directly using preestablished criteria or later on using audio-video recording systems. Main goal is to elicit and analyze emerging properties. This process is repeated until a satisfactory prototype is obtained.
- Step 3. Once a satisfactory prototype is obtained, a set of requirements for the effective development and manufacturing of the system designed are produced.

Then, what could be stability criteria? Three categories could be given, but the list is not exhaustive[2]: (1) technological issues, (2) organizational and legal issues, and (3) individual issues.

Technological Issues

Resilience engineering has become a buzz in human factors and ergonomics, expressing several models that are supposed to guide engineering design. I already expressed my reservation on this concept of **resilience**, and preferred to develop the concept of stability instead. Indeed, based on Boris Cyrulnik's immense psychiatric work on psychological resilience (Cyrulnik 2004), I have serious doubt that a concept that is so difficult to understand for people could be easy for socio-technical systems. Psychological resilience is about adaptation to stress and adversity, which can come from various kinds of issues such as health, work, finance, or emotional relations. It is often considered as a process used by an individual to cope with crisis situations, balancing negative emotions with positive ones. Resilience is about rebuilding something life critical recently destroyed or unavailable. It is about dealing with the unexpected, but after a catastrophe. With our TIS approach to HCD, we want to deal with the unexpected before it is too late and eventually after when things go wrong also. This is why we need to take the problem from a stability point of view, stability of a new TIS within the environment that will welcome it, as well as its influence on this environment.

What does technological stability of a TIS mean? In order to answer this question, let's take an example. A smartphone is a TIS that is so much used today that it deserves technological stability, that is, capability of establishing a connection with

---

[2] I challenge you to find more, and please send me an email gboy@fit.edu

either a database (e.g., the Web), another human being by voice or text, storing data (e.g., addresses, calendar events), synchronizing with other devices such as personal computers or tablets, offering navigation guidance using GPS and a geographical database (e.g., Google Maps), and so on. This constant connectivity can be considered a question of smartphone stability. When one or several of these services fails, it creates instability for smartphone users. Why? This is because we plan our daily life with smartphones today. Our smartphone is an extension of ourselves, a prosthesis that transforms us into a handicapped person if it fails. Therefore, it is crucial to anticipate these failure modes and offer recovery strategies or solutions when they occur. Anticipation of these failure modes is a matter of reliability, availability, and robustness of the various components of overall the system and their interconnections. This is where model-based systems engineering (MBSE) enters into play together with HCD. Indeed, we need to develop the best model of the overall smartphone system of systems (e.g., using SysML) and incrementally test human-systems integration in an agile way (i.e., develop and run HITLS to detect emerging patterns and possible solutions to all identifiable kinds of events).

A right mix of scenario-based design, HITLS, MBSE, and agile development is certainly an excellent choice to support investigation of TIS technological stability issues at design time.

Organizational and Legal Issues

Integration of new TISs in current socio-technical systems is likely to induce legal issues. Main topics of concern are authority (i.e., who is in charge?), responsibility (i.e., an obligation that can be individual or collective), accountability (i.e., related to ethics and governance—somebody is accountable for his or her actions—you are accountable to somebody or a socio-technical system), and liability (i.e., an obligation to satisfy some legal or regulatory requirements). Of course, depending on the nation and culture, there are various types of legal systems. The integration of TISs in our everyday lives requires more attention on liability of software in general and in specific contexts. It also poses the problem of the impact of autonomy and induced organizational changes caused by the integration of TISs. It is therefore important to identify legal liabilities at design time. They are an integrating part of TIS properties. I strongly suggest using the SFAC model (Chap. 3) as a support for this identification. This is crucial when we need to test new TISs in a real-world environment.

For example, autonomous vehicles, and more specifically self-driving cars, state the problem of new organizational road traffic rules. These rules are incrementally produced as autonomous cars are designed and developed. Autonomous vehicles should be TISs in the following sense. Anybody should be able to use such a vehicle without extensive training. Safety, efficiency, and comfort should be number one priorities. In normal conditions, self-driving cars should drive safer than any human driver of a classical car. But what would happen if anything goes wrong? Main problem is certification of such a car. If we use classical approaches to certification, we will not deliver such a car before long, since it is a brand new concept that is not likely to satisfy old certification principles and criteria! We need to release current constraining regulations, more specifically the precautionary principle, and start testing self-driving cars now. We need to consider the TOP model from the start and try prototypes as soon as we can. We need to provide innovators the necessary space for testing their innovative prototypes.

The ALIAS project outlined five leading principles[3]: (1) design according to liability (i.e., legal liabilities should be addressed in a coherent and comprehensive way at the design stage of a new concept), (2) proactive approach to liabilities (i.e., legal liabilities should be addressed from an anticipatory risk-management perspective), (3) socio-technical approach to liabilities (i.e., as system failures can only be understood in a systematic socio-technical perspective, so should be legal liabilities), (4) multidisciplinary approach (i.e., technical and legal knowledge should be integrated, to facilitate the communication between legal and technical experts), and (5) standard case-based approach (i.e., the legal case should complement the other available cases and be consistent with the generic transversal areas assessment process of SESAR[4]). Even if these principles were defined for air traffic management research, they are very valuable for an extended use for other life-critical systems. HCD always promotes proactive tests of possible futures. Therefore, it is crucial to extensively use creativity to generate possible futures (i.e., use divergent thinking) and incrementally test them (i.e., use convergent thinking). We obviously need to carry out participatory design involving technical experts, organizational and legal experts, and human factors experts. Just a reminder to say that the TOP model should support the design process from beginning to end. In addition, this process cannot be done in isolation from the legal authorities. For that matter, they should be clearly informed about what new TISs are about. Consequently, education and communication is key. A communication plan should be developed and used.

The TOP model should support the design process from beginning to end.

The following procedure could be followed: (1) understand the TIS integration concept by collecting background information and identifying SFAC-based facts and possible problems, (2) identify organizational and legal issues by identifying

---

[3] ALIAS (Addressing the Liability Impact of Automated Systems). Single European Sky ATM Research (SESAR) themes and projects: http://www.sesarju.eu/innovation-solution/exploratory-research/research-themes-and-projects (retrieved on July 31, 2015).

[4] Single European Sky Air Traffic Management Research (SESAR European Commission Program) is interested in reducing air traffic congestion, delays, flight cancelations, and charges incurred by the airlines from the air navigation service providers, increasing trajectory efficiency, improving the overall levels of automation, and making all airspace systems more predictable.

and selecting relevant organizational and legal risks, (3) perform an organizational and legal analysis, and (4) produce results from analytical findings.

SESAR already developed level of automation tables (LOAT) that provides potential failures of technology, organizations, and people (TOP) model. They make a distinction between latent and patent failures. From a legal point of view, these tables are useful to link failure risks to legal risks. This kind of risk analysis is usually fine when everything is considered as standard, but designing out-of-the-box systems will require definition of new evaluation principles and criteria.

Individual Issues

Continuing the single pilot operations example, let's identify cognitive functions for the various agents including the pilot (or another qualifier in the single pilot operations context), ground operators, and systems. Each of these agents has a set of cognitive functions providing him, her, or it with some degree of authority. Authority can be viewed as control (i.e., the agent is in charge of doing something and control the situation) and accountability (i.e., the agent is accountable to someone else). Control can be either handled directly or delegated to other agents who have authority to execute well-defined tasks. In this latter case, these other agents (should) have appropriate and effective cognitive functions and are accountable to the agent delegating. Cognitive function analysis enables rationalizing the allocation of cognitive functions among agents (Boy 1998a, b).

> **Cognitive function analysis enables rationalizing the allocation of cognitive functions among agents**.

Technical crews (or pilots) have the role and authority of bringing a set of passengers from a location A to another location B. They have the primary responsibility for safety, efficiency, and comfort of the passengers. In single pilot operations, cognitive functions of current captain and first officer are distributed among technical crews, ground operators, and new systems. In particular, technical crew cognitive functions have a set of resources distributed among ground operators and aircraft/ground systems. Ground operators have different cognitive functions that can be named dispatching, air traffic control coordination, crew scheduling, maintenance triggering, customer service, and weather forecast. All these cognitive functions can be supported by systems when they are well understood and mature. Dispatching and piloting are currently associated to develop a flight plan, find out what fuel quantity pilots should take, meet weight and balance requirements, ensure compliance with the minimum equipment list (MEL), de-conflict with other aircraft, help in case of equipment failure and, more generally, guide the flight from gate to gate.

Normal piloting cognitive functions consist in reading checklists, cross-checking life-critical information, troubleshooting and recovering from failures, fuel monitoring, and so on. Abnormal and emergency cognitive functions are triggered by specific conditions such as engine failure, cabin depressurization, fuel imbalance, and so on. Current air traffic controllers have specific dispatch cognitive functions. Their job will change with single pilot operations and will need piloting cognitive functions in the case of malfunctions in the airspace, including pilot incapacitation and its duality, total system failure. Consequently, they will need tools such as in aircraft cockpits. The whole air traffic control workstation will evolve toward an ATM/piloting workstation for single pilot operations. In addition, they will not have to control only one aircraft but, in some cases, several.

A first cognitive function analysis shows that there are functions that can be allocated to systems such as checklist-based verifications and cross-checking of life-critical information. As always, allocating functions to systems requires maturity verification. Whenever technology maturity is not guaranteed, people should be in charge and have capabilities guarantying good situation awareness. In any case, tests are mandatory. In the above-defined revolutionary approach to single pilot operations, we typically think about lower levels of control being entirely automated (i.e., trajectory control and management); human agents only act on set points, for example. We need to be careful however that the single pilot operations pilot will be aware of the crucial internal and external states of his/her aircraft environment. He/she will also need to be knowledgeable and skilled in aviation to perceive and understand what is going on during the flight as well as act on the right controls if necessary. Full automation does not remove domain knowledge and skills in life-critical systems.

Symmetrically, some aircraft systems (or artificial agents) should be able to monitor pilot's activity and health. This induces the definition, implementation, and test of new kinds of system cognitive functions based on physiological and psychological variables. Obviously, this will require sensors that could be physiologically invasive (e.g., electroencephalograms) or noninvasive (e.g., cameras). In any case, pilots will have to accept to be monitored. Pilot's activity and health monitoring can be done by aircraft systems and also by ground operators.

Other processes and technology that need to be human-centered designed and developed are related to collaborative work. In this new multi-agent world, agents have to collaborate and be supported for this collaboration. Computer-supported cooperative work (CSCW) technology and techniques need to be developed to this end. When an agent fails, for example, whether a human or a system, recovery means and strategies should be in place to continue the flight safely. It is also important, in this increasingly automated multi-agent world, to keep enough flexibility. HITLS could be used to find out the effectivity of possible solutions.

Business Continuity and Stability of Practice

How does a TIS enable or contribute to **business continuity**? Business continuity is a concept used in crisis management to denote the overall process, including procedures, which an organization uses to ensure continuity of vital functions during and after a disaster. In this book, I generalize this concept to the process of recovery to any disturbance a system may receive. We will talk about business continuity consequently to system failure or human error.

Stability in physics has been extensively studied. I already described the concepts of passive stability (e.g., pendulum) and active stability (e.g., inverted pendulum). The former does not require any external action. Conversely, the latter requires external actions. Physical stability of a TIS has then two facets: passive and active. It is then important to find out what parts of a TIS are passively stable and what other parts require external actions to keep acceptable stability. In other words, we will be looking for passively stable sub-TISs and actively stable sub-TISs.

Since a TIS involves technology, organizations, and people,[5] we need to analyze business continuity with respect to the TOP model. It is interesting to notice that if information technology (IT) can help us stabilize complex systems by defining appropriate interconnected TISs, it also introduces new kinds of instability. For example, the use of open software, IT commercial systems, integrated multi-agent information management, and international standards for interoperability introduce security vulnerability. New kinds of protection then need to be introduced.

More generally, high interconnectivity tends to provide passive stability at the global level, but requires active stability at the lower grain levels. For example, air transportation security is relatively stable at the global level, but it requires tremendous attention and action at the lower grain levels (i.e., heavy airport security checks). Could we say that current airport security systems are tangible? In this case, tangibility could be defined in terms of efficiency, cost, and discomfort for passengers. We also can say that current airport security systems are permanent crisis management systems insuring business continuity.

At this point, we need to better understand the concept of **stability of practice**. September 11, 2001 events drastically changed airport security systems. Passengers globally accepted these changes because the main issue was, and still is, in terms of life or death. We could say that September 11, 2001 events destabilized airport practices (lower grain level), but did not destabilize overall air transportation. Air traffic even keeps increasing since September 11, 2001. Therefore, people adapted to security constraints in airports and increase of flight ticket costs. However, this might not be the case for all changes of people's practices. Even if organizations and situations drastically change, practices may keep being the same for cultural reasons. For example, air traffic control practices are very similar to practices of 40 years

---

[5] This is domain specific. Sometimes technology is the only relevant part of a TIS. In many cases, a new technology has a strong impact on the organization it is used. It also may also change jobs and then have a strong impact on people.

ago. Very little changes in air traffic controllers' jobs, tools, and organizations, compared to the evolution of their counterparts in aircraft cockpits. This is due to a strong corporative culture. Of course, changes will necessarily happen because it will be impossible to manage larger numbers of aircraft with the same tools and techniques. We actually are at a bifurcation point (in the complexity science sense) where the old air traffic control model has to become a new air traffic management model. Do we have the right TISs for this change? Probably not yet! We also need to acknowledge that such as change cannot occur in one night. It has to be progressive. This is the reason why TISs will be developed incrementally and incorporated into the air traffic system with parsimony. Obviously, this does not prevent us to think globally and develop models and run simulations of possible futures. Remember that we now have the tools for doing it!

Life-Critical Systems

Life-critical systems have been described as systems dealing with safety, efficiency, and comfort (Boy 2013). Following up what I just said above, we should include security into safety. With the massive development of technology during the twentieth century, our societies are immersed into technical systems that created different human needs, but also ecological evolution of our entire planet. Consequently, we should take the concept of life-critical system from a different perspective. We should think in terms of life of our species when we design TISs of the future. We should ask questions such as the following. What will change if we design a system this way? If we cannot answer this question correctly, then what should we design instead? How can we test the repercussions of the development and use of such a system? Of course, we should take into account local and global stability metrics resulting from the various concepts that I gave in this chapter and beyond.

We should constantly remember that even if we design a fully autonomous system, this would always be a matter of people involved. There will be people who will design it, develop it, certify it, and use it. Designing a TIS is not an isolated process performed by someone in an office. It is part of a collaborative process that needs to be immersed into the real world. Solutions need to be exposed to as many people as possible, and tested as many times as possible. Participatory design and development has to be taken at different maturity levels. The difficulty is in discovering new roles that people could play in the future when a new TIS is used.

Toward a Tangible Internet of Things

Genesis of the TIS concept comes from the development and persistence of information technology. Since the beginning of the twenty-first century, we design things using computers. We use computer-aided design (CAD) tools such as CATIA,

CREO, AutoCAD, or NX. We then can design building, aircraft or cars, etc. and use them. Using computer-mounted display and CAD-generated dynamic displays, we can walk into a virtual building, fly a virtual airplane, or drive a virtual car. We then have new tools for HCD. It is now possible and most importantly credible because modeling and simulation are based on very reliable and realistic pieces of software. We can generate very reliable models that enable the simulation of realistic environments, including fluid dynamics, flexible structures, and sophisticated control mechatronics systems. Consequently, traditional approach of human factors that attempts to correct engineering flaws that generate surprises at operations time is now replaced by HCD that enables to take into account human activity at design time. Therefore, instead of worrying about automation like during the end of the twentieth century, we now have to worry about tangibility of virtual prototypes.

It is interesting to observe that automation technology has evolved toward a new type of concept, which is the cyber physical system. We already introduced this concept in Chap. 2. This concept still promotes the old approach of embedding physical objects, or things, with sensors, electronics, software, and extended connectivity. This concept is very close to the concept of the Internet of Things (IoT). IoT is typically defined as an environment where living entities and artifacts have unique identifiers and are capable of transferring data over a network without requiring human-to-human or human-to-computer interaction. IoT is a mix of Internet, microelectromechanical systems, and wireless technologies. In particular, IoT should provide designers, developer, manufacturer, users, and other actors who have an impact on systems being designed, communication, cooperation, and coordination support in design and engineering.

> **Control and mechanical engineering, computer science, and human-centered design came up to three perspectives: cyber physical systems, the Internet of Things, and tangible interactive systems that converge toward the same kind of concept that associates physical things and cognition.**

Therefore, IoT as it is conceived today requires more human-systems integration to provide a really stable and sustainable network of physical things and computing systems, not only based on economic purposes. This is why it is timely to concretely consider TISs as a long-term solution for interactive technology and society that we are constantly designing for people. It is very purposeful to link IoT and TISs because they have the same motivation, which is linking physical structures and interactive functions.

References

Boulnois S, Tan W, Boy GA (2015) The onboard context-sensitive information system for commercial aircraft. In: Proceedings 19th Triennial Congress of the IEA, Melbourne, Australia, 9–14

Boy GA (1998a) Cognitive function analysis for human-centered automation of safety-critical systems. In: Proceedings of CHI'98 (May 1998). ACM Press, pp 265–272

Boy GA (1998b) Cognitive function analysis. Praeger, Westport, CT. ISBN-13: 978-1567503777

Boy GA (2001) When safety is a matter of redundant information. In: Smith MJ, Salvendy G (eds) Systems, social, and internationalization design aspects of human-computer interaction: volume 2 (human factors and ergonomics). CRC Press, Boca Raton, FL. ISBN-13: 978-0805836080

Boy GA (2013) Orchestrating human-centered design. Springer, London. ISBN 978-1-4471-4338-3

Boy GA (2014) Dealing with the unexpected. In: Millot P (ed) Risk management in life critical systems. Wiley ISTE, London, UK. ISBN: 978-1-84821-480-4

Boy GA, Brachet G (2010) Risk taking. Dossier of the Air and Space Academy, Toulouse. ISBN 2-913331-47-5

Cyrulnik B (2004) Parler d'amour au bord du gouffre. Odile Jacob, Paris. ISBN 2-7381-1556-X

Hollnagel E, Woods DD, Leveson N (eds) (2006) Resilience engineering: concepts and precepts. Ashgate, Aldershot. ISBN 978-0-7546-4641-9

Kawano A (2012) Fukushima from the perspective of managing the unexpected. Retrieved on July 26, 2015, http://gnssn.iaea.org/NSNI/EaT/TM/lectures/MtU/d3p1-kawano-tepco/index.htm

Tan W (2014) From commercial aircraft operational procedures to onboard context-sensistive information systems. In: Proceedings of HCI-Aero 2014, Santa Clara, California. ACM Digital Library

Tan W (2015) Contribution to the Onboard Context-Sensitive Information System (OCSIS) of commercial aircraft. Ph.D. dissertation, School of Human-Centered Design, Innovation and Arts, Florida Institute of Technology

Westrum R (2006) A typology of resilience situations. In: Hollnagel E, Woods DD, Leveson N (eds) Resilience engineering: concepts and precepts. Ashgate, Aldershot, Chapter 5. ISBN 978-0-7546-4641-9

Chapter 9
Sustainability

Sustainability is a broad topic usually linked to biological and ecological systems. Sustainability science was born as a new discipline at the World Congress on Challenges of a Changing Earth in 2001 (Kates et al. 2001). In this book, I focus on sustainability of artifacts (systems that are built by people) and more specifically tangible interactive systems (TISs). What does it mean to design a sustainable TIS? Basically, a TIS should allow easy modification and maintenance. Ideally, it should be self-sustainable. Therefore, taking sustainability seriously in design is thinking about possible futures of the artifacts that we are designing. Sustainability means thinking about people who, in the future, will deal with systems that we are designing today. Sustainability means thinking about life cycle of a system from creation and design to decommissioning.

Human-Centered Sustainability

Human-centered design (HCD) cares about adaptation of technology to people and organization and more generally coadaptation of technology, organizations, and people (referring to the TOP model—Boy 2013). TIS sustainability strongly depends on TIS high-level requirements.

Advantages of the agile approach were already presented in Chap. 3. Agile design, development, and manufacturing provide more flexibility and resilience for easy technology changes and more generally technology evolution. This means that we need to have agile services that make this approach feasible. At the functional level, this is a matter of:

- Awareness (i.e., functions need to be connected to their environment and therefore require situation awareness mechanisms)
- Competence (i.e., functions require enough knowledge and information processing mechanisms to make decisions and act)

© Springer International Publishing Switzerland 2016
G.A. Boy, *Tangible Interactive Systems*, Human–Computer Interaction Series,
DOI 10.1007/978-3-319-30270-6_9

- Organization (i.e., functions need to be connected to other functions inside or outside the agent where they belong)

At the structural level, this is a matter of **human-centered** industry (i.e., engineering support should be adapted to HCD), economics (i.e., HCD feasibility strongly depends on economy and finance strategies), politics (i.e., HCD implementation requires appropriate political structures), and culture (i.e., HCD should be widely adopted by people and communities involved; and HCD culture should be created, nurtured, and maintained).

Sustainability has also to do with what we throw out in the trash. For example, when we go shopping, it is important to inspect what we have in the fridge in order not to buy a bottle of milk when we already have one. This is related to the duration of life of goods and things that we have got so far in order not to generate too much and be obliged to throw out exceeding stuff at some point. It is the same in design. Practitioners often create concepts that are usually much more tangible than theoreticians comfortably seated in their armchairs. Theoreticians throw a lot in the trash because they do not take into account enough practice (i.e., activity as already defined). Good design is an appropriate mix of creativity and operational experience.

In the country village of southwestern France where I lived during my childhood, there is still a baker who will not sell you bread if she does not know you! Why? This approach is coming from an old tradition that consisted in collecting flour from farmers. Flour quantities were written on small booklets, where bread quantity for the year was also calculated. Therefore, each farmer family had a specific amount of bread that they could get every week. Consequently, the baker was making enough bread to satisfy the global requirements of the entire village. Of course, the baker always made extra bread for exceptional visitors, but not much. Flour booklets disappeared a long time ago. However, the baker kept the notion of quantity of bread required for the village. This is why you may not be able to buy bread in this bakery even if you can see these beautiful loafs of bread displayed on the shelves.

> **TISs are always a mix of natural and artificial components, either internally or externally**.

There are always trade-offs between planning and unexpected events. Quality requires rules that people need to recognize and comply to. My bakery story is a good example of such a trade-off. In our modern western societies, **quantity** took over **quality**. This is also related to economics. We privileged quantity of cheap food over higher-cost quality food. The main problem that this approach did not, and still doesn't, take into account is related to the repercussions of absorbing such cheap food. Indeed, it ended up with obesity, various kinds of diseases, and most importantly complacency on food preparation before meals. Having a good meal is not only a matter of engagement and involvement in its preparation, but also a matter of creating a comfortable environment where all our senses can be used to facilitate social exchanges. Again, diversity of flavors, ingredients, and tools makes a difference in the way we are having meals. Taste is about culture. Good food is about health.

What I already said about food is true for anything that is prepared and developed by people for people. A good TIS needs to take into account the various repercussions of its use. Does it contribute to create changes in current cultures and environments? If yes, what are they? Some changes are good; some others are not. Of course, as we already discussed this in the complexity chapter of this book, we need to observe people's activity in order to be able to discover emergent properties (e.g., affordances) that contribute to change culture. There are always trade-offs and compromises to make. In any case, changes will come from the use of new TISs, seen as systems of systems.

Toward a Sustainable City of the Future

Talking about the city of the future, as a TIS, requires taking into account sustainability, which deals with transportation, energy, and architecture. Big cities are getting bigger, and transportation systems have to be reorganized to fit the needs of citizens. The number is the issue. In small cities, transportation can be organized "linearly" (e.g., space can be easily found for parking). In big cities, transportation needs to be thought nonlinearly because complexity comes from the number of people and their large variety of interests, needs, and constraints.

The concept of "smart city" has become a buzzword, but how could we make a city smarter? We could think about decreasing congestion and increasing safety and security, for example. A great amount of research and development has already been done on road traffic control and regulation. However, what is new today is the number! We have too many cars in big cities. This is a matter of TOP model. On the technology side, better infrastructures should be developed for highly populated cities. The **number effect** has direct implication on new kinds of people's behavior, city properties, and road rules (i.e., procedures that people should follow while driving). Technology is also about vehicles, which could be totally or partially autonomous. On the organizational side, work hours, leisure time, and grocery time, for example, should be organized to fit the needs of people living in these big cities. Various kinds of TIS could be developed to manage these new organizational setups. On the human side, people will have new living patterns; some will emerge from practice; some will have to be learned.

Let's take the example of parking in a big city. There may be many parking spaces in a city; the problem is often providing accurate situation awareness of where to park within a small periphery of the target. This goes with assistance in both navigation and specific spaces available (i.e., for small or larger cars). We can start with a task analysis of the problem (i.e., what drivers usually do when they are looking for a parking space in the city). Once a first prototype is developed, resulting activity should be observed to discover potential emergent behaviors and properties of the solution. In other words, an appropriate TIS has to be designed and developed, which could provide drivers with available parking spaces, regulations, rates, as well as connectivity with other drivers and parking personnel. They can be available on smartphone and computers as applications or Web site pages.

Another important problem is energy management. Conventional sources of energy will not be enough to satisfy the needs in 50 years from now if we continue to spend it as we do today (e.g., generating too much CO_2 in the atmosphere). Global warming is progressing constantly, and even if it could be due to geological evolution, the way we treat our planet does not help in reducing it. Consequently, we need to find tangible interactive solutions that will both take into account energy management and ecological consequences. Renewable energy coming from the wind, Sun, and tide does not produce CO_2. They are individually not sustainable. However, if we put them together intelligently, they could provide a satisfactory solution. The smart grid is a system that could enable balancing the load among various sources of energy. It could be categorized in the TIS category. If CO_2 emissions are a nightmare in most big cities, we can measure CO_2 quantity in the air. Therefore, we should use this information in a better way. A TIS could suggest to us not to drive today because the city is already too polluted and give us credits if we make this appropriate decision, for example.

TISs that will support construction of the city of the future could be considered as artifacts (A) used by citizen (U) performing tasks (T) within an organized environment (O) in various kinds of situations (S). We come back to the AUTOS pyramid that effectively supports human-centered designers. It is by continuously articulating AUTOS concepts and relations that a complex system can be designed as an integrated TIS for safety, efficiency, and comfort (e.g., the city of the future).

Natural Systems Sustainability

The discipline of reference here is ecology, which studies biological systems (natural systems). For example, forests in Amazonia are still very sustainable biological systems because people have not or barely touched them. They are healthy ecosystems. However, biological environments where people developed technology have started to be polluted, and consequently sustainability is a major issue (Bibliography of Sustainability 2015). In addition, this pollution directly affects survival of people and other biological organisms. Consequently, technology should be developed to satisfy a set of ecological constraints. These constraints are usually provided in terms of regulations and laws, which can be applied to urban, transport, and lifestyle developments. Several initiatives have been started such as permaculture, sustainable architecture and green buildings, renewable energies, smart grid, and nuclear fusion. Of course, not only technology should be sustainable, but also practices should lead local and global sustainability of our planet Earth. Unfortunately, this is not what technology-centered engineering did up to now.

Fig. 9.1 Looking for
sustainability

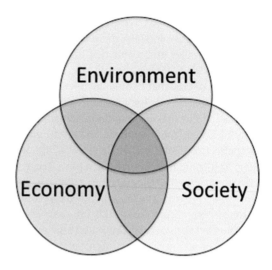

Sustainability of natural systems deals with some kind of degradation of people's health and Earth surface and atmosphere. Sustainability is at the conjunction of economy, society, and environment (Fig. 9.1). Market economy is mainly responsible for such degradation, promoting consumerism, economic growth, and manufacturing in the wild (i.e., making all kinds of products without knowledge of possible repercussions of their interactions on environment). This observation put to the front the lack of collaborative human-centered holistic approaches to the benefit of competitive finance-centered approaches. It is time to change if we want to care about sustainability of our planet Earth. Solutions are at the heart of the following requirements: increase individual and collective knowledge and consciousness on global sustainability and increase individual and collective proactivity on local sustainability. In other words, our societies should (will) go toward more educated autonomy locally and more coordination globally.

Technology Sustainability, Maturity, and Expertise

Of course, the goal is not to stop developing technology. Indeed, people developed technology since the beginning of humanity and will continue to do so. Problem is speed, purpose, and repercussions of technology development. This is the reason why HCD has become tremendously important. Its agenda needs to include an acceptable ecological stability and code of ethics based on sustainability requirements and constrains.

What is ecological stability? It is the capacity of an ecosystem to "absorb disturbance and still retain its basic structure and viability" (Sustainability 2015). HCD leads to stability thinking that takes into account the balance between human-made systems and natural systems.

The other day, I was writing a speech for a conference and thought about another presentation I gave in 1994, more than 20 years ago. It is interesting to observe how we can remember things like that. I was very happy when I found the PowerPoint file that I used in 1994 to give my talk. Unfortunately, my happiness did not last long when I discovered that I could not open the file. The reason was that the PowerPoint version of that time is incompatible today. I hear you telling me: "Why did not you upgrade the PowerPoint version incrementally?" Well, the reason is clear: I had too many files to upgrade by hand, and after I gave the presentation, I had to do something else and did not realize that PowerPoint would not be compatible several years after! You could talk about human error, but why could these files not be automatically upgraded when the operating system is upgraded from one version to another? This would provide sustainability to such presentation supports. In contrast, I found a printed photo taken during this presentation. Paper support turned out to be more tangible than software. The question now is: what are the appropriate structures and functions of an interactive system, such as PowerPoint, that we design and develop, which make it sustainable, and therefore tangible? In this case, a good answer is certainly "automatic upgrade."

Not only technology should enable us to live in a sustainable world, but also it should be sustainable itself to be easily modifiable and guaranty some kind of acceptable evolution. In other words, flexibility should be an important principle and therefore design goal.

A friend of mine provided me with another interesting example. Her son developed an integrated home entertainment system. He is a very skilled and talented person. He managed to equip their house with speakers and screens in almost all rooms. TV, films, and Wi-Fi are integrated and manageable using an iPad. The concept is very good. However, the level of maturity is not very high, and when, for some reason, the system fails, it requires its builder's expertise. My friend had many of these issues lately and does not know how to fix the failing system. She called the local company that provides TV and computer network, but they did not succeed finding out the failure because the integration was ad hoc. She spent time on the phone with her son who now lives far away on another continent. He managed to help but not on a sustainable manner because it was too difficult to provide a simple explanation and procedure to his mother. This story is very instructive for the design of TISs from a sustainability point of view. First, human-systems integration takes time and requires maturity checking before delivery (i.e., clear documentation of how the system works, can be operated and repaired in cases of failure); otherwise, it requires sustainable designer's expertise. Second, human-systems integration requires standardization to enable sustainable use and maintenance.

From Accumulation to Integration (Reducing Complexity)

Tangible interactive systems are usually being developed incrementally as we discover operational safety, efficiency, or comfort problems. For example, there are several systems that were progressively accumulated to help car drivers in various tasks, such as adaptive cruise control (ACC), global positioning system (GPS), and collision avoidance system. Each of these systems is very helpful, but their progressive accumulation requires multi-tasking attention and processing. This accumulation may then be very demanding and sometimes dangerous, even if each system was developed to individually decrease workload and increase safety, efficiency, or comfort.

The purpose of each of these systems results from incremental discovery of a driver's need. Engineers try to integrate these systems too late—typically after first delivery. This is a very complex process and sometimes very conflicting among people who request modifications and others who have to replan very complex processes. Can we discover these purposes earlier? Modeling and simulation are certainly very useful to this end. We then need to develop methods that enable us to integrate systems as early as possible during the design process. Today, computer-aided design provides very effective tools to develop virtual prototypes that can be tested with people in the loop.

Integration of TISs can be incrementally modeled, tested, and redesigned in a "tangible" virtual world. Here, the term "tangible" means that potential users can use and assess them like in the real world. This enables a design team to test human-systems integration very early and more importantly before a product is physically developed. I claim that concurrent development of **design cards** (see Chap. 3) using the SFAC model is an excellent way for anticipating sustainability issues and support designers at design time. The SFAC model should be operationalized not only by accumulating knowledge on the system being designed but also by actively testing this knowledge. Tuomi's 5-A knowledge generation model is a useful framework to this end (Fig. 9.2). It includes five main functions: anticipation, appropriation, articulation, accumulation, and action.

Useful knowledge production is not possible without *action*. For example, we learn from differences between *anticipated* behavior of the environment and the actually perceived situation. "Knowledge can also be produced by *appropriating* knowledge that exists in the society" (Tuomi 1999, page 341). For example, we learn from others who are more knowledgeable than us. Existing knowledge may be *articulated* and reconfigured in order to create new knowledge. Knowledge is *accumulated* in a memory store following an incremental process similar to Piaget's accommodation mechanism (Boy 2002).

Designing for Sustainability

Designing for sustainability requires clear explicit articulation of the various concepts, relationships among them, and their operationalization. This is the best way to develop operational and maintenance procedures and guidelines. Sharon Chinoy carried out an extensive research effort in the air traffic control (ATC) maintainability domain (Chinoy 2014). ATC maintenance is a typical domain where a gigantic number of systems have been developed and accumulated over the years since the beginning of

Fig. 9.2 The 5-A model of
knowledge generation
(Tuomi 1999, p. 343)

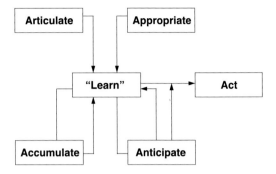

aeronautics. Systems were developed responding to specific needs and also built by different suppliers. A variety of services were developed in the wild. Today, a strong need for integration and homogenization is required. This is why a top-down study of the various components of the overall ATC system is needed. Concepts and relationships among these concepts should be elicited from what we know today. This is called domain ontology development. **Design rationale** is useful in design, but also in operations and maintenance. Indeed, people who will be in charge of operating and maintaining systems being designed should have appropriate knowledge on them. In addition, such ontology should guide the design of underlying organizations and people's jobs for both operations and maintenance of these systems.

> **Design rationale is useful for designers, end users, and maintainers to support sustainability**.

In addition to knowing what systems are about, it is also crucial to better understand their life cycle in order to plan for their sustainable (ecological) integration in the long term. Market economy worldwide considerably improved production efficiency of products and services to meet short-term basic consumer needs, but totally ignored sustainability. Tools and methods such as supply chain management, corporate reporting, and international standards supported this evolution, but did not at all address human-centeredness. Consequently, globalization and trade liberalization dehumanized work, transforming old practice into cold finance-centered processes where workers have little to say.

The United Nations Environment Programme analyzed the society, environment, and economy factors (Table 9.1) within the framework of current market economy (UNEP 2007). UNEP together with TU Delft carried out a study on developing countries requirements for sustainability. Table 9.1 provides comparisons between such requirements for developed and developing economies with respect to people, planet, and profit.

One of the main principles of market economy is individual interest leading to profit. This principle should be extended to global biological interest. Technology should be thought longer term than what we know today. In particular, the whole life

Table 9.1 Design for sustainability for developed and developing economies

UNEP (2007)	Developed economies	Developing economies
Create opportunities to meet social and equity requirements (people)	Increase urban and minority employment	Enhance number of skilled workers
	Improve safety and well-being	Reduce income inequity
	Acceptation and integration of minorities	Improve working conditions
	Reduce income inequity	Abolish child labor
		Reduce illiteracy
		Basic health services
		Clean drinking water
		Reduce population growth
		Improve status of women
		Abolish large-scale dislocation of people
Fit within the carrying capacity of supporting ecosystems (planet)	Reduce fossil energy use (climate change)	Reduce industrial emissions
	Reduce use of toxics	Wastewater treatment
	Clean contaminated sites	Stop overexploitation of renewable resources, water
	Improve level of prevention, recycling, and reuse	Stop deforestation, soil loss, erosion, ecosystem destruction
		Reduce dung and wood burning
Create equitable value for customers and stakeholders along the global value chain (profit)	Profitability	Fair share of and linkage to global value chains
	Value for company, stakeholder	Linkage of SMEs to large and transnational companies
	Value for customer	Industrialization of production, economies of scale
	Fair business model	Fair price for commodities and raw materials
		Ownership and credit opportunities for entrepreneurs

cycle of systems should be taken into account, including decommissioning. Of course, this is more general than tangible interactive systems, but since TISs have become persistent in our world, we need to take TIS design for sustainability seriously.

Evolution of the Sustainability Concept

Sustainability of natural systems is studied for a long time. In contrast, sustainability of engineered systems is very recent. Sustainability is about making sure that technical systems being designed do not induce a new lifestyle that would harm our natural environment, society, and culture.

Our world is evolving very rapidly, in constant redefinition. We live in the transient, not on a long plateau as before. The Web enables us to be interconnected worldwide. Open data is getting popularity. We can easily access various kinds of sources (both software and hardware) and various kinds of content. Is this evolution sustainable? What do we mean by sustainable in the transient? Stabilization is no longer on systems themselves but on their evolution. In other words, we need to better understand and anticipate technology evolution.

Consequently, a new theory of socio-technical systems evolution is required. Pierre Bourdieu formulated basic principles of practice theory (Bourdieu 1979, 2000). In particular, Bourdieu's concept of "habitus" that captures embodiment of the social order is consistent with the concept of tangibility developed in this book. Practice theory is compatible with activity theory and cognitive function analysis in the sense that people are considered as social beings, equipped with purposes of transforming the world where they live. People, and now TISs, are agents that belong to agencies (i.e., socio-technical systems of agents). Within the framework of this theory, TIS design should take into account properties emerging from activities that they support and sometimes require deeper understanding of the agency where the new TIS will be included.

What is the *Homo informaticus* that is emerging from this evolution? The growing number of people who extend their activities interacting with and through information technology defines this new species. TIS design should take into account both cognitive and embodied socio-technical properties. TISs tend to provide people with more autonomy and more dependency on TISs at the same time. This people-TIS autonomy also requires more coordination among them. Such coordination can be translated in terms of laws (e.g., open data management), people's lifestyles (e.g., social networks), city reorganization (e.g., permaculture and green building), and transportation means (e.g., intermodality). Consequently, sustainability is not at the individual level only but at the coordination level also.

References

Bibliography of Sustainability (2015) Retrieved on January 26, 2015. http://en.wikipedia.org/wiki/
    Bibliography_of_sustainability
Bourdieu P (1979) La distinction: Critique sociale du jugement (Le Sens commun). Editions de
    Minuit. Trans. Richard Nice in 1984, Distinction: a social critique of the judgment of taste.
    Harvard University Press. ISBN-13: 978-2707302755
Bourdieu P (2000) Pascalian meditations. Polity Press, Cambridge
Boy GA (2002) Theories of human cognition: to better understand the co-adaptation of people and
    technology. in knowledge management, organizational intelligence and learning, and complexity. In: Kiel LD (ed) Encyclopedia of Life Support Systems (EOLSS). Developed under the
    Auspices of the UNESCO, EOLSS Publishers, Oxford. http://www.eolss.net.
Boy GA (2013) Orchestrating human-centered design. Springer, London. ISBN
    978-1-4471-4338-3
Chinoy S (2014) NAS to NextGen: the evolution of socio-technical system. In: HCI-Aero'14
    Proceedings. ACM Digital Library, New York

Kates RW, Clark WC, Corell R, Hall JM, Jaeger CC, Lowe I, McCarthy JJ, Schellnhuber HJ, Bolin B, Dickson NM, Faucheux S, Gallopin GC, Grübler A, Huntley B, Jäger J, Jodha NS, Kasperson RE, Mabogunje A, Matson P, Mooney H, Moore B III, O'Riordan T, Svedin U (2001) Sustainability science. Science 292(5517):641–642. doi:10.1126/science.1059386

Sustainability (2015) Retrieved on January 26, 2015. http://en.wikipedia.org/wiki/Sustainability.

Tuomi I (1999) Corporate knowledge: theory and practice in intelligent organizations. Metaxis, Helsinki

UNEP (in collaboration with TU Delft) (2007) Design for sustainability: a practical approach for developing economies. UNEP, Paris

Chapter 10
Art

The twentieth century managed to isolate art, science, and engineering. It is time to reconcile these disciplines. I claim that design is one, and very probably the, bridge among them. Most importantly human-centered design (HCD)—the way it is defined in this book—is ready to do the job! The USA worries about the lack of interest and proficiency in science, technology, engineering, and mathematics (STEM) of its citizens, especially young people. It is time to move from STEM to STEAM, where the "A" means "arts." This chapter will present concepts and methods that can be useful to this end in the context of the design and development of tangible interactive systems (TISs).

Putting More "Steam" Into Classical STEM Disciplines

In summer 2012, I led a team project[1] during the Space Studies Program (SSP12) of the International Space University (ISU), held at Florida Institute of Technology (FIT) and NASA Kennedy Space Center, during a period of 9 weeks. The initial question was "What space can contribute to global STEM education." I continued this work with my graduate students at FIT and Ecole Polytechnique of Paris (Boy 2012, 2013). We also investigated the integration of arts into STEM. Designing new

---

[1] This team included 34 participants to SSP12-ISU, two cochair and a teaching assistant, and ten invited lecturers, including Remy Bourganel (École Nationale Supérieure des Arts Décoratifs), Guy A. Boy (Florida Institute of Technology), Jean-Jacques Favier (Centre National d'Etudes Spatiales), Caroline Hardman (National Network of Digital Schools), Leland Melvin (National Aeronautics and Space Administration), Chiaki Mukai (Japan Aerospace Exploration Agency), Carlos Niederstrasser (Orbital Sciences Corporation), Bill Nye (The Planetary Society), Cristina Olivotto (SterrenLab), Daniel Rockberger (NLS Satellites Ltd.), and the education team of NASA Kennedy Space Center. This group represented 17 countries, including Brasil, Canada, China, France, Germany, Greece, India, Ireland, Israel, Italy, Japan, Montenegro, Norway, Romania, South Africa, Spain, and the USA.

© Springer International Publishing Switzerland 2016
G.A. Boy, *Tangible Interactive Systems*, Human–Computer Interaction Series,
DOI 10.1007/978-3-319-30270-6_10

space architectures requires creativity and rigorous methods. HCD is a great direction for future education where complexity should be analyzed and not avoided because it is hard.

The current evolution of technology, organizations, and people on planet Earth fosters new endeavors in STEM education. We need to recreate this motivation and enthusiasm for the design of beautiful things that are innovative, stable, and sustainable. One of the main reasons I wanted to become an engineer was because I wanted to create new things that would change the world to be a better place and support exploration of new lands of physics and cognition. What I observe today is training of technicians to the service of powerful people whose only goal is to make money. We then need to integrate this necessary creativity part into STEM education. Information accessibility is not enough to make great things; it is crucial to further develop interdisciplinary spirit, cross-cultural cooperation, critical thinking, and synthesis.

The Cold War energized the space race, and space contributed to STEM education by providing incentives and motivation in research, development, and manufacturing. Tremendous progress in technology has been made between World War II and the end of the twentieth century. Today's space framework is heavily dependent on international cooperation in business, industry, and research. It is time to think about what we will need in the near future to build new spacecraft, organize new missions, and train people in new fields to explore our universe. Our information society is intimately interconnected; information and knowledge are now accessible anytime and anywhere (Boy 2012). "Space provides a new perspective and collaborative environment that can help challenge stereotypes, and lead to national, cultural, and gender equality. Using space to promote STEM education helps develop open-minded and creative future leaders." (Aarrestad et al. 2012, p. 67).

For me, the Apollo program was a piece of art of the same magnitude as Leonardo da Vinci's work. In his 2013 book, *Mission to Mars*, Buzz Aldrin, astronaut and Apollo 11 moonwalker, quoted this SSP12-ISU work (Aldrin and David 2013, pp. 57–60) and commented:

> *The most basic questions of humanity can attract many people of all ages to space.* – (Aldrin and David 2013)

Human Evolution and Art History

The shock wave produced by René Descartes's Discourse of the Method in 1610, propagated until the twentieth century, which could be called effective Descartes's century. It consolidated the separation between science and arts. On the contrary, it is interesting to observe that Leonardo da Vinci, who lived one century before Descartes, was certainly one of the best examples of extraordinary talented people mixing arts, science and engineering. Science and arts were not separated during his time (i.e., fifteenth and early sixteenth centuries). From that angle, the twenty-first century seems to be "back to the future," if we consider the shift from STEM to STEAM.

What science and arts share is **curiosity**. Leonardo da Vinci was extremely curious. Designing TISs involves curiosity at three levels: tangibility, interactivity, and systemics. **Systemics** could be defined as a science of artifacts mixing natural and artificial entities. In engineering terms, we often refer to "**system thinking**." An artifact is anything designed and produced by people. Let's analyze a short history of artifacts since the beginning of humanity.

Everything we do is done using our brain.[2] In particular, people create art with their brain. An art product is an artifact that is intended to support communication between the artist and other people. It expresses an intention. This is where intersubjectivity takes place. Can a piece of art create emotion, pleasure, and amazement? At this point, we are back to the concept of affordance. Is it innate (i.e., genetic) or learned (i.e., epigenetic)? We often say that intersubjectivity cannot work without education and experience, but some pieces of art do not require any education and experience to create emotion, pleasure, and amazement. A piece of art has aesthetic efficiency. It is imposed on us. We react to it using our background, both innate and learned. Jean-Pierre Changeux talks about art rules and constraints that support rational organization of a piece of art. Indeed, artists use techniques that make pieces of art engaging. Mastering these techniques is certainly based on deeper education and experience. At this point, it is important to analyze art history following the evolution of our human species. In other words, human evolution can be investigated by the observation of art productions across ages of humanity.

Art is created by artist's brain. From this point of view, the Apollo program was a piece of art created by several brains. First, in 1961 John F. Kennedy decided that Americans would go to the Moon and come back safe on the Earth at the end of the decade. This was an intention. As we already said, this was an abduction inference (i.e., project into a possible future and demonstrate that this future is tangible), exactly the same as what artists are doing. The rest is history. Neil Armstrong and Buzz Aldrin walked on the Moon in July 1969, and came back safe to Earth. But this did not happen instantly. The human brain evolved over the years since the beginning of humanity. Let's contemplate the concomitant story of human evolution and art history.

Three million years ago, *Homo habilis* started to create tools in the form of arranged pebbles, which were probably used to plow and defend their territory. We know that they had a brain of 500 cm^3 (i.e., three times less bulky than ours). Later on, between two and one million years ago, *Homo erectus*, with a 800 cm^3 brain, developed cut stones having symmetrical properties (i.e., symmetry was discovered). Then, between 600 and 200,000 years ago, *Homo heidelbergensis*, with a brain of about 1,300 cm^3, used cut stones as funerary offerings (i.e., symbolism was discovered). Between 30 and 40,000 years ago, *Homo sapiens* present on Earth since 100,000 years, with a 1,400 cm^3 brain, discovered artistic composition. *Homo sapiens* was capable of painting on cave walls perfectly recognizable animals and

---

[2] In this section, I use some of the materials produced by Jean-Pierre Changeux, a neurobiologist, member of the French Academy of Sciences, and professor at the famous *Collège de France* and Pasteur Institute (Changeux 2005, 2007, 2008, 2010a, b).

even illusion of movement. These are real pieces of art. Since then, *Homo sapiens* (i.e., us) never stopped to create many kinds of artifacts. The human brain is capable of constructing models of the world that can be used to create tools and various kinds of artifacts. Both physical and cultural environments influence this creation.

Another (shorter term) evolution should be mentioned. Newborn's brain weight increases five times to become adult. Child's brain never stops evolving during a period of 15 years, which is a relatively long period of time if we compare to the other animal species living on the Earth. Taking into account that people lived 30 years until a few hundred years ago, they spent half of their lives constructing their brain. The brain absorbs culture during this learning period (i.e., epigenetic components are incrementally integrated with the genetic components in the brain). For this reason, people do not have the same chance to acquire the same epigenetic components depending on where they are born and which education they received.

Changeux defined a few rules of art (*règles de l'art*), as he put it: "These *règles de l'art*, hypothetically viewed as acquired patterns of connections, or scaffoldings, stored in long-term memory, include, among others: novelty, coherence of the parts within the whole (Alberti's *consensus partium*[3]), Herbert Simon's parsimony[4] or the most frugal route of expression, tension between bottom-up realism and top-down abstraction, search for shared social recognition and artist's conception of the world." More generally, this is extremely important in design. This coherence of the whole is a major property of integration. These rules of art could be applied to any kind of design. The iPhone is a great example of novelty, coherence, and parsimony, which made it a revolution in the art of communication.

Short Term Against Tangibility

If technique is co-substantial to humanity (i.e., a few million years), science is more recent (i.e., a few thousand years). Technique and arts are intimately associated since the beginning of humanity. It is not the case of what we currently call science. Even if science contributed a lot in the evolution of the way we live, work, and interact among each other, it also contributed to handicap our planet.

Science and engineering are currently dominated by short-term productivity requirements. Consequently, free creativity leads to immediate satisfaction of financial needs. It is then crucial to address the question of the future of these disciplines if our goal is to support a sustainable and harmonious humanity. STEM disciplines currently support training of technicians, who are not the designers of the future and

---

[3] Leon Battista Alberti was a Renaissance Italian humanist author and artist. He is most known as an architect and extensive explorer in the fine arts (Vasari 1912).

[4] Herbert Simon, a Nobel laureate, advocated the fact that science seeks parsimony, not simplicity, and searches for pattern in phenomena (Simon 2001). He talked about the beauty in "finding pattern, especially simple pattern, in the midst of apparent complexity and disorder."

real creators. HCD mission is to define new routes for recreating a sustainable and harmonious world where people are at the center.

Software-based tools constantly support our everyday life. This is a fact that will not revert, at least for a while. Let's use them in the best way we can to support human-centered approaches to life, and more specifically design. Obviously, TISs have a major role to play. We then need to better understand how software-based tools that enable us to manipulate virtual things could help us designing tangible things.

Virtual art puts to the front illusion and immersion (Grau 2004). Illusion is not new. "Illusionary visual space can be traced back to antiquity." Oliver Grau shows how current evolution of art and image relates to interaction design, agent technology, telepresence, virtual reality, and more generally visualization. Transposing art to HCD in general, illusion and immersion are crucial concepts for human-in-the-loop simulation (HITLS) technology, where activity can be tested and emerging properties can be discovered at design time. Of course, this takes some time and money to set up in a design project, but it is extremely important for long-term stability and sustainability of products being designed and developed. Grau's framework is very interesting for the analysis of human-systems integration phenomena, functions, and structures. More specifically, virtual reality can be effectively used to enhance illusion and immersion. At this point, we can see that advanced interaction media can be used to study both physical and figurative tangibility. Physical tangibility studies require hardware-based simulation capabilities that are realistic enough to lead to credible results (e.g., force feedback, movement feelings, and everything related to physical ergonomics). Figurative tangibility studies require software-based models and simulators where functions can be tested (e.g., reaction times, situation awareness, decision-making, and action taking). Referring to the SFAC model (Fig. 3.8 in Chap. 3), physical tangibility is mostly related to structures; figurative tangibility is mostly related to functions. Summarizing, TIS design requires methods and tools that are incompatible with current short-term approaches of systems engineering.

The Art of Winemaking and Tasting

Art is not a crazy discipline where artists can do whatever they want without appropriate education and training. Artists use solid techniques, as engineers do. Then, what is the difference between a scientist, an engineer, and an artist?

Scientists are people who are designing knowledge. They use scientific methods to improve and sometime radically change our knowledge on nature, physical things, mathematical artifacts, as well as societal concepts and organizations. Scientists try to measure things, unlike philosophers who try to meaningfully articulate concepts. Engineers design, build, and maintain technology in specific contexts. They may or may not use scientific results, concepts, and methods. Sometimes technology enables scientists to discover new knowledge.

Artists are people who create, practice, and demonstrate specific kinds of art. They work with their senses. Senses are difficult to define, even if the most traditionally recognized are sight, hearing, taste, smell, and touch. In addition, people may react to a large variety of signals ranging from thermal, kinesthetic, pain, and balance to other internal stimuli. Expert wine tasters, for example, are able to recognize a wine without written information by looking at it (i.e., looking at its color, constituency, and clarity), smelling it (i.e., detecting wine flaws, fruit aromas, spices, barrel aromas, and secondary aromas), and tasting it (i.e., rolling it in their mouth to detect balance, harmony, complexity, and completeness). All these processes that expert wine tasters can detect from emergent properties of wines enable them to tell what kind of wine it is and ultimately what specific wine it is. Expert wine tasters have both experience and expertise, which are based on long-standing practice as well as incremental rationalization and categorization of relationships between these emergent properties and specific wines. I call this an art! What great winemakers are doing is even more an art because they try to design wine from a synthesis of soil, weather, grapes, chemistry, physics, and various kinds of heuristics based on expertise and experience. Again, **creativity is synthesis and integration**.

Now, you may ask why I took wine as an example to illustrate arts. For a long time, wine was made as an art, using an incrementally improved knowhow transferred from a generation of people to another. In other words, this knowhow was improved on a long period of time. I heard my uncle, who had a vineyard and was making wine in the southwest of France, saying that a new country that did not cultivate vines before needed a century to make a good wine. Now, wine has become a marketed product that needs to make money in a short period of time. Is it tangible for expert wine tasters? The answer to this question depends on the criteria that we use to assess tangibility. If the criterion is financial only, then short term is acceptable and we can engineer wine. Otherwise, if the criterion is educated taste of wine as an art, then short term is a too short answer! On this example, we can see the difficulty of assessing tangibility of a product and more specifically a TIS. Expert wine tasters may find that I overuse the concept of TIS to qualify wine, but you should admit that wine is a complex natural—but transformed by people—tangible system, which is interactive (i.e., in the human-wine interaction meaning using all senses that I described above).

Consequently, making TISs involves real issues of what kind of life they will induce when they will be used. For this reason, engineering and arts should go together to support clearly defined human-centered principles. Oenology is the science of wine. It should not be reduced to chemical engineering. It should include knowledge and knowhow of expert wine testers. In other words, oenology is the art of making and tasting wine. This discussion is about complexity, maturity, stability, and sustainability. Making wine is complex. Wine is complex. Tasting wine is complex. Remember that mastering complexity deals with familiarity. Making wine has to be a mature process. Time plays an important role in the appreciation of wine: time for the winemaker to become familiar with great winemaking practice, time for the wine to get mature, and time for the wine taster to become familiar with the various facets of wine. Enjoying wine requires mature experience. Making wine requires stable climate and constant attention coming from stable expertise. Once made, wine requires stable storage (i.e., not too much light and very little variations of temperature). Tasting wine requires stable practice. As already said, great wine cannot be appreciated without sustainable practice and culture. Of course, this does not prevent to have a variety of similar wines (i.e., the flexibility property) and invent new wines (i.e., the innovation property).

Summarizing, wine as TIS is a "natural artifact" (A) made for drinking and enjoying (U) by winemakers using specific tasks and experience (T) within a number organized communities of wine tasters (O), as well as geographical and meteorological situations (S). Back again to the AUTOS pyramid that can be used in arts as it is used in technology, wine is a good example of mixing art and technology.

The Pleasure of Creativity

Creativity comes from the inside. This claim follows Nietzsche's "will to power" philosophical concept that represents intrinsic human driving force toward many kinds of achievements. This concept that Nietzsche did not really define properly[5] was elicited from Nietzsche's notebooks (Nietzsche translated by Kaufmann 1968). "Why is all activity, even that of a sense, associated with pleasure? Because before it an obstacle, a burden existed? Or rather because all doing is an overcoming, a becoming master, and increase the feeling of power? – Pleasure in thinking. – Ultimately, it is not only the feeling of power, but the pleasure in creating and in the thing created; for all activity enters our consciousness as consciousness of a 'work'" (Nietzsche translated by Kaufmann 1968, p. 349).

Could we create things without emotion? Don Norman stated: "… positive affect enhances creative, breadth-first thinking whereas negative affect focuses cognition, enhancing depth-first processing and minimizing distractions." (Norman 2002, 2003). Norman claims that "aesthetics matter: attractive things work better." Usability and aesthetics are two different concepts. Usability engineering takes care of functionality. Aesthetic design takes care of attractiveness and pleasure. As a matter of fact, usability and aesthetics are tangibility dimensions that can be used to define criteria for testing TISs.

As already discussed, creativity is a matter of **divergent thinking** (i.e., using the right hemisphere of the brain) and **convergent thinking** (i.e., using the left hemisphere of the brain). The former deals with emotions, physical interactivity, and body itself. The latter deals with reasoning, mental activity, and mind itself. Philosophers have discussed the mind-body dualism since antiquity. Can we

---

[5] Nietzsche's notes, initially published by his sister after his death, were mistakenly considered as leading concept supporting the Nazi movement. Later on, it was established that Nietzsche's "will to power" concept was close to Schopenhauer's "will to live," which is a psychological force consciously and unconsciously used to survive (Wicks 2011).

separate our mind from our body[6]? René Descartes thought that we can and we should.[7] Engineers are still trained using Descartes's philosophy and are very much into reasoning, problem-solving, and convergent thinking, assuming that problems are well stated. The "art" of science and engineering is to incrementally transform questions to find answers. Artists are more into emotions, physical interactivity, problem stating, and divergent thinking, constantly synthesizing ideas, concepts, and matters. At this point, it is purposeful to cite Paul Valéry, a French poet, "It takes two to invent anything. The one makes up combinations; the other one chooses, recognizes what he wishes and what is important to him in the mass of the things which the former has imparted to him" (Hadamard 1954; Dennett 1978). We could take Valery's statement as the right brain makes up combinations, and the left part of the brain processes them to make something tangible. In other words, creativity is about identifying resources and integrating them into a new object.

Using the Nineteenth-Century French Example

In the beginning of the nineteenth century, the French industry realized that it needed to adapt to the upcoming industrial era and facilitate the development of practical applications of major recent scientific discoveries. It is interesting to remind that the *École Centrale des Arts et Manufactures* was created in Paris in 1829 by a businessman, Alphonse Lavallée, who wanted to train the "physicians of factories," taking the term physicians in the medical sense. The name of the school included the Arts—literally, the "Central School of Arts and Factories." This engineering school is still one of the best in France. Most brilliant engineers graduated from it, such as Gustave Eiffel in 1855, André Michelin in 1877, Louis Blériot in 1895, Armand Peugeot in 1995, and Marcel Schlumberger in 1907.

Gustave Eiffel was a civil engineer and architect. He built bridges for the French railway network. Eiffel designed and built the famous Eiffel Tower in Paris. He also contributed to the design of the Statue of Liberty in New York. André Michelin was an industrialist who founded the Michelin Tyre Company. He also published the first *Michelin Guide*[8] to promote tourism by car. Louis Blériot was a French engineer, inventor, and aviator, who made the first flight across the English Channel in a heavier-than-air aircraft. He also developed the first practical headlamp for trucks and established a profitable business manufacturing them. Armand Peugeot was an

[6] David Hodgson claimed, "my discussion of quantum mechanics has confirmed [the mind's] undeterministic character; and has also suggested that quantum mechanics shows that matter is ultimately 'non-material' and non-local, and that perhaps mind and matter are interdependent." (Hodgson 1991, p. 381).

[7] During the same period, Baruch (Benedicto) Spinoza contradicted René Descartes and stated that mind and body are the same substance. Descartes was remembered as a visionary, and Spinoza was ignored for a long time.

[8] The *Michelin Guide* is still a very famous reference that provides stars to European hotels and restaurants. These stars have a direct impact on the success of restaurants.

industrialist, pioneer of the automobile industry, and the founder of the French firm Peugeot. Marcel Schlumberger was a brilliant engineer in railways. He also participated in the design and development of the first French tanks used in World War I. With his brother Conrad, he made several inventions in geophysics and oil, which made their success. These people are examples of creative minds coming from an engineering school where the arts were promoted.

Another school can be cited that goes along the same tradition, the *Ecole Nationale Supérieure des Arts et Métiers*, founded by Duke of Rochefoucauld-Liancourt in 1780, to provide in-depth training for military dragoon officers' children. After 1800, the school became the *École d'Arts et Métiers* (School of Arts and Jobs). Among the alumni are Pierre Bézier who invented computer-aided design, Jean-Lou Chameau who became the President of California Institute of Technology, and Lucien Servanty who was the Chief Operating Officer of the Concorde program.

Again, these are examples of schools that included arts when they were created. Today, they have become institutes of technology producing great high-level technicians. It is time to restate the aim and put arts back for the promotion of creativity, emotions, divergent thinking, and great visions. This is what I contributed to design and develop at Florida Institute of Technology by setting up the new School of Human-Centered Design, Innovation, and Art. Our goal is educating and training human-systems integration architects of the twenty-first century.

Cartoonists in a Design Project

In 2006, I participated in Blue Sky meetings and workshops organized by IHMC[9] and NASA for the design of a human-driven pressurized lunar rover. A group of scientists, engineers, and human-centered designers had a series of meetings and workshops where we brainstormed, drafted, designed, and built mock-ups and prototypes. Two artists participated. They managed to draw cartoons of potential configurations and scenarios making more visual several concepts that we were elaborating (Fig. 10.1). This was participatory design at work!

For example, space suits lead to one of the design challenges. The main problem was to find a solution for the astronauts to wear these suits in a quick period of time. It typically took 45 min for Space Shuttle astronauts to wear suits for extravehicular activities. A great idea emerged from group discussions to design space suits attached to the back of the rover and having a mechanism that enables astronauts to "jump" from inside the rover to the space suit. We designed a solution that requires a couple of minutes for an astronaut to jump into the space suit.

Once ideas were more crystallized, cartoonists made an animation that captured and put alive the main configurations and scenarios (Fig. 10.2).

---

[9] Florida Institute for Human and Machine Cognition.

Fig. 10.1 Lunar Electric Rover design cartoons

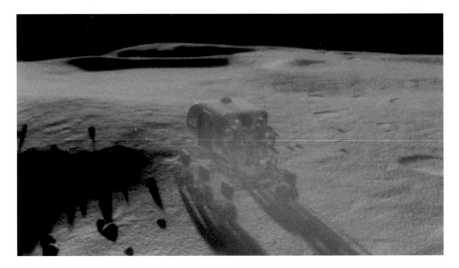

Fig. 10.2 Lunar Electric Rover design animation

In the beginning the interior was very rudimentary (Fig. 10.3), but it included enough functions for an astronaut to drive the rover.

Since then, two rovers were built and tested in various kinds of configurations and external conditions. We further developed various kinds of TISs, such as the **Virtual Camera** (Boy et al. 2010; Platt 2013; Boy and Platt 2013). The Virtual Camera was also designed and developed incrementally. We first tested it in a public

Fig. 10.3 First interior design (driving section) of the Lunar Electric Rover

Fig. 10.4 A Virtual
Camera test subject using
an umbrella to shield the
screen for better visibility,
in a park

park in Florida (Fig. 10.4). We tested the Virtual Camera together with the Lunar
Electric Rover in the Arizona desert. We also participated in a mission organized
and run by "astrobiologists and geologists from NASA Ames Research Center,
Idaho State, Idaho University and teachers mapped the lichen growth at a variety of
places around the Craters of the Moon national park using the Virtual Camera as an
assistant. One goal was to compare the ability to conduct field science with traditional tools of a digital camera, GPS device and field notebook to using one device,
the Virtual Camera. Also, collaboration using the Virtual Camera to map scientifically
important objectives was observed. Three days of field use studies were obtained
while the team mapped geologic and biological (moss, lichens) components in lava

Fig. 10.5 Collaborating during the field expedition using the Virtual Camera, in the Craters of the Moon national park

flows. Overall, the Virtual Camera was evaluated for science utility, collaboration and use for education" (Platt 2013).

The Virtual Camera is an operations assistance system that could be used for navigation and exploration purposes. We also found that it is a very interesting tool for human-human cooperation (Fig. 10.5). For example, it was used as a mediating agent enabling exploration knowledge capture and sharing. It is also a very interesting tool to explore and study human-human cooperation and human-systems integration, when the system is an interactive visualization system (e.g., a big geological database). More information can be found in Donald Platt's Ph.D. dissertation (Platt 2013).

Design, Engineering, Arts, and Science

Lunar Electric Rover (LER) and Virtual Camera (VC) are very interesting examples of a good mix of art, design, engineering, and science. We did not start with equations that we applied to a specific solution. We start with a purpose. In the LER case, the purpose was geological exploration of the Moon, where the necessity of having geologists dictated many aspects. It was an interdisciplinary endeavor from the start. We needed to put together many ideas from a variety of sources. The Blue Sky meetings and workshops were extremely rich and difficult to conduct and synthesize because lots of experience from various backgrounds needed to be mixed. However, the common denominator was motivation to succeed and make a useful and usable pressurized rover for the purpose. Creativity was the main process. Creativity was synthesis and integration of gigantic amount of knowledge and knowhow. This was collective creativity. Each of us gave his or her contribution to make a tangible whole. In the beginning, figurative tangibility was prominent

Fig. 10.6 LER test on an artificial lunar surface at NASA JSC

criterion for selection of ideas that would stay and be integrated. One thing for sure was the need for visualization. This is where artists were crucial. Progressively things became more concrete and implemented in the form of animations, computer-aided design models, and then prototypes.

In the VC case, things went differently in the beginning. In February 2009, I was observing an astronaut driving the rover on a small hill at NASA Johnson Space Center (JSC), with a crater on one side (Fig. 10.6). He was asking someone outside if he could go left, right, forward, and backward. It was just like when you try to park your car and have no visibility, you ask someone to help you by providing directional signs. I realized immediately that when this person would be on the Moon driving the rover, he would not have anybody outside help. Therefore, what would be the solution to help? The VC concept was shaped very quickly: a partial geological database that could be upgraded incrementally while exploring (i.e., using a data fusion algorithm) and an interactive visualization display. The VC project was started. Creativity was at stake. The VC could not be made without help from a variety of people, including space engineers, astronauts, computer scientists, visualization specialists, data fusion scientists, and other computer geeks. We made a team. We developed several mock-ups and prototypes before we realized that VC should be developed on a tablet. As we were developing prototypes, it went on and on discovering new patterns of use of the VC and new emerging properties to the point that the VC concept became very generic. We actually thought about using the VC concept for supporting weather situation awareness in aircraft cockpits, for example, and we did it developing the OWSAS (already described in this book). This was creativity as exploration.

Of course we can see the benefit of a liberal mind in design, engineering, and science, but what about the other way around? What can design, engineering, and science contribute in arts? The Institute of the Arts and Sciences at UC Santa Cruz

(UCSC) already offers visionary programs that promote integration of sciences and arts not only at a professional level but also at the public level. They have developed galleries, learning spaces, and events facilities, which contribute to participatory learning in any form of people of all ages. Their goal is "to explore the critical issues of our time, and share those insights with the public.[10]" The main goal is to combine power of arts and power of sciences. Doing this fusion, we need to make sure that we take the best scientists, practitioners, and coordinators to make creativity real, effective, and successful. UCSC integrates many fields such as "genomics, sustainable food systems, astrophysics, digital arts, and social justice." At the new School of Human-Centered Design, Innovation, and Art (SHCDIA), we integrate aeronautics, astronautics, nuclear engineering, medicine, automotive, robotics, education, politics, and culture. We promote collaboration among universities, but also among academia and industry and governmental agencies and our school. This new endeavor is not a dry program that has a mission to train young people with respect to procedures and rules; it is a challenge that will have to experience, test, and analyze new kinds of interaction among technology, organizations, and people. Whenever we design a system, we are responsible, and we need to better understand what these responsibilities are about. This is why we need to have lawyers in our design teams, and artists who will provide astute visualization of what long boring legal texts are saying to expert lawyers. We need to understand what we need to understand!

At FIT, SHCDIA and the Foosaner Museum of Arts, in Melbourne, Florida, provide a structure for exhibitions that could be interactive, artist and scientist residency programs, and collaborative research between SHCDIA and all departments of FIT. We also propose a project that is led by students that provide rich material for visitors to encounter the creative expression and real-world solutions. This approach provides hands-on activities cross-feed by theory and explanations. Most importantly, these activities are interdisciplinary and supervised by highly competent instructors.

We are building a home for artists who want to work with designers, engineers, and scientists to make our world a better place. This is why SHCDIA was created and is developing fast! We are working on an environmental responsive location, the Space Coast, which has a lot to do as far as pollution is concerned. We are building new approaches to return to a stable organic environment. Projects are developed to this end.

Of course, what we are doing is not the development of a new religion or a sect, or anything in that perspective. What we are doing at SHCDIA is collaboratively inventing a new life taking into account what human kind has done so far and what human kinds can do in the future. We are looking at human evolution and the science of artifacts, knowing that artifacts are built by people and a concrete expression of human intelligence. Careful analysis of artifacts is a mine of discovery of what human evolution has been so far and what it could be in the near future. Deliberately, TISs are the building bricks of systems designed at SHCDIA.

---

[10] http://ias.ucsc.edu/about

The Art of Making Tangible Interactive Systems

We need to bring together both thinkers and doers from several disciplines. Of course collaboration will be effective and sustainable if the various topics are well chosen. For example, putting together ecology, global warming, global economy, immigration in the wild, ocean transformations, and so on is a crucial topic that enters into the art of making TISs.

Today, our world is almost without borders. People communicate through the Internet anytime, anywhere, with anyone, on any topic, and so on. In the past, our interactions were constrained in a very small environment (e.g., 50 km diameter interaction in the countryside). In cities, people did not communicate well until the Internet, even those who were living close to each other. For this reason, smartphones made a big change in communication. I do not want to judge if this is good or bad, but it is! Now, we need to learn how to use these TISs to live a more flexible, mature, stable, and sustainable life.

HCD promotes getting out of the box, instead of following procedures perpetually. We need to expand our minds and generate ideas that could be provoking and suggest solutions for the future. I strongly believe that this kind of approach to creativity can work only if we carefully address deeper questions in philosophy, physics and mathematics, politics, and economy. These questions should be addressed at various societal levels of execution (i.e., government, laws, regulations, education and training, certification). We now need to accumulate as much information as we can, in the form of anecdotes, accident analysis, motivated observations of any kind, structured reporting systems, and so on. We need to develop exhibitions, which will enable public confrontations and produce precious feedback.

We saw that sustainability is an important asset in TIS design. Sustainable design and development can be illustrated by Mulligan's Social Ecology model that shifts from Elkington's intertwined dimensions (i.e., ecological, economic, and social—1997) to three dimensions (i.e., ecological, personal, and social—Mulligan 2015). Durall and her colleagues recently proposed an approach to design for sustainability by fostering reflection in the design process (Durall et al. 2015). They present design games as a participatory method that supports reflection and we exemplify it through two design cases. They show how reflection is provoked by the implementation of design games where tangible game objects help participants "to contextualize and make connections with people's previous experiences. Tangible game objects can simulate existing situations, as well as introduce new metaphors that offer a new perspective." In their study, they conclude that "good sustainable solutions do not only solve ecological problems; they encourage social sustainability by creating and increasing well-being in socio-cultural contexts for both individuals and groups. Personalized solutions are needed to support reflection and behavior changes on personal and socio-cultural levels."

In addition, a breaking idea is the development of a permanent creative place where anyone can come and create what he or she wants. There could be several levels of expression with respect to age and other relevant factors. This is why FIT SHCDIA school provides a design platform where students can come freely. This place should be a kind of shelter where people can express themselves without pressure and outside influences. HITLS and participatory design are again great support and assets. Of course, when solutions are ready for being exposed to the world, they are tested with real people in real environments. This could take the form of exhibitions, contests, even competitions, and ultimately media coverage.

Conciliating Aesthetics, Emotions, and Cognition

People have affective responses to specific visual stimuli. Visual arts use this human property to communicate emotions to trigger pleasurable experience. For example, healthy people are physically and subconsciously sensitive to and potentially attracted by symmetry. Color affords people to feel beauty and happiness, or the opposite depending on culture (i.e., affordances of colors are not necessarily innate, they can be learned and incrementally refined). For example, bright colors are likely to create positive emotions and pleasure, as dark colors are often related to negative emotions and sadness.

There is a simple rule in design: "things that you design should make sense." **Meaning is key**. In addition, they should be attractive. Engagement in human-systems integration is also a matter of aesthetical relation between people and systems. "Making sense" is not only cognitive but also embodied. What makes a great piece of art are the emergent cues that people perceive, not the individual parts assembled by the artist. Again, creativity is about synthesis and integration. It is a complex process that leads to a complex product. Complexity comes from the number of elements and interconnections among these elements. Elements and interconnections do not have to be only physical but also figurative. This is where tangibility enters into play.

It is interesting to analyze in more detail the aesthetics-functionality dualism. On one side, we could say that aesthetics and functionality of an artifact are totally independent. On the other side, we could say that they are intimately related, one determining the other and conversely. This problem brings us back to Descartes's mind-body distinction, also called "mind-body dualism." Descartes claimed that mind is the thinking part and body is extended physical part of human beings. Of course, one cannot work without the other. It is like if we represent a human being by two agents (i.e., mind and body) interacting among each other. However, this question is not trivial. We could consider that the body is a dumb extension of the mind that executes what it is told to do. We also could consider that body and mind are an integrated structure that learns skills that are embodied and knowledge that is remembered in the cortex. Aesthetics is about skills, affect, and emotions. Functionality is about knowledge, reasoning, and rationality. The same as for human being's body-mind duality, we can talk about artifact's aesthetics-functionality dualism. Designing TISs, we can say that initial design is often guided by aesthetics-functionality distinction (i.e., we design both independently and we integrate them together); and when maturity comes (i.e., technology maturity and maturity of practice), we are able to see their interdependencies. We also could have an intuition of such interdependencies from the beginning as most great artists do, but it will be the result of a long experience in designing TISs. Therefore, we could say that we start design with a positivist approach and incrementally derive toward a phenomenological approach. This is why developing prototypes and incrementally refining them through a series of formative evaluations is so important.

Tangible Graphical and Interactive Art

Technology may take a substantial amount of time to become mature to be tangible for artistic purposes. The French Lumière brothers who created film technology (Fig. 10.7). Louis and Auguste Lumière were engineers, not artists in the classical sense (i.e., their films cannot be qualified as artistic productions). Several decades later, film technology has become the support of what is now called the Seventh Art. When we go to a movie theater, we are not as impressed by the engineering side of a movie, as by its content and the feelings that it creates. Indeed, a common frame of reference was created over the years that associated technical constraints and possibilities, storytelling, and aesthetics. Movie making evolution is a good

Fig. 10.7 L'arroseur arrosé (Lumière brothers 1895)

example of a move from engineering thinking to artistic thinking, enabling the expression of situations, feelings, and thoughts.

Alan Kay's computer science concept of user illusion (1984) and Tognazzini's principles, techniques, and ethics of stage magic and their application to human interface design (1993) stated user interface's requirements for user-friendly interaction. In other words, the art of making a great user interface requires designers to eliminate "magician's strings" (i.e., programming syntax) to the benefit of what really matters for the user (i.e., content semantics).

In their collective book, Ehmann et al. (2009) proposed a tangible vision of contemporary three-dimensional design of objects and orchestrated spaces. In this book, authors make visual the intangible using "craftsmanship, physical experiences, visual environments and staged spatial installations such as art installations, interiors and architecture as well as urban interventions."

Human-computer interaction (HCI) mixed with product design, materials science, and architecture leads to reconciling the digital and physical (Wiberg and Robles 2010). Wiberg and Robles advocate "refocusing interaction design toward aesthetics and compositions." They advocate thinking of design as composition of digital and physical parts instead of keeping them apart. As a personal note, I take composition in the musical sense (i.e., a composer making a symphony). This is the reason why we need to articulate a common frame of reference (i.e., a music theory) that enables to relate physical and digital materials. Their texture model is particularly interesting, and should be extended. They claim, "texture guided the quality of composition achieved in the final design executed by a team of diverse experts." This is an interaction design approach. **Interaction design** has become a major practice in HCI (Norman 1988; Laurel and Lunenfeld 2003; Buxton 2005). Interaction design addresses the design of interactive systems (i.e., digital). HCD subsumes interaction design.

References

Aarrestad FB, Antoniou N, Bratasanu D, Bruni S, Calder-Potts G, Chen J, de Paula Silva A, Emuna N, Ferreté E, Flahaut J, Flood J, Fujita H, Gadot I, Garimella S, Grohnfeldt C, Harpur J, Hemmings DM, Laroche CM, Li H, Li X, Miles D, Okada K, Peng J, Pohl R, Reyes AM, Roos AJC, Russell C, Sandberg H, Scepanovic S, Stroh V, Wang H, Wang Y, Yamanouchi H, Xu B (2012) SPACE: a giant leap for education. SSP12-ISU team project report. International Space University, Strasbourg

Aldrin B, David L (2013) Mission to Mars. National Geographic Society, Washington, DC. ISBN 978-1-4262-1017-4

Boy GA, Mazzone R, Conroy M (2010) The virtual camera concept: a third person view. In: Third international conference on applied human factors and engineering, Miami, Florida, 17–20 July

Boy GA (2012) What can space contribute to global STEM education? A team project at ISU-SSP12. In: Proceedings of the 63rd International Astronautical Congress (IAC), Naples

Boy GA (2013) From STEM to STEAM: toward a human-centered education, creativity & learning thinking. Proceedings of the European Conference on Cognitive Ergonomics, ECCE 2013, Jean Jaures University, Toulouse, France. Also in the ACM Digital Library. http://dl.acm.org

Buxton B (2005) Sketching the user experience. New Riders Press, San Francisco, CA. ISBN: 0-321-34475-8

Changeux JP (2005) La lumière au siècle des Lumières et aujourd'hui. Odile Jacob, Paris

Changeux JP (ed) (2007) L'home artificiel. Odile Jacob, Paris

Changeux JP (2008) Du vrai, du beau, du bien. Odile Jacob, Paris

Changeux JP (2010a) The neuroscience of art: a research program for the next decade? Fifth International School on Mind, Brain and Education – Learning, Arts, and the Brain. 1–6 Aug. Retrieved on July 22, 2015. http://www.mbe-erice.org/2010-abstract-changeux.php

Changeux JP (2010b) Le cerveau et l'art. De vive voix, Paris. ISBN 978-2-84684-093-4

Dennett DD (1978) Brainstorms. Bradford Books, New York

Durall E, Uppa H, Leinonen T (2015) Designing for sustainability: Fostering reflection in the design process. No 6: Nordes 2015: Design Ecologies, ISSN 1604-9705. Stockholm, www.nordes.org

Ehmann S, Huebner M, Klanten R (eds) (2009) Tangible. Gestalten Verlag, Berlin, Germany ISBN: 978-3-89955-232-4

Grau O (2004) Virtual art – from illusion to immersion, The Leonardo Book Series. The MIT Press, Cambridge, MA. ISBN 978-0262572231

Hadamard J (1954) The psychology of invention in the mathematical field. Dover Publications, London. ISBN 978-0486201078

Hodgson D (1991) The mind matters: consciousness and choice in a quantum world. Clarendon, Oxford. ISBN 978-0198240686

Kay A (1984) Computer software. Sci Am 251(4):1–9

Laurel B, Lunenfeld P (2003) Design research: methods and perspectives. MIT Press, Cambridge, MA. ISBN 0-262-12263-4

Lumière brothers (1895) https://en.wikipedia.org/wiki/L'Arroseur_Arros%C3%A9. Retrieved on 28 Mar 2016

Mulligan M (2015) An introduction to sustainability: environmental, social and personal perspectives. Routledge, Oxon

Nietzsche F (Author), Kaufmann W (Editor, Translator), Hollingdale RJ (Translator) (1968) The will to power. Vintage. ISBN-13: 978-0394704371

Norman DA (1988) The design of everyday things. Basic Books, New York. ISBN 978-0-465-06710-7

Norman DA (2002) Emotion and design: attractive things work better. Interact Mag Ix(4):36–42

Norman DA (2003) Emotional design: why we love (or hate) everyday things. Basic Books, New York. ISBN 978-0465051359

Platt D (2013) The virtual camera: participatory design of a cooperative exploration mediation tool. Ph.D. dissertation in Human-Centered Design, advised by G.A. Boy, Florida Institute of Technology

Simon HA (2001) Science seeks parsimony, not simplicity: searching for pattern in phenomena. In: Zellner A, Keuzenkamp HA, McAleer M (eds) Simplicity, inference and modelling. Keeping it sophisticatedly simple. Cambridge University Press, Cambridge, pp 32–72

Tognazzini B (1993) Principles, techniques, and ethics of stage magic and their application to human interface design. In: CHI'93 Proceedings of the INTERACT'93 and CHI'93 conference on human factors in computing systems. ACM, New York, pp 355–362. ISBN:0-89791-575-5

Vasari, G (1912) Giorgio Vasari's lives of the artists. Retrieved on July 22, 2015. http://members.efn.org/~acd/vite/VasariLives.html

Wiberg M, Robles E (2010) Computational compositions: aesthetics, materials, and interaction design. Int J Des 4(2):65–76

Wicks R (2011) Arthur Schopenhauer. The Stanford Encyclopedia of Philosophy (Winter Edition). In: Zalta EN (ed) http://plato.stanford.edu/archives/win2011/entries/schopenhauer/

Chapter 11
Conclusion

It is time to conclude. However, this is not a classical conclusion but an invitation to go beyond what you just read. I tried to give you philosophical and technical guidance to design tangible interactive systems (TISs). You now need to design and test your own TISs. Let me remind you the most important concepts.

Articulating Human-Centered Design

Taking into account human-systems integration during the design process was a wishful thinking for a long time. In practice, human factors and ergonomics (HFE) specialists attempted and still attempt to correct engineering products. HFE is mostly about corrective ergonomics that happens too late to be really effective. Technology-centered engineering (TCE) requires such an HFE approach (i.e., user interfaces and operational guidance need to be developed). This TCE-HFE association generated the user interface concept (i.e., a layer between a system and its user). The more this layer affords users to do what they want to do, the less guidance they need (i.e., the less operational procedures, checklists, and other user guides). Of course, this depends on the complexity of the system itself and the nature of the tasks to be executed. Note that engineered products that we are talking about here can be any kind of industrial products.

> **Human-systems integration supersedes interaction design that supersedes human factors and ergonomics.**

For the last three decades, human-computer interaction (HCI) developed as a discipline in its own right. HCI mainly focuses on the design of usable computing systems. In this approach, user interfaces are produced, but the main concern is

© Springer International Publishing Switzerland 2016   207
G.A. Boy, *Tangible Interactive Systems*, Human–Computer Interaction Series,
DOI 10.1007/978-3-319-30270-6_11

interaction design (Norman 1988; Buxton 2005). One of the best examples that lead to a revolution in computing systems is the series of iPod, iPhone, and iPad. These products are easy to use because HCI has been thought, designed, and tested in a human-centered way. They are extremely well integrated, and their user interfaces afford easy access to what we need and what we want to do. They show the link between interaction design and human-computing systems integration.

This naturally leads to human-systems integration in general (i.e., where systems are not necessarily computing systems, but also physical, organic, organizational, and social, for example). In this book, I would like to insist on the fact that today design almost always starts using a computer. We sketch possible solutions using PowerPoint, for example, then a rapid prototyping application, and finally simulation software. We start in a virtual world. The difference with the past is the fact that instead of having virtual ideas floating in our heads or a piece of paper, they can now be easily sketched, drawn, modeled, animated, simulated on a computer, and used for early tests. Human-systems integration can be developed in a virtual world before making decisions and products in the real physical world. This is a real new revolution since we can test people's activity during the design process. Human factors can then be effectively taken into account at design time and not struggle correcting engineering productions once the system is physically made. The problem becomes tangibility. Indeed, tests performed in the virtual world provide useful indications on system functions, but not on the physical structure of the system (e.g., you need to physically handle a steering wheel to feel forces). This is the reason why modeling and simulation (M&S) used at design time should not be limited to software, but incrementally include hardware. 3D printing has become a solution.

Tangible Interactive Systems Design

This evolution of design and engineering leads to a new concept that integrates software and hardware: TISs. Both physical tangibility and figurative tangibility should be incrementally tested in an agile way. Typically, a new TIS is integrated into an already integrated set of TISs. For example, we have seen how we are integrating the Onboard Weather Situation Awareness System (OWSAS) into a commercial aircraft cockpit. We have seen that the realism of the cockpit simulator is key, as well as the involvement of professional pilots during the simulated flight tests.

We have seen in Chap. 3 that a TIS can be represented or documented using the design card concept, which includes structure "S," function "F," rationale "R," and activity "A" of the TIS (already defined in Chap. 3). The main problem that human-centered designers have to solve is how to integrate a new TIS into an existing TIS (Fig. 11.1).

For example, OWSAS's structure is a tablet; its function is to provide real-time weather information to the pilot; its rationale is to increase pilot's current weather

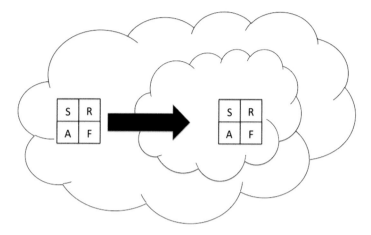

Fig. 11.1 Integration of a new TIS into an old TIS environment generates a new TIS environment

situation awareness for safety and efficiency purposes; and pilot's activity that it induces should be integrated in the overall flight management activity. Sometimes, new TISs could use the same structure as an existing TIS (e.g., OWSAS function could be integrated into the same tablet of another TIS such as the Onboard Context-Sensitive Information System: OCSIS). There are several combinations of the four TIS attributes {S, F, R, A}.[1] TIS structure and function are about physical tangibility. TIS rationale and activity are about figurative tangibility.

We have seen that tangibility of such interactive systems includes testing complexity, flexibility, stability, maturity, and sustainability.

Of course, systems that we design should be as simple as possible to facilitate their use. However, when a system is intrinsically complex (e.g., an aircraft), people using it should be familiar with its structures and functions.

Of course, automation can tremendously help people controlling or managing a complex system, but if it is not well understood, it is a rigid agent that could lead to catastrophic consequences. Consequently, TISs should be flexible (i.e., people using TISs should be able to handle maximum of situations in a flexible way).

Of course, systems that we design should be stable for standard usages, but they also enable capabilities in case of unforeseen situations. How could people or organizations recover from serious or catastrophic breakdowns?

Of course, maturity is currently taken into account using well-formatted technology readiness level (TRL) in industry, but do we really take into account technology maturity and maturity of practice? What are the processes and criteria to take these two maturity concepts into account effectively? Quality processes are totally insufficient, the way they are implemented today. Constant and deeper domain competence and expertise is required.

---

[1] Structure, function, rationale, activity.

Of course, systems are currently designed using a set of very well-thought standards and norms, but are they, though, designed and tested with sustainable human-systems integration in mind? Attention, care, active participation of domain experts, and repeated tests are required. These tests should use the SFAC model.

TISs should be considered as agents having cognitive and physical functions. Once a new TIS is being designed, prototypes should be used by appropriate people (generally experts) within a realistic simulated environment. Understanding connectivity and interactions among the various agents provides very good datasets that can be analyzed for design improvement. This is what I call orchestrating human-centered design (Boy 2013). The TIS concept is essential to take into account both physical and cognitive functions, as well as abstract and concrete structures.

Creativity, Design Thinking, and Team Spirit

Science observes and analyzes things to create knowledge. Design uses knowledge to create things. Of course, science and design should be articulated. Creativity is about synthesis and integration of things and knowledge that already exist. Creativity is always on the abstract side and the concrete side. Anything that can be expressed clearly could be translated into a concrete thing (e.g., description of a car turned into a real car or expression of grammatical rules turned into a language). Sometimes, concepts are not easy to share among a set of people, because we lack the right syntax and/or the right semantics or because people do not have the same background and/or culture. Creativity is about **design thinking** (i.e., thinking concepts abstractly by developing conceptual models and concretely by making real artifacts).

The other day, my colleague, Larry Leifer, professor at Stanford University, convinced me that the STEAM concept, which usually means science, technology, engineering, arts, and mathematics, could be interpreted differently if we write it this way, S-TEAM. Indeed, doing science with a team spirit could change everything. If we think that learning is a matter of knowledge design, then doing science with a team spirit could be **collaborative knowledge design**. One of my Ph.D. students is carrying out design and research work on tangible interactive objects (i.e., interactive cubes equipped with RFIDs). She is developing and using this technology to facilitate acquisition of reading and computing skills of kids between 4 and 6 years old (Almukadi and Stephane 2015). This is reading and computing (additions and subtractions) using their hands, manipulating cubes. Once a good result is found, an animation is provided to inform about success. My student found out that groups of kids (four to five kids) tend to collaborate by proposing to move one cube there and another cube over there, and so on until success… of the team. This kind of tangible interactive objects facilitates learning and team spirit. Without trying, incrementally creating appropriate TISs, she would never have discovered this emergent property. Without this TIS approach and an appropriate simulation environment, she would probably never have discovered this emergent property!

In the previous example, we saw that TISs being designed could be immediately tested with appropriate people in a gaming spirit also. Kids play with these interactive cubes. They have fun acquiring reading and computing skills! Results are effective.

Testing, Testing, Testing

Back to the old days of flight tests at Airbus Industrie during the early 1980s, I learned that testing is one of the most important parts of design. Testing enables fixing anything that was not well designed and document capabilities for certification purposes. It takes time to properly design and test an aircraft (i.e., from the beginning of design to certification, it usually takes around 6 years). At that time, we were not using M&S capabilities that we have today. Preparation of flight tests was based on empirical calculations using former flight tests expertise and mathematical models. Today, M&S enable testing systems very early during the design process and more accurately prepare real-world flight tests.

More generally, tangible interactive systems are typically tested in the same way (i.e., using M&S first and then real-world experimental tests). M&S provide means for testing a new TIS in a simulated environment to find out emerging properties. Not only this environment should be as realistic as possible, but also the most experienced and expert users should be involved.

Critical Thinking

Critical thinking is about finding out concepts involved in the system being designed, analyzing them, refining them, and evaluating them. Critical thinking is about rationalization. Critical thinking is about figurative tangibility. In the framework of this book, it is about finding out various contexts where a TIS being designed will be usable and useful.

Using critical thinking is looking for evidence through reality. The question at design time is to create new kinds of reality. Back to the previous section on testing, M&S and real test users are key. Appropriate scenarios and criteria are also essential. Testers need to be critical on test methods themselves and capable of adapting them if necessary. Observation and interaction are far more important than blindly following test methods. In fact, test methods should be continuously tested.

Critical thinking is about stating problems correctly, recognizing that a problem deserves to be solved and another is not an issue, and making priorities among problems. Tests usually generate lots of data. Therefore, appropriate categorization of this data is crucial. Data interpretation and recognition of dependencies among datasets are key cognitive processes. The AUTOS pyramid can be a great support doing this. Visualization is always a great tool to identify evidence from experimental datasets. Finally, never forget that critical thinking requires a certain level of maturity and therefore experience (i.e., do not hesitate to practice it as much as you can!).

References

Almukadi W, Stephane AL (2015) BlackBlocks: tangible interactive system for children to learn 3-letter words and basic math. In: ITS '15 Proceedings of the 2015 international conference on interactive tabletops & surfaces. ACM Digital Library, New York, pp 421–424. ISBN: 978-1-4503-3899-8, doi:10.1145/2817721.2823482
Boy GA (2013) Orchestrating human-centered design. Springer, London. ISBN 978-1-4471-4338-3
Buxton B (2005) Sketching the user experience. New Riders Press, Berkeley and San Francisco. ISBN 0-321-34475-8
Norman D (1988) The design of everyday things. Basic Books, New York. ISBN 978-0-465-06710-7